Advance Praise for

# The Integrated News Spectacle

"A vivid, hard-hitting study of today's news business. James R. Compton
not only shows exactly how media conglomerates are subordinating
journalism—an indispensable foundation of democratic self-
government—to a pervasive 'promotional logic,' but also explains how
news is being integrated into a 24/7 corporate-state spectacle. This is a
powerful work of demystification. Read all about it!"

Dan Schiller, Research Professor of Communications,
University of Illinois at Urbana-Champaign

# The Integrated
# News Spectacle

Sut Jhally & Justin Lewis
*General Editors*

Vol. 6

PETER LANG
New York • Washington, D.C./Baltimore • Bern
Frankfurt am Main • Berlin • Brussels • Vienna • Oxford

James R. Compton

# The Integrated News Spectacle

## A Political Economy of Cultural Performance

PETER LANG
New York • Washington, D.C./Baltimore • Bern
Frankfurt am Main • Berlin • Brussels • Vienna • Oxford

Library of Congress Cataloging-in-Publication Data

Compton, James Robert.
The integrated news spectacle: a political economy
of cultural performance / James R. Compton.
p. cm. — (Media and culture; v. 6)
Includes bibliographical references and index.
1. Broadcast journalism—United States. 2. Broadcast journalism—
Social aspects—United States. 3. Journalism—Objectivity. 4. Mass media—
United States. I. Title. II. Series: Media & culture (New York, N.Y.) ; v. 6.
PN4888.B74C66   302.23'0973—dc22   2004006667
ISBN 0-8204-7070-8
ISSN 1098-4208


Bibliographic information published by **Die Deutsche Bibliothek.**
**Die Deutsche Bibliothek** lists this publication in the "Deutsche
Nationalbibliografie"; detailed bibliographic data is available
on the Internet at http://dnb.ddb.de/.

Cover design by Lisa Barfield

The paper in this book meets the guidelines for permanence and durability
of the Committee on Production Guidelines for Book Longevity
of the Council of Library Resources.

© 2004 Peter Lang Publishing, Inc., New York
275 Seventh Avenue, 28th Floor, New York, NY 10001
www.peterlangusa.com

Printed in the United States of America

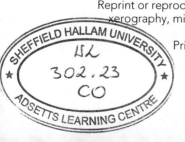

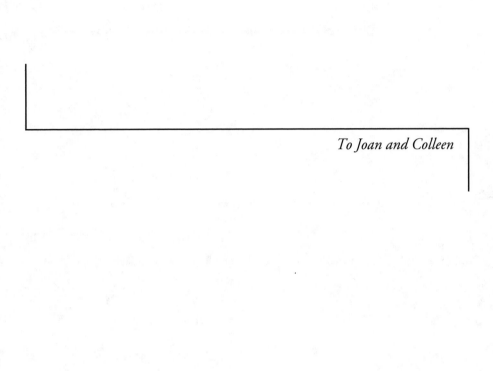

*To Joan and Colleen*

# Contents

# Acknowledgments

Many people helped me complete this book. Foremost among them is my doctoral supervisor Richard Gruneau. His lectures on "the spectacular," popular culture, and media served as a steady guide and benchmark for my own work. Rick's good humor provided me with inspiration, guidance and many laughs. My doctoral committee members at Simon Fraser University also deserve thanks. Robert Hackett, Alison Beale, and Martin Laba offered much encouragement and insight, as did my external examiner, Sut Jhally.

I owe thanks to many friends and colleagues at Simon Fraser who provided comments on earlier drafts of my work. Arthur Aginam, Diana Ambrozas, Kathy Cross, Jan Hadlaw, DeNel Sedo, David Smith, and Yeuzhi Zhao each offered challenging and stimulating observations that I found invaluable. My long-distance chats with Zhao continue to generate intellectual excitement and renew my commitment to critical scholarship. Similarly, my colleague Nick Dyer-Witheford at the University of Western Ontario offered many valuable comments on earlier versions of the manuscript. Thanks, Nick, for your advice and for your challenge to find responses to the promotional logic of spectacle.

The completion of the book was also made possible through the financial support provided by the Social Sciences and Humanities Research Council, the Faculty of Information and Media Studies at the University of Western Ontario, and the School of Communication at Simon Fraser University.

Finally, I would like to thank my wife, Joan. This book would not have been written without her patience, support, trust, and love. Her devotion to public education and commitment to equality and social justice are constant inspirations.

# Introduction

*It's the dumbest thing I've ever covered. Some people think Hell is a place where you wake up in the morning in a bed of coals. I think it's where you wake up and find out you'll be writing about Elian [Gonzalez] for the next 643 days.*

RICK BRAGG, FORMER REPORTER, *New York Times*

In recent years the opinion pages of quality North American newspapers and journalism periodicals have been bursting with self-reflexive hand-wringing, denunciations and, yes, self-loathing about the state of "the craft" (Sachs 1995; Posner 1998; Witcover 1998; Fallows 1999; Gitlin 2000a). Journalism, it is said, has sunk to new lows. Sensationalism, shoddy ethics, and brazen invasions of personal privacy—once the preserve of supermarket scandal sheets—are now commonplace features of respected broadsheets and broadcasters. The values of the paparazzi, critics wail, have spread like pond scum and sullied the credibility of all news media. According to mainstream critics, whereas, the *Washington Post*'s Woodward and Bernstein—mythologized by Hollywood for unearthing the unholy truth of a crooked president—practiced a heroic brand of "shoe-leather" journalism, today's reporters (referred to pejoratively by some as "spit catchers") are preoccupied with the cult of celebrity and the intimate details of presidential peccadilloes. Whereas fact checking is the unquestionable norm for respectable reporters, we are told today's rumormongers, such as Matt Drudge, run with the latest salacious detail concerning semen-stained blue dresses or the latest sex crime, pay for interviews and sometimes—as happened with former *New York Times* reporter Jayson Blair and *Boston Globe* columnist Patricia Smith—fabricate sources and quotes to construct an entertaining story. Hearsay has replaced reliably sourced attribution. The question "Will it entertain?" has replaced "Will it inform?" and journalism's high calling of public service has been eroded, leaving the media to settle into the muck of low-brow popular culture, the narcissism of celebrity profiles, and the pornography of violence. What happened?

First, it must be said that sensational news is not a recent phenomenon. As Mitchell Stephens writes: "Anyone who clings to the notion that the sensationalism practiced by [media mogul] Rupert Murdoch or even the most shameless present-day journalist is unprecedented could be set straight by spending a few minutes with any of a number of sixteenth- or seventeenth-century newsbooks" (Stephens 1988: 112). Stories of the strange, monstrous, and tawdry have been produced for centuries. Writers have long known how to attract an audience, and spinning a sensational yarn is one sure method. The "yellow journalism" practiced by the tabloid penny press of the early 19th century certainly contained its share of sex, scandal, and voyeurism. What is new, mainstream critics argue, is that the values of the so-called quality media have been eroded. It is bad enough for the *National Enquirer* to cover the alleged sex crimes of O.J. Simpson, but it is beyond the pale for the *New York Times*—the "gray lady" of newspapers—to cite the tabloid in its own coverage of the sensational marathon trial, as the *Times*'s David Margolick did, not once but twice (Sachs 1995).

Many media critics point to what they call the creeping tendencies of tabloid journalism. Andrea Sachs suggests the "melding" of tabloid and mainstream journalism began with the 1988 sex scandal involving Democratic hopeful Gary Hart (Sachs 1995); some suggest the floodgates burst open with the live broadcast of police chasing O.J. Simpson's white Ford Bronco along a Los Angeles freeway. Still others suggest the surging tabloid waters picked up speed with the death of Diana, Princess of Wales, in a fiery car crash within the bowels of a Paris tunnel; and they hit their apogee (nadir?) with the insatiable coverage of U.S. President Bill Clinton's sexual tryst with his young intern Monica Lewinsky. There have been other sensational stories: the death of John Kennedy Jr., the murder of little JonBenet Ramsey, the tug-of-war over a young Cuban boy named Elian Gonzalez and the scandal over murdered political intern Chandra Levy and her alleged sexual involvement with Congressman Gary Condit.

Stung by the public and in-house criticism leveled at the media, particularly following the death of Princess Diana, for which the media were blamed, many journalists have tried to protect their reputations, and that of the industry, by engaging in what Samuel Winch (1997) calls "boundary work." Journalists make the distinction between the legitimate work performed by credible news outlets (invariably their own) and the less noble work of the tabloid-influenced media and the paparazzi. It hasn't worked. Numerous polls in North America have consistently indicated the public's low opinion of journalists whom they rank, along with lawyers and business executives, as having little, if any, regard for ethics. The phrase "ethical journalist" is, for many people, an oxymoron. Mud is also thrown among rival reporters, and those hit are quick to lash back, as did *Newsweek*'s Michael Isikoff. He became outraged by

Jeffrey Toobin's portrayal of his role in breaking the Monica Lewinsky–presidential scandal (Kurtz 2000a). Veteran *CBS News* anchor Dan Rather, ironically himself a celebrity journalist who made his name as a Vietnam war correspondent, has dubbed the perceived slide of mainstream professional standards during the 1990s as "News Lite." In an interview with the *Philadelphia Inquirer,* Rather made a distinction between the "hard news" his newsroom practices and the lite news that he claims his network rivals at NBC and ABC frequently stoop to.

> [CBS is] anti-news lite. It's what we're all about. All news, all the time. Like a rock, we are hard news. I like it that the other two are going softer. We have to distinguish ourselves from them. CBS is a brand name. CBS Evening News is a brand name. We want that name to constantly be a beacon of real hard news. News lite is not our game.
> (McCartney 1997)

Rather is an extremely accomplished reporter and broadcaster whose work has been recognized by Harvard University; but his protestations have the ring of someone who is trying very hard to convince himself of his innocence. Rather was one of three U.S. network anchors who, on the weekend of January 19, 1998, were in Havana covering the historic visit of Pope John Paul II—a famed anticommunist. All three anchors cut their visit short to add their symbolic presence to a story that broke two days later on the 21st—the so-called Monicagate scandal. When Rather received his career excellence award from Harvard, he let slip a hint of his own self-loathing about the Havana evacuation: "If I really deserved this award," he said, "I would have stayed behind in Havana to cover the Pope's visit" (Gitlin 2000a). Rather's self-deprecating comment is representative of a broadly held belief that journalists themselves have a responsibility to a higher social calling. Most importantly, journalists should find the moral inner strength to resist the so-called infotainment tide. They should "just say no." At the same time, Rather is acutely aware of the fact that the scope of his free will is severely limited. "If you want to stay in the anchoring business," he told his Harvard audience, "you have two choices. You can go back to Washington and cover this breaking story or you can ask for asylum in Cuba" (Gitlin 2000a). Dan Rather, the star television-news anchor, has captured a core tension within journalism between professional idealism and the craft's material conditions of existence. Rather may regret his actions, he may indeed believe that his proper role as a serious journalist is to independently pursue the truth, inform, and enlighten his audience about important events, but on the other hand even someone as powerful as he has little choice if he wishes to keep his job.

This book explores the tension expressed by Dan Rather. It is inspired by my own work as a journalist working in Vancouver for Canadian Press/Broadcast News. I frequently found myself swept up in tabloid-like stories that had their own momentum. In 1998, I joined the British paparazzi as we chased Prince Charles and his sons,

William and Harry, to Whistler, British Columbia. The now motherless family had hoped to enjoy a private ski holiday. Like Dan Rather, I was torn between my sense that we as reporters had better things to be doing and the knowledge that I had little choice but to file the story requested of me. At the same time, I was not satisfied with the mainstream critique of tabloidization. It was clear to me that my trip to Whistler was a continuation of a much larger and complex set of factors. It was, in fact, the tail end of a global media event: the tragic death of the People's Princess. The Diana story *had* to be covered. Why? There was undeniably enormous public interest in the story. And yet this fact alone could not explain the scale and intensity of the coverage. Something else had to be accounted for.

My work as a journalist and academic has alerted me to how the news agenda, in both print and broadcast media, has become hostage to spectacular media events—what James Fallows calls an "all or nothing mentality, in which the running spectacle-story of the moment. . . squeezes everything else out" (Fallows 1999). Extreme examples of this global phenomenon include the O.J. Simpson murder trial, Monica Lewinsky's tryst with U.S. President Bill Clinton, and the mass murder at Littleton, Colorado. And yet, spectacular media events also take the form of serious news. The 1991 Gulf War and the so-called Gulf War II, of 2003, are two clear examples.

The drift toward a more spectacular media culture has been described by mass-culture critics as a process of social decay, a slide from high to low culture. Such critics see not only public/political life, but all civil society as colonized and debased by consumer culture. With the growing influence of television in the last half of the twentieth century, popular culture, including journalism, becomes a form of spectacle in which aestheticized images replace narrative as the dominant form of communication. Appeal is made to libidinal energies, not intellectual capacities. The optimists see audiences not as a collection of passive spectators, but as active postmodern subjects who create meaning through consumption. The common link between the pessimists and the optimists is that they believe the media environment to be characterized by a proliferation of commodified symbols and images.

I do not plumb the dark depths of the so-called tabloid soul. I believe this now-standard criticism of mainstream journalism misses the mark considerably. Most prominently, it mistakenly characterizes the central problem facing journalism as the substitution of entertainment for publicly useful information. Against the tabloidization thesis, a growing body of literature has developed that views media events as symbolically charged cultural performances. In this tradition, media events—such as the death and mourning of Princess Diana—are viewed as opportunities for the rehearsal of a community's most deeply held sacred values. Media events are not distractions from more important matters, nor are they examples of distorted communication.

I have difficulty with both the tabloidization and cultural-performance positions. I believe describing media events as richly symbolic dramatic performances is a vast improvement over the tabloidization thesis. However, scholarship in this tradition mistakes the part for the whole. It describes the dramatization of shared values without situating these performances within a broader historical, political, and economic context. For that reason, I organize my criticisms around the much broader concept of spectacle, associated most commonly with French Situationist Guy Debord. I critically evaluate and modify Debord's concept of spectacle in light of work by Andrew Wernick, David Harvey, Pierre Bourdieu, and others, to argue that spectacular media events can only be understood within a broader context of economic and social relations. The shortcomings of Debord's use of spectacle notwithstanding (e.g., his assumption that audiences consume mediated images passively and his total rejection of all mediated representation), I retain the concept in order to maintain a connection to a critique of power and domination. In particular, I utilize Debord's analysis of reification within consumer culture—i.e., how popular culture is increasingly subject to objectification, rational organization and control by impersonal market forces. I argue that media events are component parts of an *integrated* spectacular system of commodity production, distribution, and exchange. The book seeks to explain how "constellations" of social forces, new technologies, and institutional logics *converge* to promote economic and symbolic *synergies* that can potentially fetter the democratic use of media. At its core this book examines the *rational organization and control* of popular forms of news. I view media events such as the death of Princess Diana and the Gulf War as entry points into a much larger discussion about the underlying promotional logic that, increasingly, structures the activity of journalists and political professionals.

My approach is simple. I constantly refer the object of study—i.e., spectacular media events and their associated performances—back to the broader social totality. I argue that the integrated news spectacle can be properly understood only if we adopt a historical perspective that focuses on the *practical use* of cultural texts and other forms of cultural capital available to journalists, news organizations, political professionals, and audiences. This is accomplished first by a reinterpretation of existing scholarship in the fields of cultural studies and critical political economy of communication. Secondly, I map out the practical operation of the integrated news spectacle by reference to a combination of diverse sources, including news-industry trade publications, print, broadcast and online news stories, and government regulatory documents. These reports are mined for empirical evidence of important trends and developments in media industries. Particular attention is paid to action taken by news organizations, journalists, and political professionals to rationally organize and control popular forms of news.

In Chapter One, I critique the more generally accepted notion of tabloidization. Tabloidization is a weak analytical concept, in part, because of its adherence to a linear model of communication and the assumption that spectacular media events represent moments of displaced or distorted communication. I argue that such an account of media events fails to understand the complex ways news stories are constructed and circulated by modern news media. I then suggest that approaching news as a dramatic form of ritual takes us partway towards understanding these complexities and how news media feed off and back into popular culture. Following that, I draw attention to the main blind spots of the news ritual approach, particularly as it is practiced by theorists in the neo-Durkheimian tradition. Using the work of Pierre Bourdieu (1990, 1991), I argue that the neo-Durkheimian perspective lacks a rigorous historical analysis of power.

In Chapter Two, I suggest that the power relationships associated with media events can best be comprehended by revealing the practical application of the logic of spectacle—a logic characterized by the transposable circulation and promotion of cultural commodities. This logic is, I suggest, so pervasive that it manifests itself at both the micro and macro levels of social activity. I tease out this logic through an examination of the Princess Diana and Lewinsky-Clinton media events, among others, before explaining how the promotional logic of spectacle is embedded in news organizations' broader strategies of capital accumulation.

Chapter Three examines some of the sweeping historical developments that have helped facilitate the promotional integration of news media. I situate the integrated news spectacle within the history of the globalization of news production before examining the impact of neoliberal regulatory changes adopted by Western liberal democracies beginning in the late 1970s and early 1980s. I then turn to the development of new satellite and cable technologies and the subsequent fragmentation of audiences they helped foster. These pressures combine to give the push for profits a far greater influence over the production of news. The chapter ends with a discussion of the integrated efficiencies of 24-hour cable news and the so-called Big Story approach adopted by the all-news cable channels, such as CNN.

Chapter Four extends the discussion of the integrated news spectacle by investigating how the promotional logic of spectacle is contributing to the reconfiguration of the news industry under the banner of convergence. The chapter also investigates how this reconfiguration stands in contradiction to journalism's expressed role as a facilitator of democratic communication. It describes the specific ways in which the logic of the integrated spectacle is inscribed in the structural reconfiguration of news media through corporate and promotional convergence of formerly distinct media organizations.

Chapter Five is about the performance of politics and the politics of performance. It discusses the unique ways in which politics has become aestheticized by the workings of the integrated news spectacle. It argues that political performances are moments along the circuit of production, distribution, and consumption that form the unity of the integrated news spectacle. It seeks to establish how the promotional logic of spectacle manifests itself within mediated political performance as an objective social force. I critique Debord's understanding of political representation and his subsequent renunciation of all forms of political mediation. I argue that forms of political representation and mediation are problematic, but required in modern large-scale societies. I then explore questions of how best to judge the legitimacy of political representation. Finally, in accessing the performance of politics I utilize Pierre Bourdieu's related concepts of "habitus" and "fields" of social interaction to ask who is best capable of taking advantage of the integrated news spectacle to further particular social and political interests.

Chapter Six explores the logic of the integrated news spectacle within the context of the 2003 U.S.–led invasion of Iraq. It teases out examples of the spectacular integration of military propaganda, the corporate and commercial interests of converged-media conglomerates, mythic storytelling, and the organizational requirements of their 24-hour broadcasters.

Finally, I conclude the book by pointing to some possibilities for social actors to engage in autonomous politics in their struggle against the integrated news spectacle.

## CHAPTER ONE

# Spectacle, Ritual, and Power

*Definition of ritual: rule-governed activity of a symbolic character which draws the attention of its participants to objects of thought and feeling which they hold to be of special importance.*
STEVEN LUKES

*the public is even more fond of entertainment than it is of information.*
WILLIAM RANDOLPH HEARST

Debates about the alleged benefits and dangers of popular culture and popular forms of journalism have a long and complex history. These unresolved quarrels continue to resonate within cultural and political life today and are, therefore, worthy of our attention; but because they have received thorough treatment elsewhere (Swingewood 1977; Brantlinger 1983; Street 1997), I will restrict my comments to a brief overview of the two main theoretical assessments of popular culture before turning my attention toward developing a third, and I believe more promising, theoretical position from which to approach the study of spectacular media.

## *Judging Popular Media*

Mass-society theorists are perhaps the most widely known critics of popular culture. This critique has both conservative and radical streams. The elitist-conservative variant appears first in classical writing about Greek and Roman popular culture. Here we see the elite distaste for the masses' appetite for bread and circuses (Brantlinger 1983: 53–81).[1] However, the modern 19th-century version is steeped in a complex reaction against an emerging bourgeois commercial culture, and also liberal democracy with its attendant privileging of popular and secular values. In the influential work of F.R. Leavis, important contrasts are made between high and low culture, the sacred and the profane, activity and passivity, information and entertainment. In the conservative view of popular culture, the hallowed values and traditions of Western civilization are at risk of deterioration due the baser instincts of the masses and their demands for a more egalitarian society. In this cause the masses have an ally in popular media. Instead of cultivating reason and taste—prerequisites for constructing visions of the good life—popular media cater to cheap emotional responses "and inculcate the choosing of the most immediate pleasures, got with the least effort" (Leavis and Thompson 1948, cited in Street 1997: 151). Writing in the early 1960s, well before the creation of the multichannel cable universe and 24-hour news stations, Daniel Boorstin would revisit these themes in his book *The Image,* in which he laments the loss of a more rooted culture tied to the civilizing influence of the printed word.

> The nuance, the perspective, the contradictions of historical development and social interaction were not made for the camera eye. In the flush of TV spectaculars, wider and wider mechanical advancements, the book is still the essential civilizing influence, able to penetrate the unknowns of human aspiration. (Boorstin 1992: 148)

For Boorstin, modern society's capacity to endlessly reproduce not only cultural products like journalism but experience itself—what he calls "pseudo-events"—has created a situation in which the language of images has replaced the language of ideals. Civilizing values of traditional culture have been placed "in limbo," he suggests, amidst the multiplication of images produced, by print and electronic media. A starker contrast is drawn by Neil Postman, who also laments the ascendancy of television—a medium, he says, that inevitably trumps informed public discourse with spectacular entertainment (Postman 1985).

In the radical variant of the mass-society critique, many of the same dualisms mentioned above (high/low culture, activity/passivity, etc.) repeat themselves. Both conservative and radical versions of the mass-society critique fear popular culture and see it as a form of corruption, but for very different reasons: conservatives view popular culture as a threat to the existing social order, while radicals see popular culture as part of an ideological system that sustains a dominant social order. This radical view is epitomized in the work of Frankfurt School theorists Max Horkheimer and Theodore Adorno (1979). The importance of the "culture industry," as they refer to it, lays in its ability to paper over social contradictions and strengthen dominant interpretations of reality. Commercial entertainment and news media provide people with categorizations of the values, norms, and expectations necessary to organize and administer social life—individual autonomy is lost and a new, seemingly benign, form of totalitarianism is born. "The liberation that amusement promises is freedom from thought and from negation" (144). Commodified media, they argue—including, they would no doubt add, such spectacular media events as the death of Princess Diana, a young mother struck down in her prime—strip tragedy of "its paradoxical significance" that "once lay in a hopeless resistance to mythic destiny" (152). Where in the past tragedy signaled a kind of heroic resistance to fate, in the context of modern consumer culture it represents the individual's false identity with the tropes of celebrity culture. The ability to envision a different kind of society, a society predicated on the needs and desires of individuals, is lost—"the idea of anything specific to themselves now persists only as an utterly abstract notion: personality scarcely signifies anything more than shining white teeth and freedom from body odor and emotions" (167).

The second major theoretical assessment of popular culture is populist in nature and provides a needed corrective to the elitist pessimism of the mass-society critiques. Once again, we find conservative and radical streams. "Conservative populism," John Street argues, "is the populism of the tabloid press" (Street 1997: 151). The brash and unapologetic tabloid gaze constructs a view of the world that contrasts honest, hardworking, and so-called ordinary people with their foes: "the state bureaucracy and the established, liberal elite" (151). Bill O'Reilly, the conservative host of Fox News's *The O'Reilly Factor,* and the former anchor of the tabloid newsmagazine program *Inside Edition,* sums up his role: "My job is to bring information to the 90 percent of Americans who don't have any power" (Sella 2001). Conservative populism celebrates the ability of "average people" to make their own rational choices concerning the kinds of popular entertainment and journalism they wish to view; and it assumes that those choices inevitably will be reflected in the marketplace. The logic of conservative populism has been extended to the realm of politics in an exhaustive defence of tabloidization by Brian McNair (2000). McNair defends the blanket news-media coverage extended to such stories as the Monicagate scandal and other types of spectacular media events by attacking the "dumbing-down" thesis launched by many media practitioners and critics (Franklin 1997; Nash 1998). Yes, today's political journalism is more focused on style and image than in the past, and it has become a kind of spectacle, but this is not a problem. McNair says this turn of events is an intelligible response "to changes in the technological, economic and political environments"—by which he means the introduction of 24-hour news channels, increased market competition, and the erasure of meaningful ideological distinctions between mainstream political parties following the U.S. Democratic and the British Labour Parties' move to the political center (McNair 2000: 171). Besides, McNair argues, "sleaze" reporting of political scandals can be a legitimate "response to a particular party's, and government's, attempt to claim a monopoly on moral worth" (McNair 2000: 173–4).

The media's "commercial need for audiences, and for the raw material from which journalism can be fashioned," he argues, "are creating new spaces for the accessing and meaningful representation of non-elite voices, as well as greater diversity in the styles and agendas employed by journalists" (172). Tabloid sensationalism, by this standard, is an openly democratic influence on the political public sphere.

The populist view of popular media also has a radical stream, one that similarly emphasizes the independent agency of people to construct their own meanings through consumption. Notable examples of this view can be found in the work of John Fiske (1989) and Kevin Glynn (2000), who celebrate the expressive use of cultural artifacts in everyday life to create contradictory and oppositional meanings that resist the dominant ideology. It is through the free play of popular culture, specifically tabloid culture in Glynn's case, that a sense of the possible is unearthed. The poststructuralist work of Mark Poster (1990) emphasizes ways in which subjectivities are constituted and potentially liberated through cultural texts or language systems. Poster argues that electronic media should be viewed not as technologies that deliver or exchange messages but as "wrappings of language" that create new contexts of experience that are "unrelated to the material limitations of everyday life" and that are, therefore, self-referential (45–46). Poster rejects the insistence of the mass-society perspective that audiences are passive and argues that individuals are profoundly engaged by media (46). Sign systems, such as advertisements, news stories, and opinion surveys, constitute subjects in a manner that is independent and unanchored to the material world. Poster insists that the sign system of television advertisements, and one might add spectacular media events, is ambiguous. Subjects are spoken for by the code "as a dependent spectator, constituting the subject as a consumer. But in so doing it dissolves the autonomous subject, the rational male bourgeois" (67). By incorporating the subject into the text's sign system, Poster argues, the subject has been set free of any centered subject position. Spectacular forms of media, read as a language text, open up the possibility—however immaterial—of imagining other subject positions based on notions of gender or race; they allow a critique of hegemonic forms of subjectivity. The public that is spoken into existence through news discourse exists within a sign system that, because of its independence as a form of discourse, can be manipulated and subverted through the active use or play of the news text. Individuals can make their own meanings. Following this logic, and contrary to Horkheimer and Adorno, Princess Diana *can* be read as a tragic figure. Diana can become a symbol of feminist resistance within patriarchal society, a woman who was literally hounded to death by paparazzi eager for yet another photograph of her in an extramarital relationship for which many of her foes believed she should be punished. She was for some people the "fallen woman," who, once punished for her sins, is resurrected again as a "secular saint" or "postmodern Madonna" (Gaillard 1998; Maitland 1998). Princess Diana is, as another reading has it, an "unlikely feminist hero" who in trying to reinvent herself became a model for other women (Griffin 1999: 250). Of course, in these examples I have not exhausted the possible readings of Diana's death and the public mourning that followed; these various readings are what constitute the Diana text. It is then for audiences to construct meaning out of spectacular media events by relating each narrative back to their own lives.

Instead of mourning or celebrating popular culture, I want to rethink the terms of debate of journalism's relationship to entertainment and democracy. In the case of modern news media—highly visible elements of popular culture—such an analysis would integrate the insights of cultural theory into an understanding of the day-to-day work routines of journalism and its economic and material context. Any analysis of journalism as a cultural practice must understand its historical conditions of existence; but it must also remain sensitive to journalism's core storytelling function—its ability to facilitate the construction of meaning, which may, depending on the context and the uses to which the story is put, serve interests of power and domination, strengthen bonds of solidarity within society, weaken them, or allow for forms of countervailing politics. It must strike a balance between structure and agency; and consequently, it must allow for an analysis of the process of social integration that avoids reactionary responses of dismay or uncritical complacency. Popular culture cannot be judged in such a categorical fashion. "Popular culture can, in the way it offers forms of identity, become engaged with politics, in particular with the politics of citizenship, the right to belong and to be recognized" (Street 1997: 12). Conversely, and highlighting the deepest fears of Horkheimer and Adorno, John Street reminds us, "Popular culture's ability to focus passion and to express defiance also allows it to become a form of political management" (13). A news story, as with all popular culture, is in itself *politically ambiguous*. Its status as a cultural artifact can be progressive or reactionary depending upon the context and the uses to which it is put. News stories are enmeshed within a troika of values associated with modern Western societies, familiar values that have been given differing emphasis in the works cited above; they are *freedom, equality* and *order/solidarity*. As Denis McQuail argues, these three values form the core principles at stake in debates about democratic communication and they often come into conflict with one another (McQuail 1996: 70–76). Complete freedom to communicate is hard to reconcile with equality of communicative opportunities; while equality can put limits on freedom and clash with hierarchical or otherwise oppressive forms of order. And yet, whereas diversity of experience is crucial, modern society would cease to exist were it not for some level of shared values, understandings, and solidaristic experiences that allow for the reproduction of society over time. All three values are essential for large-scale modern societies and must be balanced against each other. The freedom to communicate, equality of communicative opportunities, and the social harmony required to pursue free and equal communicative experiences are all indispensable. Danger arises when any one value is hypostatized and privileged over the other two. What is required is a method of examining how news stories are used and under what historical circumstances. Before doing that we must first steer our way through some existing debates concerning the uses and abuses of news media.

## Entertainment Versus Information

Conservative and radical critics of spectacular journalism make a distinction between entertainment and information. The contrast between the two categories of storytelling is at the heart of the normative debate over journalistic professionalism. Critics such as Bob Franklin (1997) worry about the increasing substitution of what he calls "newszak" for coverage of government affairs and international relations, which he documents as being on the decline in Britain's print and broadcast media during the 1990s.

> Entertainment has superceded the provision of information; human interest has supplanted the public interest; measured judgement has succumbed to sensationalism; the trivial has triumphed over the weighty; the intimate relationship of celebrities from soap operas, the world of sport or the royal family are judged more 'newsworthy' than the reporting of significant issues and events of international consequence. Traditional news values have been undermined by new values; 'infotainment' is rampant. (Franklin 1997: 4)

Entertainment is here associated with distraction and passive spectatorship, while information is associated with facts and engaged analysis. Entertainment diverts our attention from the weighty topics of the day, such as health care, education, and poverty. Entertainment is an indulgence, while information is the currency of responsible civic action and the basic building block of politics. One U.S. study, for example, found that 75 percent of respondents to a survey could identify Linda Tripp's role in the "Monicagate" scandal, while only 13 percent knew Clinton had signed the Republican-sponsored Welfare Reform bill. Moreover, the same study found that respondents tended to assume Clinton took a so-called liberal stance on most issues, when, as his support for the Welfare Reform bill indicates, these impressions were often contradicted by his political record (Lewis, Morgan, and Jhally 1998).

The antimony between entertainment and news is strongly anchored in the liberal-democratic tradition, which believes news media should facilitate a rational exchange of information between government and citizens. More recently, Jürgen Habermas's (1989) conception of the public sphere has been used as an ideal standard of comparison by both liberal and radical intellectuals concerned with preserving a process for the free development and rational exchange of critical public opinion. For Habermas, the potential of critical public opinion has been subverted as the result of colonization by consumer culture. The public sphere, ideally a domain of critical debate in which not only government but all forms of authority are challenged through the free exchange of rational discourse among formally equal citizens, has become a theater of promotion in which authority is displayed for the public's passive consumption using the tricks of modern public relations. Entertainment is always bad—it distracts citizens from living the good life and it supports forms of social domination. Habermas's bleak portrayal of the "refeudalization" of media continues in the tradition of Horkheimer and Adorno, and therefore carries with it many of the faults of mass-society theory—it is unnecessarily elitist and, as Habermas himself later admitted, it underestimates the ability of audiences to resist forms of domination and power (Habermas 1992: 439). Nonetheless, the potential danger of confusing entertainment with news *is* real; as Jostein Gripsrud argues, perhaps the most dangerous aspect of the substitution of entertaining tabloid-like stories is that they offer melodramatic explanations of the world that emphasize the irrational, the emotional and the personal, over the complex, the abstract and structural. "Modern society," Gripsrud argues, "*is* an abstract phenomenon. It does not present itself as a 'whole' to the 'naked eye' or to our everyday experience. The relationships between the various developments in various areas—economic, social and cultural, nationally and internationally—can only be understood in highly abstract, theoretical terms" (Gripsrud 1992: 91). The spectacle of starving African children may well elicit an emotional response among Western viewers whose purse strings are loosened long enough for international aid organizations to successfully solicit donations, but the images of emaciated young bodies cannot *explain* the combination of political, economic, social, racial, and environmental forces responsible for the crisis.

While it is certainly true, as Habermas argues, that journalism would be incapable of sustaining free and equal participation in critical debates about public policy if it were entirely preoccupied with the distraction of pure entertainment, another qualification is required; it does not necessarily follow that an entertaining news story is without democratic value. Good storytelling—stories that grab our attention and excite the imaginations of a broad range of people, as well as challenge established commonsense truths—should be at the core of journalism. James Curran (1996) makes a series of related points aimed at traditional liberal critics, but his remarks also can be applied to conservative and radical critiques of news. First, these critics, he suggests, overemphasize the role of rationality in individual decision making. Individuals have idiosyncratic and selective ways of consuming the news (Neuman, Just, and Crigler 1992 cited in Curran 1996) and may have moral, psychological, and material reasons to accept or reject competing explanations of social reality (Bennett and Edelman 1985: 161; Edelman 1988). Second, Curran argues that an "untenable distinction" is made "between information and representation. . . . Missing from this analysis is a recognition that ideas and *systems of representation* are part of the discursive arsenal which competing groups use to advance their interests" (Curran 1996: 101). In other words, they are constitutive elements of modern politics. The news media, in his view, must take account of these different forms of rhetoric and discursive strategies if they are to open up public discourse and ensure that all views are considered. Using dramatic narratives that incorporate vernacular language can broaden access to political discussion. And surely, we can accept this point without taking the more extreme position adopted by McNair (2000) that tabloidization enhances democracy.

Finally, Curran suggests, entertainment genres, such as fiction, can provide "cognitive maps that structure and interpret reality, and provide a commentary upon our common social processes" (Curran 1996: 102). It is this last point that I wish to explore in more detail with respect to news stories and cultural performance. Rational procedures of public decision making cannot be rejected outright without falling into the postmodern abyss of complete relativity; but at the same time, one must account for the empirical reality that news, and spectacular news in particular, is situated within a cultural system of communication that does not always engage in the rational exchange of information and argument.

### News as Dramatic Ritual

We must pay heed to the fact that spectacular news stories such as Monicagate absorb a disproportionate amount of journalistic resources, deflect public attention from important issues, and contribute to a misinformed public. Journalism's core purpose should be about providing important and useful stories to citizens, so they can, as Gripsrud puts it, "collectively influence or change their social situation" (Gripsrud 2000: 286). This is, after all, the essence of politics. Nevertheless, news is not only about the linear transmission of information. Such a model of communication focuses attention on the content transmitted, its quality and character, whether it has been altered as a result of the transmission, and, if so, it asks whether the alteration is the result of organizational work routines (Fishman 1980; Ericson, Baranek, and Chan 1987, 1989) or if it was instrumentally manipulated to insert a particular managerial or ownership bias (Herman and Chomsky 1988; Winter 1997)—all important issues. Nevertheless, a linear model of communication occludes an understanding of the means by which meanings are forged and shared within culture. A linear model of communication cannot grasp the intricate and complex manner in which meanings are produced, circulated, consumed, and reproduced within culture—and yet, the linear model is implicit in the critiques of tabloidization. The often prurient ingredients of these stories—the licentious behavior, betrayal, and public shame associated with many political scandals, for example—do not sufficiently explain why these stories resonate throughout civil society and are, in turn, reproduced on such a grand scale.[2] These stories, in other words, are not simply examples of inappropriate or distorted information flow. If we are to understand the significance and scale of spectacular news stories—Why it is that a presidential peccadillo involving a young intern, a blue dress and cigar, could so completely involve a 24-hour news channel that MSNBC would eventually be nicknamed the All-Monica-All-the-Time network?—we must first comprehend the general media culture that all news stories feed *upon* and feed *back into*. Examining news stories as ritual forms of communication takes us partway to that goal.

News is not only about the dissemination of information; it is a dramatic "portrayal of the contending forces in the world" (Carey 1992: 20). Communication is not merely about transmitting information to isolated, formally free; and equal individuals who use data to make rationally informed judgments in isolation, or through intersubjective rational argument, as Habermas's theory of communicative action would have it; "communication is a symbolic process whereby reality is produced, maintained, repaired, and transformed" (23). There is, as James Carey argues, a ritual element to news in which "communication is directed not toward the extension of messages in space but toward the maintenance of society in time; not the act of imparting information but the representation of shared beliefs" (18). Research in this tradition owes its origins to the pioneering work of Emile Durkheim. "There can be no society," posits Durkheim, "that does not experience the need at regular intervals to maintain and strengthen the collective feelings and ideas that provide its coherence and distinct individuality" (Durkheim 1995: 429). Civil society, in this view, is also a cultural space in which collective identities are forged as an essential precondition for the proper functioning of stratified and complex modern societies.

David Chaney argues that mediated forms of public life—that is, forms of dramatization, such as news and entertainment—provide us with the tools necessary to "tell ourselves about ourselves" (Chaney 1993: 3). "The spectacle," argues David Chaney, by which he means the dramatization of collective life as opposed to its direct experience, "is more than a representation of social life; it functions as the practical medium through which order is sustained and the collectivity given an appearance" (42). Researchers in the neo-Durkheimian tradition are interested in phatic communication—the ways in which cultural performances can strengthen social relationships through storytelling. The ritual perspective on media is summarized nicely by Jostein Gripsrud.

> The media are storytellers, reiterating stories that, like ancient myths, serve as ways of thinking about existential and social matters individuals and groups have to deal with in their everyday lives. Such a function overrides distinctions between genres, such as those between news and other ostensibly informational genres on the one hand and those explicitly dedicated to entertainment on the other. (Gripsrud 2000: 295)

Investigations of ritual performances do not focus on the way the world is reported. In this tradition, news stories "are less reports, selecting and distorting a set of events in the real world, than accounts put together after the manner of literature according to a sense of what is necessary and appropriate" (Elliott 1980: 171).

This growing body of literature views cultural texts, such as the 24-hour news coverage of the deaths of Princess Diana and John Kennedy Jr. or the custody battle over young Elián González, as resources that people use to narrate their social lives— to tell stories about themselves and their collective life together. Cultural artifacts— such as news stories—are read as texts that provide richly symbolic experiences, which in turn are used by people to make sense out of the seeming chaos of modern life. They have "existential utility" (Sparks 2000: 27–28). Stories, in short, are used for purposes of social integration and stability. The view is shared by veteran journalist Trina McQueen, who defends the predominance of spectacular news stories—what she calls "hot stuff"—on the grounds that these types of stories provide people with the opportunity to explore moral and ethical issues. "Perhaps," says McQueen, "when we gather in the lunchroom to discuss O.J. or Paul Bernardo or Paula Jones or Alan Eagleson [a National Hockey League player's agent embroiled in scandal] or Diana, we are really discussing our moral options and ourselves" (McQueen 1998).

A uniquely Canadian ritualized narrative of national unification in death was enacted through media coverage of the memorial services for former Prime Minister Pierre Elliot Trudeau. "He enthralled us all" trumpeted the banner headline in the *Globe and Mail*. In the edition announcing Trudeau's death, no fewer than twelve pages were devoted to repeating the basic myth articulated on the paper's front page, a myth readers are told that helped shape the modern Canadian identity: "He was— is—our one mythological prime minister, our one mythic hero. . . . Pierre Trudeau. . . was the divine enhancement of the earthbound Canadian" (Valpy 2000a). Similarly, the televised funeral of Canadian Olympic curling champion Sandra Schmirler presented itself as a moment to rehearse mythically foundational tales of small-town Canadian life.[3]

Of particular interest is Daniel Dayan and Elihu Katz's (1992) cultural-anthropological work on "media events." Here we have researchers working in the neo-Durkheimian tradition who are specifically concerned with large-scale, live-televised events, such as British Royal weddings, the funeral of John F. Kennedy, and the visit of Pope John Paul II in Poland, events that are global in reach and impact. Dayan and Katz offer an extremely circumscribed definition of media events. They restrict their research to live events that are organized and preplanned outside of the media themselves, often by governments. Media events monopolize media attention during their duration, and in doing so, Dayan and Katz argue, break life's everyday routine to create a sense of special occasion; media events are "high holidays of mass communication" in which citizens take time out of their regular schedules to join together as part of a collective televisual audience. Once again, as with other work in the neo-Durkheimian tradition, Dayan and Katz take pains to emphasize how these "great ceremonial events celebrate order and its restoration" (9).

Three narrative "scripts" for media events are identified: contests, conquests, and coronations. Each script is a representational form corresponding to one of Weber's three types of authority: legal/rational, charisma, and tradition. Contests include election debates, sporting events, and televised senate hearings, which Dayan and Katz refer to as "rule-governed battles of champions" (26). Examples of conquests include Pope John Paul II's trip to Poland and Egyptian president Anwar Sadat's historic journey of peace to Israel in 1977. Finally, coronations are heavily involved in ceremony and usually involve funerals and parades (26). The televised funeral of Princess Diana fits their admittedly "parsimonious" definition perfectly. Despite their differences, say Dayan and Katz, each of these scripts, or types of media events, celebrates reconciliation—with the rule of law, one's opponent, or universal experience.

Dayan and Katz put great stock in Victor Turner's concept of the "liminal" experience in ritual. The liminal stage is the in-between stage of ritual, when the structure of society is temporarily suspended. It is a moment when rules may be bent or broken and social reality is not understood as taken for granted, but is, instead, open to possibilities of what could or should be; as Turner says, liminality marks "the scene and time for the emergence of a society's deepest values in the form of sacred dramas and objects." It is a time, he argues, of "radical skepticism" in which the daily reality is suspended and "where people are allowed to think about how they think, about the terms in which they conduct their thinking, or to feel about how they feel in daily life" (Turner 1984: 22).

Media events, insist Dayan and Katz, contain their own liminal moments of cultural reflexivity. Cultural performances, such as royal weddings and presidential inaugurations, remind "society of what it aspires to be rather than what it is" (Dayan and Katz 1992: ix). They are moments of utopian introspection and longing. Michael Ignatieff makes a similar argument regarding the significance of the memorial service for Princess Diana, televised live around the world.

> The campaign for a people's funeral for a people's princess became a great popular uprising, not just against the Royal Family but against the indignity of dying and the impoverishment of our memorial rituals. The public wanted something grand for her because they wanted something better for themselves than hospital deaths and dry-eyed cremations. The popular uprising that forced an unwilling monarch to pay public tribute to Diana was actually demanding the right to define the protocols of public mourning. (Ignatieff 1998)[4]

Her tragic death, Ignatieff argues, became "the catalyst" for individuals' "suppressed emotions."

Here we have an example that meets many of the prerequisites set out by Dayan and Katz: the event was televised live, it was organized by nonmedia organizations and the event clearly did mark off a special moment in time in which many people became disengaged from their everyday routines to partake in a shared, if heavily mediated, experience. Where Ignatieff, differs is that he observes a level of conflict over publicly held values that is not accounted for by Dayan and Katz.

I will return to this important distinction in a moment. But first I want to suggest that Dayan and Katz's focus on live-ceremonial events handicaps their analysis, as does their reliance on a functionalist theoretical explanation of the uses to which such media events are put. In their pursuit of a rigorous social-scientific definition, Dayan and Katz exclude an examination of how media events, as they narrowly define them, are situated within a broader system of news production and civil society—a civil society stratified along social cleavages such as class, race, and gender. Secondly, while a great deal of the televised media coverage of the Diana event was live, most of it was not. Surely, a crucial aspect of these media events is the extent to which cultural performances so thoroughly resonate throughout the entire mediascape, in print as well as broadcast. As Paddy Scannell notes, the "aura" attributed to media events by Dayan and Katz is hard to sustain in a market-oriented media environment increasingly characterized by pay-per-view and pay-per-channel access (Scannell 1995: 155). Media coverage of Diana's death was important, not only because it provided a shared live televisual moment infused with emotional images of secular rituals, and "spontaneously" erected shrines in her honor (Walter 1999). It was important because it fueled news and current-affairs coverage for weeks following her death and still continues to resonate today throughout popular culture in various ways from annual stories marking the anniversary of her death to the continuing coverage of her eldest son, Prince William, and the sale of kitschy Diana memorabilia (Kear and Steinberg 1999, Merck 1998). The unprecedented scale and intensity of the media coverage—that is, until it was matched and eventually surpassed by subsequent media events such as the death of John F. Kennedy Jr., the shooting deaths at Columbine high school in Denver, and the child custody battle of Elián González—cannot be captured using Dayan and Katz's, admittedly, "parsimonious" definition because it excludes an examination of the dialectic between the real-world event, its mediated construction and civil society.

One notable attempt to extend the Dayan and Katz model to include an analysis of the relationship of media events to civil society is provided by Jeffrey Alexander and Ronald Jacobs (1998). Alexander and Jacobs believe Dayan and Katz's model to be a sound corrective to the implicit and false assumptions of the mass-society critique discussed earlier; those assumptions include: passive audiences, a single public, and an exclusively rational model of communication (26). In other words, Alexander and Jacobs reject a strictly "cognitivist" understanding of communication.

> . . . while the Habermasian notion of the public sphere has been important for recognizing the centrality of discourse, it errs by hypostatizing a notion of communication as being involved singularly with rational processes of reaching consensus. . . . Civil society

is a cultural space in which different individuals and groups 'narrate the social' (cf. Sherwood 1994) and where citizens actively construct their own understandings of real and ideal civil society by filtering overarching discourse and narratives through multiple public spheres and communities. (Alexander and Jacobs 1998: 29)

Alexander and Jacobs emphasize the cultural plurality of civil society in which competing groups attempt to *narrate the social* by drawing upon the available stock of explanatory narratives and frameworks—stories that serve to explain collective and historical experience. The media are crucial players in democratic life, and while one of their tasks is to circulate information to ensure that citizens are properly informed, another, perhaps more important role, they argue, is to facilitate rituals of communication—the representation of shared beliefs as opposed to the transfer of messages in space. The function of cultural performance, they argue, is not to impart ideology, but to produce and maintain shared definitions of reality that, in turn, make possible not only the maintenance of community and social order but pluralistic politics itself.

[S]ocial actions, movements and identities are guided by narrative understandings. Furthermore, by connecting their self-narratives to collective narratives, individuals can identify with such imagined communities as class, gender, race, ethnicity and nation. (31)

Alexander and Jacobs are interested in preserving a theoretical understanding of political agency within a liberal-pluralist framework; power in their view is diffuse and observable in the competitive struggle by disparate groups and organizations within civil society to have their narrative interpretation of events gain authority. Nonetheless, each of these competing narratives through their articulation and repetition are constitutively linked to the broader cultural environment, which is always referenced by competing groups and made use of by audiences in the construction of meaning. Two fundamental components, or "structural levels," according to Alexander and Jacobs, make up the cultural environment: the "deep structure" of the "common semiotic system" used to interpret communication, and the "temporal structure of common narrative frameworks through which public actors chart the movement of themselves, and others, in real historical time. These two cultural environments simultaneously constrain and enable public actions in civil society" (30). Together, say Alexander and Jacobs, they form the constitution of meaning. Rearticulating Durkheim's work in the *Elementary Forms of Religious Life,* Alexander and Jacobs argue that the common semiotic code typifies actors and events into binary elements such as the sacred/profane, citizen/enemy, democratic/anti-democratic, etc. "This 'common code' not only allows for a degree of intersubjectivity among public speakers, but also provides a relatively stable system for evaluating events and persons."

Within "American civil society," for example, "the semiotic code is organized around the sacred signs of rational and controlled motivations, open and trusting relationships and impersonal, rule-regulated institutions" (30).

Narratives help individuals identify their place within civil society, with whom they share allegiance and to whom their interests are opposed. Narratives, therefore, help guide and structure the activity of social actors. Alexander and Jacobs argue that the oppositional readings of media coverage that resulted from the Watergate scandal and the 1991 beating of African-American motorist Rodney King by Los Angeles police officers were actualized, in part, through the liminal quality of these narratives. As ritualized narratives, they invoke the sacred binary codes latent within civil society that motivates individuals and movements to social action. The semiotic and narrative structures provide the constitution of meaning through which "the utopian vision" is articulated (38). And, certainly, the invocation of a utopian vision is an integral part of Ignatieff's analysis of the public reaction to the death of the Princess of Wales and media coverage of the mourning of Pierre Trudeau and Sandra Schmirler (cf. Alexander 1988).

### Remembering Power

The value of Alexander and Jacobs's neo-Durkheimian reading of media culture is that it draws our attention to the complex interrelationship between civil society and media culture that is played out through cultural performance, an analysis that is missing from linear models of communication. However, serious shortcomings remain, due in large part to implicit functionalist assumptions about social integration and its relationship to power and domination. In other words, the ritual view of communication sketched above, while important in certain respects, is not sufficiently sensitive to social relations of power.

First, at the heart of the neo-Durkheimian position is a basic assumption that a society's deep-seated values—those that, in Alexander and Jacobs's view, form the "deep semiotic structure" of the sacred and profane—exist prior to social activity. "This semiotic structure," they say, "develops not so much through the agency of individual *speech,* but rather through the incremental changes inherent in the historicity of *language* (cf. Saussure 1964 [1916]). In other words, while the semiotic code is always in a process of incremental flux, it appears to a language community as immutable" (Alexander and Jacobs 1998: 30). So, while Alexander and Jacobs stress how disparate social groups compete to have their narrative explanations of temporal events gain credence and authority using forms of cultural performance, they discount suggestions that the semiotic structure used in the formulation and execution of these narratives is in any way socially constructed. *Value consensus, just is, that's all.* The functionalist assumption that ritualized expression and performance is evidence of preexisting, or a priori value integration is quite simply tautological. "The first question," as Steven Lukes suggests in his critique of neo-Durkheimian readings of political ritual, "is whether, to what extent, and in what ways, a society *does* hold together" (Lukes 1977: 63). As Lukes says, neo-Durkheimians too often assume that there are few "divergences in the interpretation of such values within a society" (62). There are some notable exceptions within the news-as-ritual tradition. James Carey (1998) modifies Dayan and Katz's model to include media events that are not purely integrative. There can also be, argues Carey, rituals of excommunication, or shame and status degradation. The former define "the permissible range of social discourse," while the latter delimit "the consequences for transgressing this range" (55). The 1998 impeachment of U.S. president Bill Clinton and the subsequent public ridicule he endured following the publicity of his extramarital affair with Monica Lewinsky surely fall into this category. Carey's intervention into the debate is welcome to the extent that it acknowledges social deviance and, importantly, that cultural performances are used to reassert dominant values and cultural boundaries of acceptable behavior. I want to argue that "visualizing deviance" (Ericson, Baranek, and Chan 1987) *is* one of the core contributions made by news workers to the reproduction of social order; but Carey still leaves unanswered the question of the origin of these underlying values. Whose values are they? How are they produced? Do some people's narratives count more than others? If so, why, and whose interests do they serve?

John Langer's (1998) work on ritualized tabloid televison narratives goes partway to answering some of the questions I have posed; in particular, whose values are represented and served. Langer is concerned with social relations of power and how they are manifested within tabloid metanarratives. Langer agrees that communities are constituted through ritual and that order is regulated by revealing the dramatic structure of stories. He goes further to suggest that, through their repetition, tabloid stories—what he calls the "other news"—reveal a subsystem that works through the flow of news broadcasts and generates "a commentary on causality and its disintegration" (142). The flux and uncertainty of modern life is powerfully accented by the "other news" with its emphasis on "remarkable" occurrences, "victims' stories," and "disrupture and disorder." Through repetition in media reports, the "mythic structure" of these stories reveals itself while providing a resolution to the contradiction between "permanence and change." Langer's analysis can be applied to the coverage of the mourning of John F. Kennedy Jr. Audiences are given the opportunity to rehearse the myth of Camelot—in which the Kennedy clan represents a nation's idealism and collective hope for a better future, while simultaneously embodying the tragedy of dashed dreams that must be borne stoically. MSNBC invoked this contradiction and its mythic resolution when quoting President Clinton's response to the accident while he presided over a ceremony honoring the U.S. Women's World Cup soccer champions—an interesting cultural performance in itself that tapped into the well-known narrative of the "Kennedy curse" and mixed it with a seemingly unrelated pop-culture event to produce a sorrow-inflected pean to American national identity and social purpose.

> "We can come together in sorrow or in joy if it reflects the values that we honor most," Clinton said as he greeted the soccer team on the White House south lawn that was once John F. Kennedy Jr.'s home.
> "This is one of those moments. The Women's World Cup champions here at the White House brought America to its feet, had us screaming our lungs out with pride and joy." Clinton. said. But, he added, "we all know this is both a moment of celebration and a moment of sadness for the United States, and our thoughts and prayers are with the families of John Kennedy and Carolyn and Lauren Bessette." (MSNBC.com 1999)

The tragedy, said Clinton, united Americans "as a national family." The tragedy of the so-called Kennedy curse—the myth of the wealthy and powerful family that is at once blessed with civic virtue and cursed by the dogged shadow of death—was invoked in almost every media report of the fatal plane crash. Even the *Globe and Mail,* Canada's self-proclaimed national newspaper, felt the need to reproduce the myth: "By now, after more than a half century of tears, the rituals of tragedy are agonizingly familiar to the Kennedys, and to the country that has made them its most celebrated and benighted family" (Cohen 1999a). For Langer, then, the repetition of these myths resolves the contradiction of the constant upheaval of modern life and the need to soldier on regardless. Rich people die in sudden tragic deaths, too. To this extent, Langer is in agreement with the position taken by Alexander and Jacobs—myths embody deep-structure of the sacred and profane; but where Langer departs is in his emphasis on power. Borrowing from John Thomson (1990), Langer suggests that ritualized tabloid stories are ideological to the extent that they create meanings "in the service of power."

> The other news offers modes of explanation and sense-making which displace and mask the social, political and historical context in which events occur and can be made to mean. The personal and the impersonal become naturalized forms of expression and intelligibility within a news discourse which deflects attention from what is perhaps a more crucial factor in explaining the conditions of mastery and its nemesis—the structure of domination and subordination. (Langer 1998:150)

In this regard, Langer argues, ritualized tabloid stories contribute to a "retreat" from the world of social activity. Recurrent stories about natural disasters and other tragedies work to suture individuals into narrative structures that suggest people should resign themselves to fate. "If control 'out there' is not possible, as tabloid television reiterates on a daily basis, perhaps it can be attained in the realms of the private and the personal, an increasingly large part of which, as it turns out, has now been incorporated into the processes of commodification and consumption" (167). Langer says these myths help to "naturalize" consumerism "as part of everyday consciousness and practice" (167). This is an extremely important argument that I want to return to and extend; but first, I want to outline the problems associated with the structural/functionalist approach detailed above—namely that it is ahistorical.

### Historicizing News Ritual

Langer's assessment of the "other news" is, as mentioned, an improvement upon the work on news rituals by Dayan and Katz and Alexander and Jacobs, because it acknowledges the existence of social relations of power. It points to the structural needs of consumer culture that benefits from narrative forms that emphasize personalization over structural determinants. Nevertheless, Langer's method suffers from the same functionalist assumptions. Where neo-Durkheimians assume that ritualized expression and performance is evidence of preexisting, or a priori value integration, Langer, with his neo-Marxist–inflected structural analysis, suggests that ritualized narratives and cultural performances are themselves evidence of structural domination. Together they form flip sides of the same tautological coin; missing is an investigation of the historically situated *processes* contributing to narrative production, distribution and use of cultural texts within the context of consumer culture. The focus on narrative forms does not refer back to historically situated social actors and narrative production. The constitutive features of narrative forms are separated from their material existence and become reified. They become mythical narrative structures whose socially constructed origins remain occluded. To return to the central question I have posed, if we wish to understand why particular narrative forms—those of the All-Monica-All-the-Time variety—have increased in intensity and scale within the news media, we must investigate the historical processes involved in the transformation. We must investigate the complex multidimensional relationships among narrative forms, cultural performances, and social and economic structures.

Ronald Jacobs (1996) has put forward his own multi-dimensional research proposal in which he considers "production, reception and content as interdependent and overlapping 'moments' of the communication process" (376). Jacobs's focus is on the empirical investigation of these overlapping moments. News workers, he argues, rely on "literary archetypes" that are "crucial to the 'performance' of the news. . . . During each step of news production—discovery, research, production, enactment—events [are] constructed as parts of stories"; this holds for the perceived newsworthiness of an event through to the research and performance of the story by television anchors and reporters. At all levels, says Jacobs, the public, as the "implied audience," is taken into consideration (384).

Narrative forms are used to structure news production (Darnton 1975, Schudson 1982), and the contribution made on this point by cultural-text theorists is welcome.

But Jacobs's multidimensional methodology remains blind to the broader social totality in which these narratives are produced, articulated, and read. Again, narrative archetypes are accepted as forms that exist prior to experience, and as a result, have no social history of their own (383). The story form of the self-reliant hero, for example, may have existed for centuries and have appeared across many different cultures, but that does not mean that its particular revival in news discourse under the guise of human-interest profiles of successful entrepreneurs has no historical existence, or that it cannot be linked to particular social interests; the same can be said for its semiotic partner, the profane narrative of the welfare bum.[5] In other words, the narrative form cannot be severed from its social content. It is the linkage to a broader social totality that can help us answer why some narratives gain acceptance over others. For this we need historical analysis. We need to understand the historical and social factors that have led major news organizations to privilege particular narrative forms, i.e., the deaths of Princess Diana and John F. Kennedy Jr. We need to understand, as Lukes suggests, how and why things happen as they do. Victor Turner's concept of liminality draws our attention to processes in the cultural sphere that, as he and his intellectual descendants argue, allow human beings to dramatize the sacred and profane and in doing so hold those ideals up to collective scrutiny. However, as Renato Resaldo (1989) argues, "Turner's conclusions emphasize principles of social structure more than the human processes he so thickly dramatizes" (96). In other words, while Turner's concept of liminality is used to suggest the possibility of cultural reflexivity, it is more often used to emphasize a more conservative view of societal integration.

Pierre Bourdieu's concept of the "habitus" provides us with a middle path that allows for the existence of background normative assumptions about what is, or should be—the existence of a normative order—without separating them from material reality as reified ideals of the sacred. The individual and collective practices of everyday life, says Bourdieu, are conditioned at the level of the habitus, by which he means the complex accumulation of experiences accrued through an individual's or group's practical and historical engagement with social structures, such as the economy, class, race, family, gender, etc. Out of these experiences are produced, what he calls "transposable dispositions . . . which in their turn are the basis of the perception and appreciation of all subsequent experiences" (Bourdieu 1990: 53–54). Deep-seated values do not preexist society; instead, they hold a dialectical relationship to society, they contribute to the production of society at the same time that they are products of society. "Nothing is more misleading," says Bourdieu, "than the illusion created by hindsight in which all the traces of a life, such as the works of an artist or the events at a biography, appear as the realization of an essence that seems to pre-exist them" (55). Individuals, groups, and movements hold deep-seated values, but they are the product of historically situated practical experiences. Sacred values are always invoked within "social fields" that have their own historical conditions of existence.

❖

An extremely high-profile and dramatic example of the public rehearsal of so-called deep-seated values followed the inconclusive ballot results of the 2000 U.S. presidential election—itself a spectacular media event, minus any sex or death (the seduction of power and loss of a political life aside). At one point, an unofficial tally by the Associated Press gave Republican George W. Bush a slim statewide lead of 300 votes against his Democratic rival, Vice President Al Gore. With the election's outcome hanging on Florida's 25 Electoral College votes, both candidates invoked sacred narratives to woo public opinion and gain the moral high ground over their opponent while court battles continued to determine whether hand recounts would be allowed. Gore spoke solemnly of the sacred obligation "to respect every voter and every vote." Bush, on the other hand, appealed for Gore's concession on the grounds that the health of the U.S. republic—a value that apparently trumps the rights of individual voters to have their ballots counted accurately—hung on resolving the dispute quickly. Bush "believes the time has arrived," said one Republican spokesman, "for our nation to begin the process of moving forward" (Cohen 2000a). The importance of Bourdieu's concept of the habitus is that it allows for social agency in the use of culture while acknowledging the existence of social structures that are historically situated. The post-election spectacle of two competing candidates trying to narrate their particular versions of social experience needs to be understood within the context of the massive multimillion-dollar war chests accumulated on both sides for the purpose of fighting this public-relations battle. In addition, it must be noted that the spectacle was initiated by competitive pressures among the U.S. commercial networks. After retracting their earlier award of Florida's Electoral College votes to Gore, NBC, CBS, CNN and ABC all prematurely declared Bush President Elect, a while after Fox News's election-night decision desk recommended calling Florida in Bush's favor. That decision was further complicated by news that John Ellis—the head of Fox's decision desk—is Bush's cousin, a committed Republican whose comments in support of the Bush campaign have appeared in the *Washington Post*. It was also reported that Ellis had made phone calls to the Bush camp during the course of the ballot count on election night. As Tom Rosensteil, director of the Project for Excellence in Journalism, notes, Fox's "marketing slogan 'We report, you decide' is obliterated by the fact that one candidate's first cousin is actually deciding, and then they report"(Kurtz 2000b). The information is crucial in light of the use by the Bush camp of the premature election call to act as if the election had been won and then taken back. On one occasion Bush referred to his wife as the First Lady elect and assured the public that he was taking the appropriate steps to ensure that his administration would be ready when the time came to assume power.

How cultural texts are produced and performed is clearly historically contingent. A news story's description of competing normative values, such as individual and collective rights, is also historically contingent. One of the more delicious ironies of the U.S. presidential debacle is that a Republican presidential candidate who supported a platform of individual and states' rights was now using a federal court to block hand recounts of ballots in Florida on the grounds that they were unreliable.[6]

What neo-Durkheimian cultural text theory lacks is an explanation for why some people's understandings, or readings, count. One must not only attend to the potential meanings of cultural texts, but also to how they were made and by whom. In other words, the cultural critic must ask who has the ability to promote the narrative of Olympic communalism—as President Clinton did in his response to the death of John F. Kennedy Jr.—to what purpose that text is put, and whose interests are served? Cultural texts and the performance of ritualized narratives are constitutively connected to struggles over the definition of reality—what ought to be taken seriously or taken for granted. It is in this sense that they must be understood as sites of political struggle (Gruneau 1999: 48). "The business of judging popular culture," as John Street says, "is part of a political process, one involving the exercise of power and the attempt to legitimate that power" (Street 1997: 176). Was Bill Clinton, by invoking and combining the myth of Olympic communalism with the myth of Camelot, able to rehearse another metanarrative—that of the legitimacy and fairness of American society in the face of the deeply unfair personal tragedies that befall individuals? Was Clinton's performance used to preserve an ideologically partial view of sacred, fundamental American values—those of fairness and justice—despite growing empirical evidence that in the United States people of color are more likely to be incarcerated and sentenced to death for their crimes than their formally equal white citizens, and that during the last 30 years the economic divide between the rich and poor has increased substantially? Or, as Alexander and Jacobs would have it, was Clinton simply rehearsing narratives that are deeply rooted in the deep structure of the sacred and profane of American society?

Darnell Hunt (1999) incorporates political struggles over the definition of reality into his modified model of media events. In his study of the O.J. Simpson murder trial, Hunt largely accepts Dayan and Katz's model and views the highly publicized trial of the former football star accused of slaying his wife, as a ritualized "high holiday" in which the sacred ideals of the U.S. justice system—fairness and impartiality—were also on trial, while the public took advantage of the liminality of the event to sit in judgment of the system (46). Nonetheless, Hunt is clearly not satisfied with the model's inability to incorporate an analysis of political struggle. Hunt draws upon Antonio Gramsci's (1971) concept of hegemony, which argues for a conception of civil society that is shaped both by consent and historically specific levels of coercion. Hunt does this to argue that news rituals, such as the O.J. Simpson trial, contain both integrative hegemonic narratives and counter-hegemonic narratives that are used by competing social actors. The model allows for a multiplicity of readings, but, importantly, it acknowledges that *not all readings are equal.* "In other words, as popular trial, the Simpson case generated a range of narratives, each competing for dominance, but some gaining the upper hand in the struggle to set the conditions of belief (e.g., those hypermediated by mainstream news media)" (Hunt 1999: 28). The O.J. Simpson trial, as media event, tapped into existing cleavages in American society such as class, gender, and race that were played out in narrative form by news and entertainment media as both fiction (made-for-TV movies) and fact (news coverage), and, argues Hunt, their dominance extended along a line of continuum from most plausible (narratives that affirmed Simpson's guilt) to most implausible (narratives that affirmed Simpson's innocence) (28–29).

# CHAPTER TWO

## The Nature of Spectacle

*The intellectual historian may (at his risk) pay no attention to economics, the economic historian to Shakespeare, but the social historian who neglects either will not get far.*

ERIC HOBSBAWM

*We are now at the point where we are covering the spectacle we create, which is sort of artificial to begin with.*

JACK GERMOND, FORMER COLUMNIST, *Baltimore Sun*

### Aesthetics, Fascism, and Totality

Dayan and Katz reject Walter Benjamin's (1968) famous warning that aestheticized politics can lead to fascism. Benjamin argues that fascism offers people the ability to express themselves instead of the ability to act upon the world through practical engagement. Fascism mobilizes the power of the imaginary, through mass spectacles and myth, to suture the individual into an aestheticized collective identity, usually embodied in the person of a charismatic leader. It opposes bourgeois forms of politics and the unseemly irritation of fractious debate. Instead, it offers an intellectual, spiritual, and psychological "convergence." Fascism offers a "reconciliation of reason and emotion, history and myth, language and image, fascism unifies the divided tracks of human cognition and experience by means of the effective logic of the symbol, the imaginary" (Koepnick 1999: 160). Fascism, with its colorful mass rallies and heated oratory, replaces a politics of debate—the open and democratic accommodation of disparate interests—with the "beauty of the whole" (Falasca-Zamponi 1997: 27–28), a beauty that coincides with dominant interests. Fascism reconstructs "cultic spaces of social integration, to stir hopes for innerworldly redemption, and thus to recast the political as a site at which unestranged authenticity comes into being" (Koepnick 1999: 161).

The extent to which the culture of fascism appears to overlap with contemporary large-scale media events and their valorization of myth is striking. Many critics characterized the public mourning of Princess Diana as a kind of "feeling fascism" that forced those who did not share the grief to silence themselves (Walter 1999: 20). Christopher Hitchens, journalist turned reluctant "royal watcher," felt the sting of the "Diana backlash" after he challenged her "canonization" as "yet another time when everything depends on how people 'feel' and not at all on what, if anything, anyone thinks" (Hitchens 1998: 51). The critique of the aestheticization of politics, therefore, presents a serious challenge to Dayan and Katz's neo-Durkheimian analysis. The media events they describe, with their emphasis on heightened emotions and social integration through moments of shared collective experience, appear to give modern form to Benjamin's fascist nightmare.

Tony Walter rejects those who label the mourning of Diana as "the tip of a fascist iceberg" as being ignorant of long-held "social rules following a death" (Walter 1999: 33). The required silence of people like Hitchens, says Walter, is the norm following any death. Speaking ill of the dead is simply not done, at least not until a respectable period of time has passed and the deceased is safely buried. Yes, says Walter, there are social norms that impose temporary restrictions upon the behavior of individuals, but these norms are what grant those who wish to mourn the freedom to do so. Besides, critics eventually found themselves quoted by the media anyway.

Dayan and Katz are aware of the potential association between fascism and media events; and consequently, they are at pains to disassociate their work from such recriminations. They argue that media events are not, despite suggestions to the contrary, "latter-day versions of the mass rallies of fascism" (Dayan and Katz 1992: 18). They offer four reasons: (1) Western broadcasters are independent of government and can choose not to cover events. (2) Individuals usually are not isolated and alone while watching media events, but instead share and discuss the experience with others often in the comfort of their homes. Such a context, Dayan and Katz suggest, is not conducive to "translating aroused emotion into collective political action" (19). (3) Live media events would fail as rituals if audience participation was withheld. For example, what makes the coverage of the death of JFK Jr. work is the fact that audiences *are* deeply involved in the mourning ritual. And finally (4) oppositional or counter-hegemonic readings are possible (19). "Danger lurks," they say, only when liminal moments are substituted for political structure (Dayan and Katz 1992: ix). This, I suggest, is a major misunderstanding. I want to argue that *the neo-Durkheimian focus on liminality and ritual discourages an understanding of the underlying structure of spectacular media events*. It is the structure, the inner logic, of the spectacular mediascape, not liminality, that has been substituted for political structure.

Many media events *are* ritualized performances that create opportunities for social integration as well as counter-hegemonic meanings; the public struggle among disparate groups to lay claim to the legacy of Lady Diana as well as the narrative of racial oppression that was a key component of the televised O.J. Simpson murder trial are but two examples. And modern politics is nothing today if not a form of performance. If there was ever any doubt on this score, surely the U.S. presidency of Ronald Reagan disabused those who would cling to a purely rational account of political communication. Nevertheless, the neo-Durkheimian focus on the maintenance of social order and liminality lacks a complete analysis of *how* cultural texts are made, how they are used and to what purpose. In order to answer these questions we need to understand the mechanism through which cultural texts are produced, organized, and circulated among members of civil society and throughout the broader mediascape. And importantly, we need to think through how this system of cultural and economic distribution stands in relation to the norms of news professionalism. As we have seen, some work in the neo-Durkheimian tradition makes this very point (Alexander and Jacobs 1998). Nevertheless, the focus of this research remains fixed on specific media events themselves—i.e., the O.J. Simpson trial, the beating of Rodney King, Lady Diana's wedding, and finally her funeral.

This research *mistakes the part for the whole*. Individual media events are singular moments of a much larger social and cultural process—a complex integration of cultural, organizational, economic, state, and material interests. At the same time, news media are complicated cultural institutions, which, through their use of storytelling, do enjoy a degree of autonomy from the dictates of profit and ownership. As Hackett and Zhao note, "Media genres and professional codes impose their own disciplines; audiences, with their expectations of media fare, are also part of the media system" (Hackett and Zhao 1998: 7). This is the message from cultural-text theory I wish to preserve. The professional norms of journalism are not "entirely self-generating" forms of "discourse." They have their own material conditions of existence (7). The integrated spectacle is constituted through these conditions of existence; and the tension felt by a growing number of reporters between their duty of professional service and the demands of economic and organizational obligations are the result of the spectacle's contradictory relationship to the norms of news professionalism.

Instead of making the easy comparison of spectacular media events with fascist spectacles, we need to investigate the historically contingent ways in which aesthetics (e.g., beauty) are perceived within the news spectacle, and by whom. This is the scholarly project advocated by Walter Benjamin: "In critiquing the aestheticization of politics, Benjamin's aim was to show how political presentation interacts with historically contingent patterns of perception, and how imperatives of power and money may colonize the specific ways of what and how we see" (Koepnick 1999: 237). In the case of beauty, for example, we need to ask what is considered beautiful, by whom and in whose interests?

## *Media Logic and Representation*

News is not a straightforward representation of reality. Despite the insistence by some stubborn practitioners, this point is now a commonplace observation. Nor is news a straightforward distortion of reality. News is socially constructed and is the result of a confluence of factors, including: traditional news values, organizational work routines, reporter-source relations, the introduction and use of new technologies, and the political economy of news production itself (Tuchman 1978; Gans 1979; Fishman 1980; Ericson, Baranek, and Chan 1987). And yet, despite this established body of research, the sticky question of representation remains. How we understand representation affects the kinds of expectations we will have about the limits and possibilities for news media in general and for large-scale media events in particular.

Journalism, insist David Altheide and Robert Snow (1991), is dead. We are now in the "postjournalism era" because news media are no longer capable of representing a social reality independent of their own internal logic and organizational behavior. News formats created for radio and particularly television—complete with their own entertainment values, pacing and syntax—have been adopted by independent organizations within civil society as well as the state. These organizations package their own values and interests into *entertaining* narratives replete with interesting characters and visuals that meet the institutional and organizational requirements of news media. That is to say they meet the requirements of media formats. "The journalism enterprise, especially TV news, essentially is reporting on itself; it addresses events that are cast in its own formats and frames of relevance, rather than attempting to understand the events in their own terms, and then trying to communicate the complexities and ambiguities of 'real world' conditions" (51). In the end what is considered aesthetically beautiful, that is, good TV as well as good public-relations work, amounts to the same thing—the reproduction of established media formats. The assumption is at the core of media production and is most evident during election campaigns when reporters essentially cover little else but scripted announcements by hopeful candidates. The success or failure of campaign events hinges on the proper application of formats, not necessarily policy content.[1]

But Altheide and Snow wish to make a broader and more significant point: that media logic has become part of everyday life. "Our point is that media are powerful because people have adopted a media logic. Since people perceive, interpret, and act on the bias of the existing media logic, that logic has become a way of life" (252). And, striking a decidedly Durkheimian chord they suggest that media logic is at the heart of social change and "the collective consciousness that binds society together" (252).

A chilling example of the personal adoption of this so-called media logic came April 20, 1999, when a student named James used a telephone to provide a bizarre color commentary of a shooting spree by two trench-coat clad teenagers at Columbine High School, in Littleton, Colorado—a tragedy that left 12 of his fellow students and a teacher dead. James barricaded himself in one of the school's rooms with a TV set, and then contacted Denver-area television station KUSA. His color commentary was immediately picked up by CNN and in Canada by CTV. "I'm trying to be a little bit quiet so they can't hear me from inside," he told the anchors (Saunders 1999). "It seemed," says puzzled reporter Doug Saunders, "oddly like a scripted event . . . as TV reporters, anchors and victims repeated lines and performances that have become alarmingly familiar on live newscasts" (Saunders 1999). Moreover, many of the reporters who covered the Columbine massacre noted how surprised they were at how open and comfortable most students and family members were with being asked to repeat their stories over and over again for the benefit of the hungry media horde that descended upon Littleton (Onion 1999; Seigel 1999).

While Altheide and Snow's analysis of the working of "media logic" goes partway toward describing the incestuous and recursive quality of today's mediascape, it falls short of helping us capture the underlying structure of large-scale media events. It is true that news media are influenced by an inner logic. An analysis of media logic rightfully counters the claims of critics who narrowly assess Monicagate or the mourning of Diana as the latest examples of tabloidization, a sensationalistic corrosion of what is in essence an unquestionably good institution whose core purpose is the facilitation of open communication. Altheide and Snow also note that these media formats are affected by a particular history involving the development of new technology and commercialization. But this history is never fully investigated; instead, their method, adapted from Georg Simmel, focuses on the identification and description of social forms, i.e., news formats. They attempt to show how content flows out of form, and that media formats have their own constitutive logic that is played out by practitioners in the fields of entertainment and politics. Again, this is partially true. "Princess Diana was not 'attractive' nor even simply photogenic," argues Jenny Kitzinger, "she was, above all, 'telegenic'" (Kitzinger 1999: 69). The images of Princess Diana were constructed using the techniques of television. In particular, moving images were "essential to producing the Diana mythology and shaping the 'national shock and mourning'" (69). The image of the "People's Princess" was constructed, in part, through meticulous attention to camera movement, framing, and sound. Her gestures and movements—while stroking a sick child's knee or casting a shy glance—contributed to the portrayal of a caring yet vulnerable princess (69). The problem, however, lies in clinging too tightly to a mediacentric perspective. In other words, those who rely strictly on media forms fall into the same trap as those who direct our attention to the constitutive features of narrative forms: these forms are separated from their broader social and material existence and become reified. It must be emphasized that news media's definition of the beautiful, that is, good TV, is historically contingent. "Professional and popular definitions of 'the best' television production practices are not inherent in the technological possibilities of the medium, nor in universal aesthetic categories; rather, they are socially produced and culturally variable" (Gruneau 1996: 12).[2] The extent to which these media practices are accepted and internalized by individuals is also contingent. The citizens of Taber, Alberta, where a similar fatal shooting incident occurred a week after the Columbine massacre, had a much more hostile attitude toward the media than did the residents of Littleton.[3]

Altheide and Snow recommend that people "reject all claims by others—and us— that focus only on the inappropriateness of media culture for our lives. It just is, that's all. . . . Journalism, as we know it, cannot be salvaged; it must be replaced with a different expectation and a different format that will permit independent representations of culture, events, and issues" (252). Altheide and Snow are seemingly blind to the contradictory position that individuals must submit to the inevitability of the "one way" to represent the world—to media logic—while at the same time commit themselves to search for an independent method of representing culture. In the end, they are trapped within a circular logic that asks critics to evaluate the media by their own internal standards. By taking this position, Altheide and Snow abandon the ideological "kernel of truth" within journalism discourse that historically has paid tribute to the defense and development of independent communication among citizens. It is this commitment to some form of social responsibility (no matter how ideologically freighted) that has afforded news media their legitimacy and their claim to independence from government. In essence, then, Altheide and Snow advocate a submission to a reified objective standard of everyday life—a set of expectations, rules and guidelines that stand above individual and collective experience, and that must be obeyed. After all, it just is, that's all. Or, as Guy Debord might have put it: Altheide and Snow have accepted the spectacle's own account of itself. They have mistaken the part for the whole.

### *Spectacular Representation*

In his essay *Comments on the Society of the Spectacle,* Guy Debord says, "There is no place left where people can discuss the realities which concern them, because they can never lastingly free themselves from the crushing presence of media discourse and of the various forces organized to relay it" (Debord 1988: 6). This is a bleak assessment to be sure, and it no doubt correctly captures how Debord would have felt toward media events such as the Littleton massacre. That is not to say that the media and their representations constitute the entirety of what Debord means by the spectacle. Far from it. The "mass media" can be only understood as the spectacle in a "limited sense." They are, he says, "its most stultifying manifestation" (Debord 1995: sec. 24).[4] The media represent, in a partial way, the workings of the entire society, a society in which people never directly experience life, but instead contemplate it in a passive way via images constructed and administered by others. "The whole life of those societies in which modern conditions of production prevail presents itself as an immense accumulation of *spectacles*. All that was directly lived has become mere representation" (Debord 1995: sec. 1). Certainly, it is safe to assume that Debord would not have been surprised by the media circus that was the O.J. Simpson murder trial, if he had lived to see it; nor would he have been startled by the cry of media pundits who, in his words, stick to "vain generalities or hypocritical regrets" about the examples of media excess. "That modern society is a society of the spectacle now goes without saying," wrote Debord 20 years after the initial publication of *Society of the Spectacle* (Debord 1988: 2).

Conservative critics of media representation such as Daniel Boorstin (1992) catalogue the media's "increasing reliance on dealers in pseudo-events and images" (204)—that is, public-relations experts and media organizations themselves. Boorstin argues that far from being superficial, the trend signifies "a world where the image, more interesting than its original, has itself become the original. The shadow has become the substance" (204). The sentiment expresses a great deal of what Debord means by the spectacle; but according to Debord, Boorstin fails to capture the true essence of the spectacle because of his belief in an "honest product" or commodity and the insistence that private life still provides a potential refuge from the excesses of media images (Debord 1995: sec. 198). The problem, in Boorstin's view, is our own moral weakness and desire for sensationalism. After all, "the image is what people want to buy" (Boorstin 1992: 204). This, of course, is the argument used by many who defend the offerings of the news media on the basis of consumer sovereignty. The media provide wall-to-wall coverage of tragic accidents and sexual trysts involving celebrities and presidents (increasingly seen as one and the same), because it is what the people want—sex sells. But this has been true for centuries. Such a banal insight does nothing to further our understanding of the scale and intensity of large-scale media events; and, in any case, sex is not a problematic moral activity for Debord.[5] Sensationalism in itself is not the core problem, as many of the critics of tabloidization assume. The very word conjures up moral indignation and a weariness with the public display of tawdry stories taken from private life. This is the root of much of the angst displayed over President Clinton's dalliance with a young intern. Debord, however, is less concerned with *the representation of private moments of seduction in the marketplace than he is with the market's seduction of private life.* Debord rejects conservative and liberal interpretations of spectacle (Lasch 1978: 218–236; Sennett 1978: 264–268) that call for independent standards of morality, ethics, and civility as bulwarks against the erosion of the public sphere by the subjectivizing and privatizing forces of mass consumer culture. Boorstin's ultimate failure, says Debord, lies in his belief that one can "isolate an industrial rationality, functioning on its own, from social life as a whole" (Debord 1995: sec. 200). Debord believes the commodity *form* has penetrated deep into everyday life to create a false sense of reality. The spectacle "is not something *added* to the real world—not a decorative element, so to speak. On the contrary, it is the very heart of society's real unreality" (sec. 6).

## Commodities, Meaning, and Spectacle

Debord's notion of the spectacle is a reformulation of Marx's concept of the "fetishism of commodities"—a process in which commodities take on so-called mystical qualities (signifying sex appeal, love, social status, etc.) that are separated from their use-value (the product's ability to serve real human needs). In the market, commodities have exchange value in relation to each other or in relation to money, which represents them abstractly; their value is not based on their true source—human labor. Value is, therefore, perceived in a "phantasmagoric" form as a relation between things instead of a relation between people. The world of real social relations (wage labor, relations of production, gender, race, and class divisions) becomes occluded in the fantastic realm of commodities, which in turn alienates individuals from their real social existence. But where Marx posited that capitalist society entailed a "downgrading of *being* into *having*," that is to say the reduction of social life to the false equivalency of the purchase and sale of commodities, the spectacle, according to Debord, marks the historical moment that "entails a generalized shift from *having* to appearing: all effective 'having' must now derive both its immediate prestige and its ultimate raison d'être from appearances" (sec. 17). The commodity form has become pure image, an arbitrary image that can be used, discarded, and reused countless times under varying circumstances while connoting disparate meanings. The spectacle is "the world of the commodity ruling over all lived experience" (sec. 37). Media events are for Debord, then, particular historical manifestations of the commodity form; investigation into their social significance must begin with the commodity, and not with their fetishized "gloss."

Media events are *produced* as commodities; and as with all commodities consumption (that is, the point at which the meanings of spectacular media events are absorbed, forged, and/or struggled over) is related to production—the former presumes the latter and vice versa. (Marx 1978: 236). In fact, to understand what Debord means by the spectacle, one must understand the complex relationships that form its unity among the various moments of production, consumption, distribution, and exchange. The explication of these relationships will form the bulk of this book. Debord's theory of the spectacle, however, suffers from its highly abstract formulation. There is a tendency in Debord's writing to dismiss the products of cultural production—in our case cultural performances, or media events—as fetishes, as mere ideology; in doing so Debord occludes a full investigation of the inner working of the spectacle. In other words, Debord's abstract formulation of the spectacle complicates his own method of analysis.

Debord assumes that individuals are easily duped by the proliferation of aestheticized images. But this assumption is simplistic. As we have seen, news can be understood as a ritualized narrative form, whose meanings are open to contestation and are determined through a complex process of social struggle and mediation. For example, it is too easy to categorize the enormous public outpouring of grief following the death of Princess Diana as the inevitable outcome of the spectacle's impoverishment of everyday life. Modern society is highly fragmented and the division of labor has multiplied as a result of increased specialization in the workplace; as well, there is a real sense in which many of the mourners *actually* did know more about Lady Diana—her hopes, fears, and desires—than they did about their own neighbors, not to mention the larger unity of a globally integrated economy marked by cleavages of race, gender, and class. But that is not to say we must necessarily agree with Debord when he asserts that within the spectacle "the individual's own gestures are no longer his own, but rather those of someone else who represents them to him" (sec. 30).

The sentimentality of Elton John's song "Candle in the Wind," revised by the singer for Princess Diana's funeral, cues our emotional responses to her death. Judith Williamson (1998) writes that "we live a lot of our emotional lives by proxy," through the real and fictional stories of celebrities as told to us by the media. But, as she suggests, the images of thousands of people who traveled long distances to Buckingham Palace and to the Paris tunnel where Diana was killed may signify "an attempt to grasp something more solid—a run on the bank of the real" (26). That is to say, the media coverage of the public mourning of Diana cannot be simply reduced to the alienated spectacular integration of a society atomized by capitalist division of labor. The ultimate meaning of these stories is not solely determined by the spectacle's representation of the real, but by the individual and collective struggle of people to make sense of life. The meanings of mediated commodities must appeal to *real* needs and concerns of audiences. They must "resonate" in some way with audiences' own experiences. Commodities "come alive" because audiences "breathe life into them" (Leiss, Kline, and Jhally 1990: 310). Audiences bring their own needs and desires to news texts. They are attracted to cultural products, like news, because the media promise to address or resolve real-world needs (fear of crime, shrinking pay checks, or ecological pressures); as Williamson notes, the "outpouring of grief over Diana's death suggests how much we fail to express in our actual day-to-day lives" (Williamson 1998: 28). At the same time, it is this desire for satisfaction that opens up the possibility for contradiction. "These desires," Hans Enzenberger says, "are not—or are not primarily—internalized rules of the game as played by the capitalist system. They have physiological roots and can no longer be suppressed. Consumption as spectacle [viewing the funeral procession of Princess Diana for example] is—in parody form—the anticipation of a utopian situation" (Enzensberger 1974: 112). News commodities contain the promise of satisfying our concerns about society and political life, but to the extent that they fail to do so a rupture is created; whether that rupture is the result of the liminality of the media event is an open question. Again, the communal mourning behavior and the British public's demand that the Royal family make some sort of public gesture of grief toward the loss of the so-called People's Princess may have been such an occasion (Ignatieff 1998; Walter 1999: 24). In other words, news texts, as promotional commodities, hold partial truths. Their use-value or meaning is *malleable* and open to contradiction.

The malleability of commodities notwithstanding, this surfeit of meaning also contributes to the production of spectacle. As mentioned above, there are numerous readings of Princess Diana, from postmodern Madonna and object of "cathartic grief" to crass celebrity icon (cf. Kuhn 1998); no single reading needs a complete victory over any other to serve the requirements of the spectacle. Contradictory meanings coexist within media spectacles, and struggles over their meaning can contribute to the further expansion of the media event itself. The struggle over whether O.J. Simpson was a victim of racial stereotyping or a successful manipulator of those stereotypes for his own defense fueled seemingly endless debate among media pundits. Questions linking President Clinton's marital infidelity to his competence as president performed the same function for CNN's *Crossfire* and CNBC's *Hardball* and *Rivera Live;* all of these programs benefit from the indeterminacy of meaning. The more meanings that can be attached to a commodity, the better—the more marketable the commodity becomes; similarly, value increases with the amount of conflict (a core news value) attached to a media event. The discursive struggle in the media to brand young Elián González as a kidnap victim or, conversely, as a symbol of liberation from Communist oppression was a bonanza for the 24-hour news agencies that followed the story's every twist and turn. Viewers can tune in to the coverage of Lady Diana's funeral out of heartfelt respect or out of an amazed condescension over the media excess. Both serve the need to create an audience; and the contradictory needs of these audience fragments can be met through the different kinds of coverage attached to the event. After all, news organizations routinely run stories probing whether media coverage is appropriate or excessive. These stories are now a regular component of media events as they serve two immediate purposes—first, they forward the story and second, they are used by journalists as part of their "boundary work" through which reporters make ritualized distinctions between legitimate work routines (usually their own) and unscrupulous conduct (Winch 1997; Bishop 1999; Berkowitz 2000). The reviled tabloid paparazzi came under particular scrutiny during the Diana coverage; and, Christopher Hitchens's caustic commentary about the mourning of the "People's Princess" aired on numerous TV talk shows.[6] What is important is that meaning be created and that it resonate within civil society. Without meaning, the transaction cannot be completed and production will not occur—one presumes the other. What is crucial is that meanings generate sufficient interest so that they are consumed. Debord's point is that once consumed those meanings have been partially tamed.

## The Logic of Spectacle

While Debord's work suffers from its overly abstract articulation and a lack of historical analysis, I believe that the concept of spectacle is still valuable. But if we are to salvage the concept of spectacle, we must ferret out the *practical logic* of commodities and investigate how this logic relates to media events. We must understand how media events *use* the spectacle in order to comprehend how the spectacle *uses* media events We must understand how the use of commodities—and by extension media events—is structured.

Debord builds on Marx's work by adapting Georg Lukács's (1971) concept of reification—whereby everyday life, through the process of commodification, is objectified and made subject to rational control and administration. The commodity becomes the "universal structuring principle" of human society (85). It is this crucial insight into the operation of the spectacle that I wish to preserve; and, as I said above, it can be done without adopting Debord's overly pessimistic assumption of self-alienation. We can first understand the historical roots of reification before turning our attention to the ways in which this logic is applied to media events.

The historical origins of what Debord and Lukács would later characterize as reification lie in the nature of self-performance in modern consumer culture. It is a culture born from the upheavals of modernity—the historical shift away from a preindustrial and traditional society. A number of interrelated themes present themselves. First, the rise of urban centers and the shift from a feudal to a market-industrial society created enormous upheavals, including a crisis of subjectivity. The secure order of values that had served to anchor one's place within society was rent apart. In premodern times one's identity was linked to family, religion, law, and place, but with the rise of modern society this seemingly more stable, but nevertheless oppressive, order gave way to atomization. People were forced to choose their own identities, and the privileged site for this activity was consumer culture. Along with the loss of a fixed identity, individuals were forced to negotiate their place within multiple "public and private spheres, each with their different roles" and "norms" (Slater 1997: 84). The instability of this new social experience was further complicated by an aching epistemological doubt created by the Enlightenment's replacement of traditional authority with reason. In the modern world the Enlightenment's promise of truth was itself insecure because it too was open to critique, and therefore provisional. Finally, and crucially for our present discussion, modernity placed "mediated experience at the center of social life" (Thompson 1995; Slater 1997: 84). More and more complex, and sometimes contradictory, life worlds were revealed to people as a result of improved transportation (trains, planes, and automobiles) and communication structures (print, radio, and television); and because these structures were dependent upon commercial revenue for survival, *everyday experience itself became commercialized*. These newly revealed "lifestyles" became possible choices of identity that, through the extension of marketing, advertising, and other cultural industries, were related to people as potential consumer choices (Slater 1997: 84). "In the consumer society, marketing and advertising assumed the role once played by cultural traditions and became the privileged forum for the transmission of such social cues" as taste and class (Leiss, Kline, and Jhally 1990: 57–65). In this sense, choice of dress, food, and entertainment signaled one's place and standing in the world.

With the collapse of social supports for identity formation, selfhood became a lifelong project of individual development. One was now expected to enrich oneself through mental and physical pursuits conducted largely in the sphere of consumer culture. This aestheticization of everyday life was "the project of turning life into a work of art" (Featherstone 1991: 66). Jackson Lears (1983) suggests this "therapeutic ethos" was an anxious response to the insecurity caused by urbanization and marketplace relations. Products, ranging from cosmetics to self-help books and other promoted cures for personal ennui, were offered to assuage "longings for reintegrated selfhood" through the promise of, among other things, "intense experience."

> A dread of unreality, a yearning to experience intense "real life" in all its forms—these emotions were difficult to chart but nonetheless pervasive and important. They energized the spread of the therapeutic ethos, underlay the appeal of much national advertising, and mobilized a market for commodified mass amusements. They formed, in short, the psychological impetus for the rise of consumer culture. (6)

For Lears, the rationalization of everyday life—the effort described by Max Weber to systematically extend bureaucratic instrumental control over all social environments—had produced a powerful reaction in the therapeutic ethos.

It is in this modern context that performance became vital for self-realization. In the highly bureaucratized world of modernity, success, and social mobility became less dependent on the *quality* of the work one did than on how one was *perceived* by others. Success for the "other-directed" self became dependent upon "impression management" and the ability to manipulate others (Lears 1983: 8; Riesman 1961 cited in Slater 1997: 90). "In the emerging other-directed society of managers and professionals, advertisements increasingly assumed *the importance of creating a pleasant social self*" (emphasis added) (Lears 1983: 25). Of particular importance is that modernity, with the help of commercially based cultural intermediaries in the fields of marketing, advertising and popular entertainment, was *merging public image with inner life*. Don Slater cites the work of American sociologist David Riesman to argue that in order to "maintain a career" in the modern world, "one must market one's personality through the same kind of 'product differentiation' that characterizes commodities (Riesman 1961, cited in Slater 1997: 90). This advice is applicable to someone looking for a job as well as to a politician seeking votes. In modernity, personality had become a product for sale like any other commodity. The aestheticization of everyday life was achieved by the objectification of the commodity form. And, as is the case with most commodities, an individual's exchange value (how one was perceived) dominated his/her use-value (what he/she could produce). This assessment is at the heart of Debord's critique of the spectacle.

The all-encompassing environment of the spectacle envisioned by Debord is linked to the impersonal network of market exchange. In order to bridge the gap between anonymous consumers and producers commodities are aestheticized through marketing, advertising, and other forms of promotion; they are associated with arbitrary meanings that are in turn appropriated by modern social subjects in their quest for self-realization. The quest for self-realization is bound to rational calculation, but most importantly for Debord, it is embedded in a system structured in domination. *Social identities, mediated through market transactions, become essential to economic competition and rational organization; they become objects of rational and strategic action by commercial interests and institutions.* It is in this sense that personal autonomy is under the constant threat of domination. Debord's argument is that the logic of commodity relations has become coextensive with all social relations. The aestheticization of commodities serves to arouse and influence consumer demand, but more than that it pervades all social life. We conduct our lives according to *its* rules, not our own. "The individual can use his knowledge of these laws to his own advantage, but he is not able to modify the process by his own activity" (Lukács 1971: 87). In other words, one learns the rules of promotion as a prerequisite of participation in consumer society; one presumes the other.

There is then a central tension in consumer culture between the promise that consumption is "the privileged site" of autonomous identity formation and the incorporation of the meanings of subjectivity into the circulation of economies and capital accumulation. It is a struggle between instrumental strategies of social control and free self-formation (Slater 1997: 31). The result of this lack of independence, according to Debord, is a contemplative stance toward the world, a world increasingly represented in the form of image. The rules apply to all, including PR specialists, reporters, and social activists. Even academics and other critics of the spectacle must play by its rules if they wish to reach a broader public (Debord 1988: 2). Anti–World Trade Organization protesters dressed as endangered sea turtles at the WTO's 1999 meeting in Seattle were communicating using the language of the spectacle, as was Princess Diana when—in attempting to manage her own image—she campaigned to eradicate land mines, AIDS, and homelessness (Bhabha 1998: 106). "Just as the logic of the commodity reigns over capitalists' competing ambitions, and the logic of war always dominates the frequent modifications in weaponry, so the harsh logic of the spectacle controls the abundant diversity of media extravagances" (Debord 1988: 2). Aestheticized images, including media events, are thus, for Debord, "the indispensable packaging for things produced . . . as a general gloss on the rationality of the system" (Debord 1995: sec. 15). The "beauty of the whole" is not a shiny fascist boot recursively put in the side of public life; it is the practical result of the spectacle striving to realize itself according to its own internal rules and logic. "It is," Debord says, "the omnipresent celebration of a choice *already made* in the sphere of production, and the consummate result of that choice" (sec. 6). To understand spectacular media events, we must understand how the logic of the spectacle manifests itself within media events as an objective social force within production. The logic of the spectacle is a constitutive element of the production of spectacular media events; its influence resonates throughout the media system and carries implications for all those who are caught in its web, whether they be willing participants or critics.

### Practice, Promotion, and Spectacular Media Events

In order that we may further clarify what is meant by the logic of spectacle, I want to turn to the work of Andrew Wernick (1991). Wernick is careful to eschew any association between the aestheticization of commodities and an illusory reality imposed upon "real" life. In his work, the *use* of arbitrary meanings is shown to be a cornerstone of what I am choosing to call the logic of spectacle. Wernick has extended the critical analysis of marketing to include a range of cultural, economic, and political domains. In doing so, Wernick is extending an argument made by Debord and others (Lukács 1971; Horkheimer and Adorno 1979; Lefebvre 1991; Slater 1997) that the logic of consumer culture has permeated an increasing proportion of social life. What makes Wernick's work particularly useful, however, is that it is grounded in an analysis of practice. Instead of relying on abstract analysis or the insight of the critic, Wernick delves into the practical workings of "promotional culture." The focus on practice also prevents Wernick from veering off into the stylistic excesses found in some postmodern theorists of spectacle such as Jean Baudrillard (1981, 1995). So, while he does not critique the unreal from the ideologically secure position of the real, Wernick also refrains from highly abstract speculations of "hyperreality" and the law of "the code"—academic discussions that have become increasingly disengaged from the more prosaic goal of explaining why one set of historical circumstances follows another. For our present purposes this exercise involves attempting to explain why stories of mythic stature have become subjects of large-scale media events on a scale, intensity, and frequency not previously experienced.

Wernick's first point is that market production and promotion are "integrally conjoined" (15). The promotion of commodities is not a separate activity that is added externally following production. Promotion is constitutive of the production process itself. The style, flair, and feel of media events contribute to their material construction; conversely, a media event's production is a key element in its ability to act as a promotional sign. This dual relationship forms two conjoined "endpoints."

Advertising transfers meanings on to a product from the outside, through repeated ima-gistic association. Through design, on the other hand, that same signification is stamped on to it materially. The result is a dual-character object, the *commodity-sign,* which func-tions in circulation both as an object-to-be-sold and as the bearer of a promotional mes-sage. (Wernick 1991: 15–16)

Wernick is describing the logic of an "integrated system of production/promotion" (16). The bathos that marked the mourning of Princess Diana may have reached out to a real sense of grief among her admirers—a grief rooted in a sense of modern mal-aise and personal unconnectedness—but it was also a promotional strategy that, from the very beginning, was integral to the production of the media event. The massive media response to her death, the blanket coverage, and the repeated probing by re-porters designed to elicit an emotional response from mourners, was not entirely spontaneous; as Peter Ghosh suggests, it was preplanned and calculated based on the knowledge of "a pre-existing media audience of enormous dimensions, established over a number of years" by the tabloid press (Ghosh 1998: 42). John Morrison, BBC Editor, TV news programs, reveals the corporation's plan: "we had worked to a fic-tional scenario involving the death of a leading royal in a car crash in a foreign coun-try recently," said Morrison in an interview a week following Diana's death. "It proved amazingly prescient" (42).

Ghosh goes on to argue that the media response to Princess Diana's death was, in a sense, "over-determined" (43). A number of factors were at play: (1) As mentioned, there was an existing audience of enormous potential that the BBC and other media organizations around the world tapped into. (2) The media were not the only organ-izations interested in utilizing Diana's image. Many observers agree that Tony Blair's New Labour Party successfully managed to associate itself with the image of Lady Diana, and along with that a more sensitive and caring populism (Holt 1998: 185; Wil-son 1998: 120), when on the Sunday morning of her death Blair held an impromptu news conference declaring her to be the "People's Princess" (Ghosh 1998: 42). Prin-cess Diana was and still is the perfect commodity-sign—her image was produced as an advertisement for herself and it acted as a site of promotion for other interests, in this case New Labour, which succeeded in draping its policy turn to the right with Princess Diana's commitment to "feel-good charity" (Holt 1998: 197). And (3) To these factors can be added the growing disenchantment with the Royal family in Brit-ain and its developing legitimation crisis following the monarchy's "annus horribi-lus." The seeds had been sown for a full-blown media event.

Princess Diana was a fulcrum point for what Wernick calls the "vortex of promo-tion." Wernick suggests that cultural products, including media, serve at once to pro-duce an interwoven set of "promotional" and "nonpromotional" messages. "In the or-gans of print and broadcasting, information and entertainment are the flowers which attract the bee. In this sense, too, the non-advertising content of such media can be considered, even semiotically, as an extension of their ads" (Wernick 1991: 182). All commodities, in his view, are produced both as commodities for sale and as advertisements for themselves. They are commodity-signs. The logic of promotion is inscribed within all sorts of commodities and has infiltrated the cultural and political domains as well as the economic. Previously distinct boundaries of social and economic activity are blurred while individuals are caught in a swirling *vortex* of promotional circulation. "Each promotional message refers to a commodity which is itself the site of another promotion. And so on, in an endless dance whose only point is to circulate the circulation of something else" (121).

Wernick is not suggesting that all culture is now a superstructural gloss attached to commodity production. The key point here is that culture, production, and promotion are constitutively linked. The interdependence of culture and production means that promotional strategies—the images and narrative forms that constitute media events—must derive their significance by making reference to "an understood cultural code; and in such a way that the values in terms of which the product is endorsed are endorsed by those to whom they make appeal" (37–38). It is in this sense that the "deep semiotic cultural code" of the sacred and profane to which neo-Durkheimians such as Alexander and Jacobs refer is constitutive of spectacular media events. The much celebrated "authenticity" of Princess Diana resonated for many because of a perception that the British monarchy had become tired, uncaring, and out of touch with the concerns and trials of everyday people. Princess Diana's image signified a utopian moment in a world that could and should be better than it is. At the same time, Princess Diana's image was constructed and aestheticized using the techniques of storytelling, video production, and through the rearticulation of others, such as Tony Blair, who actively used and/or struggled over her image to enhance their own promotional strategies. "One might as well be blunt about it," wrote Associated Press reporter Dirk Beveridge, in one of the many "Diana packages" assembled by news rooms for the first anniversary of the fatal accident, "the death of the Princess of Wales created a rare commercial opportunity that business people weren't going to miss." A year after her death, the image of the "People's Princess" supported "a mini-industry estimated at 100 million pounds (about C$250 million [US$165 million]) or more" (Beveridge 1998).[7] By the first anniversary Elton John had donated US$32.6 million (£20 million) from sales of his remake of "Candle in the Wind." To make a large profit would have been considered bad form. The money instead goes to charities that the Princess supported; meanwhile, John's sagging career receives (intended or not) a massive promotional boost. Even David Hasselhoff of *Baywatch,* a man known more for his beefcake than his vocal talents, tapped the Diana spectacle by performing a song at a tribute concert for the late Princess entitled "Bless a Brand-New Angel." The song had been written for the funeral of one of the show's characters (Dowd 1998). Clearly, the connection between the death of a celebrity princess and a fictitious TV character more devoted to exposing skin than the "paradoxical significance" of tragedy, is arbitrary in the extreme. What brought them together is integrated promotion; it is the grease that lubricates the machinery of the spectacle and allows its reproduction and expansion well beyond the spectacle's initial boundaries. It is promotion that is used by disparate interests to attach themselves to the spectacular fulcrum point of the moment.[8]

The lucrative potential of spectacular logic is driven home satirically by Michael Posner, who, following the media coverage of the Princess's funeral, wrote a mock licence application for a new 24-hour specialty channel devoted to "all funerals, all the time."

> Looking ahead, I see big numbers for Castro, Reagan and especially the Pontiff. Such levels of viewership speak not only to the character of the departed, but of the latent, unrequited public appetite for ritual, ceremony and even spiritual meaning in contemporary life—a vacuum The Funeral Channel would go some distance toward filling. (Posner 1997)

The bite of the gag is lessened, however, when one learns that the major networks in Europe and North America are busily competing for prime camera positions at the Vatican and other locations around Rome in anticipation of the Pope's final day. According to one report, "CBS—for an unconfirmed sum—outbid its rivals for the exclusive use of the terrace of the Atlante Hotel overlooking the Vatican" (Valpy 2000b). CNN's daytime audience almost quadrupled during its coverage of the funeral for country-music star Tammy Wynette. The funeral for Sonny Bono, former pop star turned politician, doubled MSNBC's daytime audience (Valpy 2000b). The live round-the-clock television coverage of Pierre Trudeau's funeral also drew a big audience for both CTV and CBC. John Moody, the Fox network's vice-president for news, sums up the potential of these funereal media events: "We know that these things [funerals] attract viewers. We know that when a well-known person is memorialized and the high points of his or her life are presented to an audience, you are going to draw people who loved them or hated them" (cited in Valpy 2000b). Note how contradictory meanings among audience members are assumed and, indeed, desired. In such a context, "Death TV," or as Maureen Dowd says, "DTV," is already a reality. We live in an age when it is getting more and more difficult to do satire; although, the show does go on. Following comedian Chris Farley's unexpected death from a drug overdose, *Saturday Night Live* held a "death-curse extravaganza" using interview clips of deceased stars John Belushi and Gilda Radner (Dowd 1998).

The key here is that it is the commercial logic of the spectacle which, to a large extent, is the prime driving force behind media production, not the liminality of the ceremony; although, as I've said the meanings of liminal moments can be used for promotional purposes. The commercial logic of the spectacle not only creates new sites of promotion; it points the way toward a workable business plan. One such plan has been operationalized by Infinite Design Software, the Burlington, Ontario, company that launched www.funeral-cast.com. North America's first Web site devoted to webcasting funerals (Luciw 2000). In the post-Diana media age, "chasing grief" (Pogrebin 1998) is increasingly seen as a lucrative news/business strategy.

### *Promotional Fulcrum: The Micro Level*

News stories packed with emotion, pathos, and melodrama are not new. What is new is the scale, intensity, and increasing frequency of media events. One of the important contributing factors to this trend has been the spectacular and "integrated" expansion of the logic of promotion within both the economic and cultural spheres. Let us look for a moment at the origins and development of the Clinton-Lewinsky scandal. From its very beginning the scandal was about the construction of a news story that could be promoted for profit and/or for the further promotional benefits that could accrue to the drama's various players and their disparate interests.

"I had all kinds of Clinton stories that I had tried to peddle," Lucianne Goldberg told *Brill's Content* (Brill 1998: 123). For five years Goldberg, a New York–based literary agent, had been trying to dig up stories about Bill and Hillary Clinton that she could turn into tell-all books about America's famously troubled First Family. Goldberg's hard work finally paid off January 18, 1998, when Internet gossip columnist Matt Drudge leaked a spiked *Newsweek* article about Clinton's now infamous tryst with a young intern. The material for the story was constructed by Goldberg, who steered the process from its inception. Goldberg admitted she coached former White House secretary Linda Tripp—herself someone who, Goldberg says, was shopping around book ideas—to tape conversations with her friend and coworker at the Pentagon, Monica Lewinsky. The tapes, containing the admission from Lewinsky that she had an affair with the president, were then made available by Goldberg to *Newsweek* reporter Michael Isikoff, who told her he needed something official before he would run the story; to that end, Goldberg says she advised Tripp to convince Lewinsky to send the president love letters using a courier service. Lewinsky agreed, and the courier service obliged Isikoff by making itself available for an interview. Isikoff discovered later that the courier service was owned by Goldberg's brother's family. *Newsweek* editors were not entirely happy with the story and decided to hold it, but Drudge's scoop of *Newsweek's* own story prompted the magazine to play catchup by publishing Isikoff's account online. Goldberg denies being the person who first tipped off Drudge, but admits she confirmed details for him over the telephone. "Monicagate" exploded in the mainstream media three days later, on January 21, when Jackie Judd of ABC News reported an unnamed source who told her Lewinsky could be heard on a tape saying that the president encouraged her to deny the affair.

The mainstream media now had the legitimizing hook they needed. The story is not, we were told, about sex, but about the honesty and integrity of the U.S. president. The media's interest having been piqued and "legitimized," the office of the special prosecutor, Republican politicians, and the religious right fed and magnified the story with a series of leaks and stories designed to further their own partisan interests. Evangelist Jerry Falwell produced a video titled *Circles of Power* detailing Clinton's so-called moral and ethical failures, while his counterpart Pat Robertson interviewed Paula Jones (whose civil suit against Clinton opened up the Lewinsky-Clinton scandal through the funding of the right-wing Rutherford Institute) on his nationally televised program (Thompson 2000: 157; Delli Carpini and Williams 2001: 176).

The importance of the scandal is symbolically highlighted by the three major networks (ABC, NBC, CBS), which by now had pulled their anchors from Havana where they'd been reporting on Pope John Paul II's historic visit to Cuba. MSNBC began its nearly 100 days of All-Monica-All-the-Time coverage. It is the story that the all-news cable network uses to establish itself as a 24-hour provider of news and information. MSNBC's *The Big Show with Keith Olbermann,* running the logo "The White House in Crisis," provided perpetual coverage and saw its ratings skyrocket. MSNBC publicist Kyle Kaino said the audience for *The Big Show* was 148 percent larger in October 1998, a peak month for the scandal, than it was a year earlier. MSNBC reported that the number of households tuned in to the cable network's prime-time lineup that month was up 137 percent, compared to a year earlier (Shepard 1999). Chris Mathews, the bombastic host of MSNBC's *Hardball,* along with his always-eager CNBC prime-time mate Geraldo Rivera, feasted on a banquet of rumor and political spin. But MSNBC and CNBC were not alone in wanting to tap into the spectacle. CNN and the fledgling Fox News Channel also devoted enormous resources to the story. As Olbermann, no longer an MSNBC host, put it: the networks were devoted to "covering this story 28 hours out of every 24" (Gabler 1998). The scale and intensity of the coverage was a bonanza for telegenic pundits such as Ann Coulter, a conservative constitutional lawyer who became a regular guest on CNBC's *Rivera Live* and a celebrity in her own right. The story also propelled Matt Drudge from relative obscurity to a household name synonymous with celebrity and political gossip; Drudge became a media star almost overnight. Scores of stories were written about the man who a month earlier *Vanity Fair* had dubbed the "Walter Winchell of the Web" (Conant 1997). Drudge, however, used the public vilification he received at the hands of politicians and media practitioners to his advantage. Drudge's claim that only about 70–80 percent of what he publishes is true did not scare off the Fox News Channel, which soon offered him his own television talk show; and by July 1999 he signed a deal with ABC to host a syndicated weekly radio talk show. Drudge's brand strength encouraged ABC Radio executive Geoff Rich to boast that "never before has a national talk show debuted in so many top markets" (Associated Press cited in EXTRA! 1999). From the very start, the Clinton-Lewinsky scandal was a story that was rationally constructed and administered by individuals and organizations concerned with promoting their own interests and who did so using the logic of promotion—the wheels of the media machine are greased by creating a commodity-sign that can be used as a site of promotion for disparate interests, whether they be personal, political or commercial.

Monica Lewinsky, like Princess Diana before her, was a fulcrum point for the spectacle's vortex of promotion. Tapping the Monicagate spectacle is good business. What is by now the standard round of blue jokes fills out the repertoires of late-night stand-up comics.[9] Restaurants and radio stations scurry to organize Monica Lewinsky look-alike contests in which grinning women pose holding Freudian cigars (Cohen 1999b). And in September 1998, Italian fashion design-house Gattinoni announces that it is negotiating with Lewinsky's lawyers to have her make a catwalk appearance in a Milan fashion show. Lewinsky, says a publicist, would wear a Gattinoni designed blue dress. DNA tests of a navy-blue GAP dress owned by Lewinsky discovered traces of semen matching the DNA of President Clinton (Reuters and Associated Press 1998). Collectible experts are quoted in the press saying the infamous size-12 gown—of which Lewinsky later regained possession—could fetch in excess of US$1 million at auction (Straub 2001).

The big coming-out event, however, occurs March 3, 1999, when Lewinsky is interviewed by Barbara Walters in a two-hour special edition of ABC's newsmagazine *20/20*. The interview, the first of two (Lewinsky was also interviewed by Channel Four in Great Britain), was timed to coincide with the launch of her new book, *Monica's Story,* an account of her time with the president and its repercussions. It is written by Andrew Morton, Princess Diana's biographer. Close to 74 million people tune in to watch Lewinsky tell her version of the story on *20/20*. ABC, acutely aware of the potential riches to be gained from the enormous audience, expands the program from one to two hours and charges US$800,000 for 30-second advertising spots. The estimated windfall is US$35 million (Cohen 1999b). Not surprisingly, the *20/20* broadcast helps expand the spectacle even further. The broadcast sparks a run on the Club Monaco lipstick worn by Lewinsky. An ABC publicist reports receiving "hundreds and hundreds of e-mails asking about her lipstick" (Province 1999).[10] Soon, Lewinsky's much-discussed weight problem comes to the attention of Jenny Craig, which has inked a deal with the 26-year-old former intern to represent the company in a US$7-million television campaign promoting its weight-control program.[11] Sarah Ferguson, the Duchess of York (in Toronto February 11, 2000, promoting the Canadian launch of an animated television series based on her children's books entitled *Budgie the Little Helicopter*), is quoted by Toronto scribes as being sympathetic toward Lewinsky and her latest choice of employment (Vancouver Sun 2000). The Duchess, no stranger to the glare of the media spotlight, happens to be a spokesperson for Jenny Craig's competitor, Weight Watchers.

Not to be outdone, while the Duchess is in Toronto, producers for MTV are in Ottawa staging a promotional circus for *The Tom Green Show* involving Lewinsky, Canadian comedian Tom Green and, as one newspaper put it, "a couple of sack-like purses" (Vancouver Sun 2000). In total, twenty TV cameras, six news organizations with two live satellite feeds in tow, converge on an Ottawa restaurant named the Little Beaver. They have been lured there with hints that Green and Lewinsky will announce their engagement. The nuptial declaration does not happen; instead, a mute Lewinsky (apparently her hair is a good enough signifier) joins Green on top of the restaurant's roof where, according to one report, he "'rambled some nonsense' about Ottawa being the 'fabric capital of the world'" before waving the purses for the cameras (Vancouver Sun 2000). The purses are part of Lewinsky's new collection available for sale at various high-end apparel stores and over the Internet (www.therealmonica.com). A year and a half after Lewinsky launches her book, Hillary Clinton announces she intends to tell her side of the story in book form. Simon & Schuster is so bullish that the publisher gives Clinton an US$8-million advance. Lucianne Goldberg, her expert status on the scandal confirmed, is quoted as saying: "Hillary writes a dirty book. I think it would be an enormous bestseller" (Whitworth 2000).[12] The protean circulation of the Lewinsky commodity-sign is truly dizzying, and with the Goldberg quote, has come full circle. And it is all covered by the mainstream media, who are also eagerly attempting to wring value out of the various moments of promotional circulation.

Lewinsky would later sign a deal, reported to be worth close to US$1 million, to participate in an HBO documentary about the presidential tryst. Having by now mastered the promotional language of the self-help industry, Lewinsky is quoted as saying it was time to add to the *Monica's Story* tale. "The book, that captured that time for me," she told the *New York Times*. "The last couple of years have been such a time of intense growth and perspective for me. I want to do something that really reflects the way I felt then, the way I feel now" (Rutenberg 2001a). Living in New York, Lewinsky's attendance at Oscar parties and various gatherings, such as the opening of a Chanel store in Manhattan's Soho district, is chronicled by celebrity gossip scribes (Straub 2001). Lewinsky is now a bone fide regular on the city's promotional party circuit, organized by "event publicists" such as Lizzie Grubman (French 2001).[13]

An intuitive understanding of the logic of promotion allows Donato Dalrymple to grab his 15 minutes of fame in Miami. Dalrymple is the man initial news reports refer to as "the fisherman," who, on Thanksgiving Day 1999, pulled young Elián González out of the sea after the boat he and his mother used to flee Cuba capsizes. Truth be told, Dalrymple is not a fisherman. He cleans houses for a living and that day on the water was his first time out fishing on his cousin's boat. There is even some dispute as to whether he pulled the young boy from the water or simply assisted. Michael Leahy, a *Washington Post* reporter who interviewed Dalrymple, writes perceptively that it was this "moniker" of the fisherman that "made him sound like a character born of Hemingway, and he looked the part: broad-shouldered, barrel-chested, salt of the earth, with tattoos covering his arms and a passionate bark to his speech" (Leahy 2000). His sudden fame and prestige as the "savior" of Elián allows Dalrymple—the man Oliver North calls a hero, but whom Leahy contemptuously dubs "The Cleaner"—to contemplate a campaign for public office: "Yeah, I could see myself walking through that door and maybe running for mayor or that lower office, you know, what is it? Commissioner or something?" (Leahy 2000). Elián González is yet another tragic fulcrum point for the vortex of promotion. While a custody battle between his father and his Miami relatives rages in court, he is paraded in front of the media daily. Their cameras, desperate for more fodder, hungrily consume his image. At one point, the Miami relatives release a video of the boy stating that he does not want to return to Cuba—it is a propaganda moment worthy of Joseph Goebbels. "Elián," writes the *New York Times*'s Frank Rich, "has been sacrificed to the media gods, who extract a fresh slice of video meat daily. His performance has been gleefully facilitated by the Miami relatives, who purport to have the boy's best interests at heart, and eagerly disseminated by entertainment corporations that saw a ratings winner" (Rich 2000a). Rich goes on to quote an unnamed network executive who states bluntly "Elián's not a political symbol; he's a very sexy kid in a soap opera. . . . For TV, it's plain-old voyeurism, and for voyeurism to be really fun, it has to include good-looking people. Those gold chains are a look. The way he's been dressed, he could be a 16-year-old hanging out with Gloria Estefan." It didn't take long for the entertainment division at CBS to take a cue from their news colleagues and announce plans for an Elián mini-series (Rich 2000a).[14]

## *Spectacular Storytelling and Flexible Production*

The cultural texts stemming from the mourning of the Princess of Wales or the ritual of excommunication endured by U.S. President Bill Clinton are promotional commodities that have been aestheticized through marketing and advertising. It is true that these cultural texts can be appropriated by individuals who yearn for a deeper sense of community, or who feel shared social values are being threatened. However, the key point I have tried to develop is that these narratives—mediated through a particular set of market transactions—have become constitutive of economic competition and rational organization; they have become objects of rational and strategic action by commercial and political interests. It is in this sense that popular culture has become reified and susceptible to forms of domination.

Media events of the historically specific variety under discussion are well suited to a global trend toward "high-volume flexible production systems" characterized by flexible forms of management, labor performance, and increased intensity in the speed of production and turnover time (Castells 2000a: 167). New technologies and forms of information processing, driven by the desire among competing organizations to increase profitability, "act upon all domains of human activity, and make it possible to establish endless connections between different domains, as well as between elements and agents of such activities" (78). The semiotic transposition of spectacular news stories from one seemingly unrelated domain to another—where the fiery death of a British princess in a Paris tunnel is linked via a promotional network to the promotion of a U.S. TV show about well-toned lifeguards—contributes to the expansion of the spectacle. With the addition of new media technologies, says Philip Graham, we have entered into a historically unprecedented phase of "hypercapitalism" characterized by "the almost immediate production, consumption, distribution and exchange of valued categories of thought and language—knowledge commodities—on a planet-wide scale" (Graham 2000: 139).

According to David Harvey (1989) this "regime of flexible accumulation" has had a significant impact on popular culture. Flexible accumulation has contributed to a greater emphasis on the fleeting and the ephemeral, on fashion and lifestyle, and, in turn on the speedier production of cultural meanings attached to commodities. The need for faster turnover time in consumption, argues Harvey, "has led to a shift of emphasis from production of [durable] goods . . . to the production of events (such as spectacles that have an almost instantaneous turnover time)" (Harvey 1989: 156–157). In Harvey's view, new forms of spectacular promotion become a decisive element in the quest for increased capital accumulation. In other words, *aesthetic production has become integrated into commodity production* generally. More worrisome, says Harvey, is that this flexible system of production carries with it a shift in the form of domination. Ownership and the "direct control over the means of production and wage labour" are not the principle means by which domination is enacted and secured. "What stands out," instead says Harvey, "is sheer money power as a means of domination." Such a system of asymmetrical money relations is predicated on "the need to mobilize cultural creativity and aesthetic ingenuity, not only in the production of a cultural artefact but also in its promotion, packaging, and transformation into some kind of successful spectacle" (Harvey 1989: 347).

Cultural performances are subject to the logic of promotion. Moreover, spectacular stories are integral to the profitability of 24-hour news organizations. CNN, MSNBC, and the Fox News network survive on the timely arrival and speedy, efficient exploitation of large-scale media events. These news organizations need spectacular media events to survive. Spectacular stories and their personalities increasingly have become central to the business of journalism on three levels: (1) they are transposable; (2) they are efficient; and (3) they become anchors for broader strategies of capital accumulation. I will develop these three aspects of spectacular storytelling in greater detail in Chapters Three, Four, and Five. But for now, I want to briefly sketch out their importance.

1. Transposibility: Spectacular stories and character types are easily inserted into the news flow because they utilize widely shared themes of everyday life: the tragic loss of a mother, the plight of a terrorized young boy, and the infidelity of a husband resonate easily and powerfully across cultural, class, and demographic boundaries. Conversely, narratives that seek to explain complex social, cultural, and economic phenomena demand much more from audiences. Given the relatively short length of most news pieces (a minute and a half to two minutes for TV, 600–800 words for most newspapers), audiences are required to fill in the blanks of most narratives; that is, readers must make the story meaningful by referring to their own store of cultural and social information—their own horizon of interests. This point runs parallel to the basic position of neo-Durkheimians such as Alexander and Jacobs (1998). But because these narratives are easily understood by diverse audiences, they can flow effortlessly back and forth through seemingly disparate cultural spheres and sometimes between real life and fiction. Consequently, the dramatic tension strived for in theater can be applied to the production of media events.

Channel surfers could be forgiven, the week of November 12, 2000, for thinking they were witnessing an adaptation of Luigi Pirandello's play *Six Characters in Search of an Author*,[15] in which the traditional boundaries of real life and drama become problematized and thrown into question. On November 15, George W. Bush interrupted prime-time programming to make a live televised statement in support of his efforts to end manual recounts of U.S. election ballots in Florida. The unusual break in network programming followed a similar address to the nation by Vice President Al Gore earlier that evening. Both men were courting public opinion while their lawyers continued a prolonged legal dust-up following the inconclusive election results. Bush's televised address broke into the CBS miniseries "American Tragedy," the story of the O.J. Simpson murder trial. One of the characters in that drama is Harvard Law professor Alan Dershowitz, who advised Simpson's defense team. Meanwhile, for those viewers flipping to the real-time presidential drama unfolding on the 24-hour cable networks, Dershowitz (the flesh-and-blood version) could be seen providing a strident argument defending demands by Democrats for ballot recounts in three Florida counties. Celebrity legal pundit Greta Van Susteren, who gained notoriety during the Simpson trial, was also back on CNN providing commentary on the intricacies of civil procedures. "All that's missing from the scene outside the Palm Beach County courthouse," writes Caroline Baum "is the Juice himself, driving in his white Bronco, and Monica Lewinsky's first lawyer, William Ginsburg" (Baum 2000). Three days later Will Ferrell of *Saturday Night Live* would satirize Bush's performance "by declaring in Bush-speak, 'Tonight I am victoriant'" (James 2000).

*New York Times* writer Caryn James suggests the "dueling news conferences" that aired live throughout the week contributed to a surreal conflux of drama and politics. "Along the way, it often intruded on fictions that seemed more plausible than the reality being reported. The result is one large political conversation in which drama, comedy and news mingle freely on screen, informing and shaping the off-screen political reality" (James 2000).

2. Efficiency: At the level of production, the "vortex of publicity" allows for the increased efficiency of individual news workers and the entire system of newsgathering and dissemination. Spectacular images and narratives can travel with little friction between different media and their various program formats. The flexibility of these images and narratives allows for their efficient reuse or recombination in a variety of programs, publications, and Web sites. Consequently, news staffs can handle a much higher volume of information than would otherwise be the case. The production requirements of 24-hour news stations provide a good example. The all-news networks rely on spectacular stories to fuel their production. Spectacles such as Monica Lewinsky's tryst with President Clinton, the massacre at Columbine High School in Denver or the war in Kosovo, Afghanistan, and Iraq provide the raw material for continuous programming with the added benefit of increased efficiency and flexible use of network labor. Speaking in 1999, Jeff Zucker, the executive producer of NBC's *Today* show, now president of entertainment, explained how most foreign correspondents use to "leave 90 percent" of their material unused after filing for the nightly news and his own program. However, that situation has changed now that formally "surplus" information is being "repurposed" to support the production of numerous programs on the 24-hour cable network MSNBC, CNBC, and the Internet (Kurtz 1999a). In addition, increased labor flexibility is required from reporters who are expected to provided a steady stream of "live hits" during the course of the broadcast day. The Tribune Co. has been the leader in North America in extending this logic to the integration of its combined newspaper, broadcast, and Internet properties. In addition to their regular duties, scribes at the *Orlando Sentinel,* for example, routinely file live reports for the company's local 24-hour cable television station.

The analysis stemming from the concept of flexible accumulation helps us explain the intricate ways in which spectacular cultural products can serve disparate interests in both the economic and social realms. The story of the NATO bombing of Kosovo in 1999 was a boon to Republican presidential hopefuls eager to gain name and face recognition. Many appeared as guest pundits on shows such as MSNBC/CNBC's *Hardball,* providing the program with much-needed high-profile experts while at the same time providing themselves with national exposure (Kurtz 1999b). This confluence of interests provides an interesting example of what Wernick means by the "vortex of publicity." Both the presidential hopefuls and the cable programs they appear on act as promotional signs for each other. The increased circulation of spectacular images about the war serves to raise the profile and value of both the networks and candidates. In the early days following the NATO bombings, MSNBC's ratings were up 103 percent.

Finally, the flexible-accumulation argument directs our attention to the financial and cultural capital required to participate in the spectacle. Republican presidential hopefuls can insert themselves into the circulation of images precisely because of their financial wealth and cultural capital. Peace activists who lack similar resources may find it more difficult to have their views broadcast.

3. Anchors for broader strategies of capital accumulation: The ability to "repurpose" information content, in tandem with new technologies such as global satellites and the Internet, helps news organizations grow in ways previously unthought of. For example, 24-hour cable news networks such as CNN, MSNBC, and Fox are not viable ventures without the ability to repurpose information. Spectacular stories are perfectly suited to this purpose. Media events such as Monicagate provide 24/7 news organizations with their largest audiences; but their chief importance lies in how these aestheticized events provide fulcrum points that allow integrated media properties to profitably administer their promotional system on a global scale. As systems of production and consumption become more and more integrated, audiences are divided into niches and shared among the various strands of the integrated system of production and distribution—among broadcast, print, and new media. This was the underlying logic behind the US$182-billion AOL–Time Warner megamerger. The stunning announcement, January 10, 2000, prompted a rush of similar cross-media mergers that year in the U.S. and Canada, deals that suddenly made convergence a frequent front-page story in newspapers across the continent. To be sure, the development of new media technologies is crucial to media convergence and integration. But the driving force behind the mergers has been a desire to take advantage of the promise of promotional integration. At the news conference announcing the deal, AOL Chief Executive Steve Case bragged to reporters that the newly merged company "will offer an incomparable portfolio of global brands," including CNN, TBS, TNT, HBO, *Time, Sports Illustrated,* and *People* magazines (Leibovich 2000). In July 2000, a press release issued by CanWest Global Communications trumpeted the broadcaster's C$3.5-billion purchase of Hollinger Inc.'s major Canadian newspaper titles. The deal, while tiny compared to AOL's blockbuster move, gave the company unprecedented control over the news Canadians receive, and it raised media concentration in the country—already at dangerous levels—to new heights. The combination of CanWest and Hollinger news and entertainment brands, including the *National Post* newspaper, is formidable. "Our goal," said CanWest CEO Leonard Asper, "is to employ all of these assets to provide maximum linkages between advertisers and their customers. We also intend to create new interactive opportunities for buyers and sellers to transact business, thereby generating new revenue streams for our company. More than ever before, with this transaction, CanWest is now content rich, advertiser friendly and e-commerce ready." In a couple of years' time, a heavy debt load and a slumping economy would hammer the share prices of both companies. Case would be forced by shareholder pressure to resign his position as head of the company. But the seed of promotional integration had been planted.

Corporate media convergence is the partial realization of what Debord came to call, much earlier, the integrated spectacle. It "is characterized," says Debord, "by the combined effect of five principal features: incessant technological renewal; integration of state and economy; generalized secrecy; unanswerable lies; [and] an eternal present" (Debord 1988: 4). Debord's view of the integrated spectacle is characteristically bleak. During the Cold War, he believed there to be two variations of the spectacle: diffuse and concentrated. In countries such as the United States, Canada, and France, where the commodity form is able to roam freely, we find the diffuse spectacle. The concentrated spectacle, on the other hand, is epitomized by Stalinism and its valorization of state bureaucracy. "The relatively feeble economic development of these countries, as compared with that of societies ruled by 'diffuse spectacular power,' is compensated by *ideology*" and the requirement that people identify with a charismatic leader (Jappe 1999: 9). In the twilight of the 20th century, Debord abandons the distinction for the term *integrated spectacle*.

We can, I think, make use of this term without adopting its more paranoid aspects. In Debord's hands the term is used to critique the "man behind the curtain" whose control of all public knowledge and whose lies cannot be answered or exposed. There is no answer to the spectacle, says Debord, quite simply because the circularity of the spectacle "is the only thing to which everyone is witness. Spectacular power can similarly deny whatever it likes, once, or three times over, and change the subject; knowing full well there is no danger of any riposte, in its own space or any other" (Debord 1988: 6). And yet, as we have seen, social and political struggles are waged within the confines of the spectacle. The racial politics of the O.J. Simpson trial is but one example (Hunt 1999; Glynn 2000: 66–99). And as John Thompson observes (2000), the increasingly mediated visibility of political life can spell danger for politicians unable to keep secret potentially damning information. Bill Clinton's private indiscretions come to mind. Debord's pessimism gets the better of him; and yet, there is still some usefulness in the concept. My use of the term *integrated spectacle* is informed by Krishan Kumar's observation that flexible specialization does not necessarily mean the abandonment of centralized control of production (Kumar 1995: 60–61). As the move toward vertically integrated corporate media mergers indicate, flexible production strategies can be used by large global corporations as well as small cottage industries. The key strategy, as Leonard Asper makes abundantly clear, is to accommodate economies of scope with economies of scale.

# CHAPTER THREE

# Steps towards Spectacular Integration

*The big problem in cable is that nobody watches unless there's a big story.*
ERIK SORENSON, FORMER MSNBC PRESIDENT

## Beginnings of Integrated News

Today's highly integrated and globalized media environment may be historically unique, but the process driving its creation is not unprecedented. The globalization of news is a 19th-century phenomenon first made possible by the confluence of the telegraph, state patronage, and the development of transnational news agencies. When referring to the process of globalization, I am using John Thompson's (1995) definition, which includes three factors: (1) activities that take place on a global and not merely a regional scale; (2) activities that are coordinated and organized on a global scale; and finally (3) that these activities involve a high degree of interdependency among different regions of operation (150).

Transnational news agencies came into existence in the 1830s. In 1835 Charles Havas established the first news agency in Paris. By the 1840s Havas was joined by two rival newsgathering operations: Reuters in London, and the Wolff news agency in Berlin. From the beginning, the development of these agencies was associated with the development of the telegraph and the commercial penny press, both of which also came into existence in the 1830s. "The press," explains Robert Babe, "required the immediacy of the telegraph to obtain dispatches about faraway events that had occurred within the previous twenty-four hours. The telegraph, on the other hand, was financially dependent on the daily press as its single largest customer" (Babe 1996: 285).

The birth of news agencies coincided with the birth of general-interest newspapers dedicated to selling audiences to advertisers. It also coincided with the colonial expansion of the major European powers: Britain, Germany, and France. To control these vast regions, the colonial powers relied on naval power and the speedy communication provided by cable and telegraph. It is at this moment that we see the first instance of electronic communication being used to centralize the management and control of the flow of commodities on a global scale. "The critical change," says James Carey, "lay in the ability to secure investments. There was no heavy overseas investment until the control made possible by the cable" (Carey 1992: 212). The news agencies followed the cables laid by their home countries as they too colonized vast territories and then proceeded to carve out regional monopolies. An agreement finalized in 1870 gave Reuters control over the British Empire and Holland; Havas gained control over the French Empire, Italy, Spain, and Portugal; while Wolff controlled Germany, Scandinavia, and Russian territories By colonizing electronic space, the news agencies monopolized news transmission and became the prototypes for future global communications organizations (Thompson 1995: 155; Rantanen 1997: 616–617).[1] Thompson summarizes the significance of news agencies as threefold. First, they generated the systematic gathering and dissemination of news and information on a global scale. Second, the triple news cartel carved up the world for themselves, and, in doing so, created "a multilateral ordering of communication networks" across the globe. Third, through their close relationship with newspapers, news agencies were part of a growing communication network that reached a significant number of people (Thompson 1995: 154). To this list we can add a fourth significant impact. The 19th-century news agencies also played a key role in making news into a commodity to be bought and sold in national and international markets. The commodification of news, in turn, is closely interconnected with the broader development of the commodification of place, space, and time.

### Commodification of Place, Space, and Time

There is a well-established body of theoretical work that maintains that modernity along with the development of electronic communication has fundamentally changed the significance of time and space for everyday life (Meyrowitz 1985; Harvey 1989; Ferguson 1990; Giddens 1990; Carey 1992; Thompson 1995; Rantanen 1997). Put simply, one of the principal characteristics that separates modern from premodern societies is the ability, due to improved transportation and communication, to overcome the limitations of time. In traditional societies, social relations were embedded in situated locales and carried out largely through face-to-face communication. In modern societies, these relationships undergo fundamental change. No longer are social relationships predicated on shared locales; social relationships are now spread over multiply interconnected geographic areas. Space and place are rent apart as the local and the global become increasingly interconnected via communications technologies and the process of capital accumulation. Improvements in transportation and communication technologies contribute to what Harvey (1989) calls "time-space compression," a process in which the limitations of space and time are eliminated or reduced significantly as they become objectified and subject to management and control. The telegraph's contribution to this process lay in its separation of communication from transportation. Prior to the telegraph, the speed of communication was tied to the speed of transportation. In James Carey's words: "The telegraph ended that identity and allowed symbols to move independently of geography and independently of and faster than transport" (1992: 213).

Of central importance is how the production of new social spaces through the elimination of time is constitutively linked to social relations of power. On this point David Harvey argues persuasively that the ability to objectify, organize, and control space through the elimination of time is "an important means to augment social power. In material terms this means that those who can affect the spatial distribution of investments in transport and communications, in physical and social infrastructures, or the territorial distribution of administrative, political, and economic powers can often reap material rewards" (Harvey 1989: 233). The implications for the production and commodification of news are substantial. The ability to command resources of communication gave news agencies and other media institutions the ability to extend "economic (and political) dominion over time and space" (Ferguson 1990: 154). Commenting on the role of the telegraph in this regard, Tehri Rantanen notes that: "The telegraph profoundly changed the relationship between news and time, because the value of news could be measured against time that had become quantified" (1997: 610). In the 18th century it took a minimum of 48 days for the British Crown to communicate with its colonial subjects in America. The development of news agencies and the telegraph shrank that time to hours. (Stephens 1988, 220 cited in Rantanen 1997: 610). As Elliott and Golding (1974) suggest, the value of commodities is based, in part, on their originality and the speed with which they can be produced and delivered to market; consequently, in highly competitive media industries a premium is placed on beating your competition to market. And, this "necessity of gathering, processing and distributing information as quickly as possible has implications for the type of commodity produced" (Elliott and Golding 1974: 248, cited in Ratanen 1997: 610). The advent of the daily newspaper is tied to the business community's need for up-to-date information and the telegraph's ability to deliver it. And the success of news organizations depended upon their ability to control and exploit the emerging relationships among place, space, and time.

Electronic news contributed to the changed nature of space in the 19th century. Electronic news linked far-flung markets, and in doing so, changed the nature of the news experience. News was no longer predominantly about social relationships connected to places and experiences with which people shared some familiarity through direct face-to-face encounters. People became engaged in what John Thompson calls "mediated quasi-interaction"—a process whereby individuals, stretched across time and space, share symbolic forms of communication which are distributed monologically (Thompson 1995: 84–87). With the telegraph, people were presented with news from distant locales around the globe, news that was not directly related to their everyday experiences. Quoting Anthony Giddens, Rantanen argues that place had become "phantasmagoric" (Rantanen 1997: 609). Increasingly, the news commodity found itself less and less connected to real material relations that were experienced directly (e.g., news of local officials or tariffs on various goods that had originally been traded directly in the marketplace); the news commodity became dematerialized as it represented social relations, now experienced discontinuously and at a distance. The news commodity, time, and space had become abstract and subject to organization and control by news organizations interested in maximizing exchange-value. And as Rantanen suggests, the main criteria used to evaluate the value of news became time and place (Rantanen 1997: 613).[2] A news story's exclusivity was predicated on its place of origin and the speed with which it could be delivered. The age of a story contributed to its exchange-value, the newer the better. As a result, there is a built-in imperative, beginning in the 19th century, to produce news as quickly as possible so as to add value; and of course, the news agencies' exclusive use of stories resulting from their monopolized regions contributed greatly to improving their bottom line. The clichéd phrase "This just in" has a traceable historical origin that is shared with the commodification, distribution and exchange of the news commodity.

Importantly, the process of commodification—increasingly subject to the control of monopoly news agencies—contributed to the development of a new style of news presentation. The advent of the global news market created the need for the speedy delivery of news from distant locales to newspapers, which in turn used stories to attract general audiences for advertisers. These production requirements contributed greatly to the creation of the "universal news style." The complex process of commodification had also changed the nature of news events in the electronic age. "In the global news flow," says Rantanen, "places could easily become *phantasmagoric* [my emphasis] non-places, that only refer to an *event* [my emphasis] that has taken place there and lose their local authentic identity" (618). These socially constructed mediated events, in other words, were subject to intensive commodification through the use of abstract representations and "expert systems" of organization well before the advent of CNN. The decontextualization of media events is in essence the process first described by Marx, in which products are abstracted out of their real conditions of production, and represented and valued using standardized yet arbitrary symbols of exchange, including money. Exchange-value is privileged over use-value. The uniqueness of these new mediated events is linked to the control of space and time, as well as the means of symbolic aestheticization, that is, dramatization, promotion, and advertising. The result was that the value of media events became integrated, early on, with the process of commodity production, distribution, and exchange.

## Human Interest and Commercial Interests

The fast pace of modern life marked by collapsing spacial boundaries and the discontinuity of everyday experience carried with it opportunities and challenges for capitalist production, and in particular, for the production of news. As mentioned above, individuals accommodated themselves to the rationality of the new modern consumer culture by making their lives into renewable projects. Individuals utilized the resources of aestheticized commercial products and services in a continual process of self-identity construction. News organizations, as major advertising vehicles, were also forced to accommodate themselves to these changes. So in the 19th century, while individuals were actively using the symbolic goods produced by consumer culture in their personal projects of self-identity formation, news organizations increasingly began to speak to consumers in the personalized voice of the human-interest story.

During the interwar period of the 20th century, important economic changes occurred in the news industry that, when combined with these broader cultural shifts already being experienced at the level of the individual, contributed to the proliferation of so-called human-interest stories in an attempt to universalize the appeal of newspapers. James Curran, Angus Douglas, and Gary Whannel (1980), citing the British experience, list a series of economic factors that collectively exerted pressure on popular newspapers to increase the proportion of human-interest stories. First, because of the high fixed costs associated with producing the first copy of a paper, there was enormous incentive for newspapers to take advantage of economies of scale by increasing circulation. The more copies sold, the cheaper the unit cost of each subsequent copy because the fixed cost could be spread over each unit. Meanwhile, overall production costs rose steadily during this period (1921–1939) as successful publishers reinvested increased revenues (due to expanded advertising) back into editorial (whose size grew in proportion to advertising space). This, in turn, applied further pressure on newspapers to universalize their appeal in order to boost circulation. Second, the push to universalize appeal was augmented by the growing incentive to tap into an expanding national advertising market. Those papers with national distribution were at a distinct advantage (due to economies of scale) over regional papers in the cutthroat competition to woo large-scale firms and their national advertising patronage. Third, and importantly, the development of new and sophisticated market-research techniques in the 1920s and 1930s brought to light the importance of women consumers, a group that previously had not been targeted by newspapers. Subsequently, newspapers reoriented themselves to account for the newly expanded definition of what constituted an appropriate audience. However, while there were rising incentives to increase distribution (to working-class women for example), this was softened by continuing differences in purchasing power among classes. The willingness of advertisers to pay more for access to elite affluent consumers meant that publishers of popular newspapers were encouraged to de-emphasize their attraction to working-class audiences. To this end newspapers universalized their appeal with content that was attractive to men, women, and different regions and classes (289–292). Personalized human-interest stories were perfectly suited to this purpose.

During the interwar period, therefore, various economic incentives along with improvements in technological distribution contributed to the creation of overlapping markets for news at the local, regional, national, and global level; and the transposability of the news commodity became increasingly important for news organizations in their drive to universalize their audience and expand circulation. The more people a news item could speak to, the more valuable it was. It is in this sense that the phantasmagoric nature of news became critical. The ability to distribute a given news event across various geographical regions coalesced with acute market incentives to speak across geographic, gender, and class boundaries. News agencies figured in this development; and in the late 1920s, control over the organization, distribution, and exchange of news across space and time contributed to the production of one of the world's first truly spectacular media events: the cross-Atlantic flight of American pilot Charles Lindbergh.

On Saturday, May 21, 1927, Charles Lindbergh became a heroic figure of the modern age. That morning Lindbergh completed his unprecedented solo flight across the Atlantic from New York to Le Bourget airfield in Paris. He was greeted by a huge crowd of well-wishers estimated at between 150,000 to 200,000 people. Overnight, Lindbergh became an international media star, a darling of both the general public and the upper-class elite who contrived to share in his fame. Despite Lindbergh's status as a media darling, historian Modris Eksteins (1989) disputes claims that his fame was the result of a "spectacle-craving public" or that it was a media fabrication. Eksteins places the event in a broader cultural context to argue that Lindbergh satisfied the needs of two different worlds. The first was old and based on the values of rigor and decorum; the second world was new and based on an emergent modern sensibility. On the one hand, Lindbergh's solo flight signified the best of the 19th century's celebration of "individual achievement based on effort, preparation, courage, staying power" (250). Conversely, the audacity of Lindbergh's daring flight, accomplished without the aid of a radio, spoke to a "modern sensibility. . . . enchanted above all by the *deed*." In the new modern aesthetic, "The purpose was immaterial. The act was everything" (251). Lindbergh's flight was the accomplishment of an individual who had acted for himself. It was the deed of an individual whose actions, following the end of the First World War, resonated with large numbers of people who had real doubts concerning the inevitability of rational historical progress and government's ability to administer for society's needs.

The new modern sensibility referred to by Eksteins—what he calls "the journey to the interior"—was in sync with modern consumer culture. However, to suggest, as Eksteins does, that for the most part "the press followed the excitement rather than created it" (250), is to underestimate the importance of the global circulation of the news commodity. To argue that the various meanings attributed to the Lindbergh flight met the needs of two overlapping Zeitgeists—one 19th century, the other early-20th-century modern—does not exclude an examination of the underlying economic value the story held for news organizations gearing themselves towards the new global market for news. The Lindbergh story was all the more valuable because of its wide appeal. It was a highly transposable commodity that news agencies could be sure would appeal to disparate audiences around the globe.

The decisive importance of the transposability of the news commodity is made patently clear by Helen Hughes's (1936) celebrated study of the media's sensational coverage of the kidnapping of Lindbergh's 19-month-old baby boy in 1932. Hughes notes that the Lindbergh kidnapping story was known by American newspapermen at the time as "the greatest human-interest story of the decade." The story was featured on the front page of the *Herald-Tribune* every day except one in March of that year; while the venerable Gray Lady of print, the *New York Times,* devoted half of page one and two full inside pages on the first and last days of the story. It even topped coverage of the Sino-Japanese war (35). When the story ended 72 days later with the tragic news that the baby's body had been found in a pile of leaves near Lindbergh's home, *Editor and Publisher* declared: "From a circulation standpoint the finding of the body was the biggest story since the Armistice and in some cases, the biggest story of all time" (cited in Hughes 1936: 36). The reason was due to the story's universal appeal to the rich, poor, and people of various racial origins. Everyone could empathize with the loss of a child, and because the tragedy involved the child of a hero, the story grew to enormous proportions. "It is not important because of calling for a redirection of action; there is nothing at all to be done. But the importance of the news, to the commercial press, lay in the universal interest it awoke" (35). In other words, the story's use-value was next to nil, but its exchange-value in the newly integrated global market for news was phenomenal. During the first ten days of the coverage, newspapers in New York and Philadelphia reported circulation gains of between 15 and 20 percent (36). It was precisely this function that placed the human-interest story at the center of strategies to develop a mass-circulation press.

Hughes sees the penny press as an extension of the early modern forms of popular street literature. It "was an industrial form of the circulation of gossip" (Sparks 2000: 19). The business strategy of the penny press, in the words of one of its practitioners, was to make one human-interest story "the talking point" for the day by "directing the attention of wide circles of people to one event for one day with magnetic power. . . . In this way circulation is attained, which then brings the most important desideratum advertisements" (cited in Hughes 1936: 50). And, if updates to the story can grip the attention of readers and raise circulation for 72 days, all the better. In the Lindbergh kidnapping story, we see an early precursor to the mourning of Princess Diana. It was a story of immense popular interest that dominated news coverage for weeks and had members of the public searching for ways to express their sorrow. It became a promotional fulcrum point around which grief was commodified, coverage was organized, and circulation expanded. The machinery of the early penny press and the international wire services ensured that the story, and its myriad updates, would be transmitted quickly and globally. In this way, the provincial gossip of the abduction of a baby is mixed with the celebrity star system and techniques of modern news production to become a huge world story. It is a commodity that has been revalued by a historically specific labor process to meet the changing needs of the market.

The phantasmagoric character of the Lindbergh kidnapping story—that is, the extent to which it was decontextualized and socially constructed to meet the needs of different media's promotional interests—is also made clear by Hughes's important study. Hughes notes that all forms of newspapers, not just the commercial penny press but also the Communist press, were attracted to the universal appeal of the Lindbergh kidnapping story. She compared the coverage given by a variety of newspapers in Berlin that indicated that the form of the story was not a function of the intrinsic nature of the event, but instead, corresponded to the needs of each particular newspaper (54). For example, even the city's Communist Party organ, *Die Rote Fahne* (The Red Flag) could not pass on the opportunity to tap into the interest generated by the Lindbergh story. Hughes describes the coverage as a sermon in which Lindbergh is portrayed as a bourgeois "fetish of the American patriots" (39). Conversely, the personalized coverage of the commercial penny press was a result of a business strategy conducted by large-scale news organizations to build up circulation. Both, however, were promotional.

The Lindbergh story, both in its heroic and tragic phases, was the result of a complex historical process involving the *convergence* of the state, technological development, and the exigencies of economic relations. It is an early example of the integrated news spectacle, albeit on a smaller scale and intensity than exists in today's media environment. The integrated news spectacle needs to be understood as a complex dynamic involving the process of commodification along with managerial and bureaucratic attempts to harness the spectacle's power. The media spectacle of the Lindbergh story (not to be reduced simply to the public's interest in the story) resulted from the unique segmentation of time and space made possible by an earlier convergence of state resources, technology, and capital. Since then, further historical developments have occurred within the state, technology, and capital triumvirate. Before we can explain the proliferation of spectacular media events in the twilight of the late 20th century, we need to trace these developments and relate them back to the specific ways in which the news commodity is produced, distributed, and exchanged.

In order to understand today's modern integrated news spectacles (i.e., the All-Monica-All-the-Time phenomenon) we need to be sensitive to changing dynamics among "constellations" of social forces, new technologies, and institutional logics that form their historical and material context.

## Setting the Scene

In most Western nations, the state has played a pivotal role in the development and structural transformation of the news industry. The first newspapers were overtly political, subsidized, and regulated by the state and political parties. The era of the politically partisan press ended with the development of a commercially funded press in the early 1800s. In turn, the formation of the original oligopolistic international news cartel was made possible with the power of three colonial governments: Britain, France, and Germany. These governments conferred territorial markets upon their national media organizations (Reuters, Havas, and Wolff) at a time when global trade was increasing in importance and there was a need for swift communications regarding world news and events. Western-based news agencies became wholesalers of news and information to regionally based newspapers, some of whom would eventually expand their circulation nationally to meet the needs of burgeoning national advertising markets.

Following the demise of the partisan press in Britain, Canada, and the United States, the state continued to perform an important regulatory function for the economy as a whole, and, in particular, for electronic communication industries that had become increasingly important to the process of capital accumulation. At the risk of over-simplification, the state is charged with two basic functions: it must promote the interests of capital through fiscal and regulatory policies designed to reproduce suitably skilled labor and a secure investment climate while simultaneously performing the role of arbitrator for wider social interests that can, and often do, come into conflict with capital accumulation. Rianne Mahon argues the role of regulatory agencies, such as the Canadian Radio-Television and Telecommunications Commission, is to resolve this conflict in a way that accommodates dominant elite interests within the context of more vaguely defined "national interests" (Mahon 1980: 160). Certainly, the creation of strong public broadcasters in Britain and Canada during the 1920s and 1930s attests to the success of broadly defined national interests having been taken seriously by government. Indeed, news has long played a role in the "project" of modern nationalism—the very idea of "national" news embodies this project. But, this more socially minded outcome of state involvement in media regulation has not always been the case, particularly in the United States.

In the mid-1920s, during the infancy of the radio industry in the United States, the two main private networks, the National Broadcasting Company (NBC) and the

Columbia Broadcasting System (CBS), were supportive of government efforts to regulate the industry. The now-dominant advertising-supported business model had not yet fully developed, and private broadcasters were concerned that chaos would spread if the government did not step in to regulate the distribution of spectrum frequencies. That attitude changed, however, once the fledgling private broadcasting industry was on a stable economic footing. Once it became clear that private broadcasters had secured a stable business climate, they began intensive lobbying efforts to limit the ability of government to establish public-interest guidelines. In 1934, the U.S. Federal Communications Commission (FCC) was created, and a limited government regulatory framework was established that allowed for government regulation only if it could be shown that industry self-regulation and the marketplace had failed (McChesney 1991).

In the 1980s and 1990s, the United States government, following a tremendous lobbying effort by influential corporate media conglomerates, began to dismantle the limited regulatory framework that had governed the broadcasting industries in that country since 1934. Of particular importance has been the 1996 U.S. Telecommunications Act, which removed barriers to entry and consolidation among media industries and the telecommunications industry. These moves have had an incredible impact internationally because of the significance of giant U.S. communication companies.

The U.S. government showed some interest in liberalization in the 1970s. The Nixon administration's "open skies" policy, which liberalized the satellite and cable industry, was perhaps the first important step. It ensured that satellite technology, which had been under the control of governments, would be made available to private enterprises. The policy would prove vital to the development of satellite-television broadcasting in the 1980s (Parker 1995: 30). But it was under the Reagan administration of the early 1980s that the major transition occurred. Reagan's early appointment of Mark Fowler as chairman of the FCC signaled the beginning of a shift in policy toward a re-regulation of communication industries.

The process of re-regulation is more commonly referred to as deregulation. But as Vincent Mosco (1996: 202), among others, has argued, deregulation is a misnomer because of its implicit assumption that corporations have been freed of regulatory ties, when in fact a form of government regulation has been replaced with market regulation. In other words, government regulations established to meet public-interest and service goals were targeted for elimination and replaced by market standards of performance. There were two basic approaches to the 1980s re-regulation: (1) the removal of ownership limit restrictions; and (2) the removal of general content regulations. In the 1980s, these twin pillars of re-regulation would react with phenomenal developments in communication technologies to forge the foundation of today's integrated media environment.

## The State, Ownership Limits, and the Push for Profits

The trend towards liberalization of media industries in the 1980s and 1990s was part of a worldwide trend towards neoliberal trade policies. Throughout Europe, Canada, and Australia, public enterprises were privatized, government regulation of private industries was lessened, and government expenditures on social welfare and other public services were drastically reduced. In Europe, steps were taken to reform broadcasting industries that had been dominated by government-owned broadcast monopolies. European governments did two things: (1) they introduced competition by issuing private broadcast licenses; and (2) they ordered government monopoly broadcasters to commercialize by becoming more dependent on advertising (Parker 1995: 30). In Canada, the Canadian Broadcast Corporation (CBC) saw its annual grant from Parliament shrink. By 1996–97, the parliamentary grant (C$854 million) accounted for approximately 75 percent of the CBC's funding, the rest ($250 million) being made up with advertising revenue from television. CBC Radio remains, for the moment, free of advertisements (Taras 1999: 128–129).

In the United States, FCC rules that had placed national limits of five AM, FM and television stations per company were relaxed in 1985 to allow 12/12/12. Those same limits were increased to 30 AM and 30 FM stations in 1992, and with the introduction of the seminal 1996 Telecommunications Act, national ownership limits for radio had been practically eliminated (Fairchild 1999: 553). U.S. broadcasters were handed a further freebie in 1996, when the U.S. Congress gave them $70-billion worth of digital spectrum space without any reciprocal obligation. No public auction was held. In essence, the U.S. Congress gave private enterprises billions of dollars' worth of public property so that it could be sold back to the public in the form of high-definition and interactive programming.

In 1999, as part of a mandatory review of ownership restrictions required by the 1996 Act, the FCC made it easier for a single entity to own more than two TV stations in a single market, a move that increased the ability of dominant broadcasters to further expand their market share. The FCC would go further; it signaled that it had plans to ease restrictions on cross-media ownership (Labaton 2000; Goodman 2001). In April 2001, The U.S. federal regulators voted to eliminate the "dual network" rule, which had blocked one television network from buying another. The decision effectively allowed multimedia conglomerate Viacom to retain ownership of the UPN network. The FCC had formerly demanded that Viacom divest itself of the UPN network as a condition of its 2000 purchase of CBS (Stern 2001). And two days after the September 11, 2001, terrorist attacks in New York and Washington, the FCC announced proceedings to review regulations limiting ownership limits for cable companies. Predictably, in the wake of the attacks, there was little news coverage. In June 2003, the Republican-controlled FCC voted to raise the limit on how many broadcast stations one company could own. One company would be allowed to own stations that reach 45 percent of U.S. households, up from 35 percent. Cross-ownership restrictions were also lifted to allow combinations of newspapers and broadcast stations in one market. Public opposition was fierce, despite the paucity of media coverage, and eventually a bipartisan coalition in the U.S. House voted to maintain the 45-percent limit, leaving intact the cross-ownership waiver of newspapers and broadcast stations. A bipartisan struggle ensued over the legislation. An appeals court in Philadelphia ordered an emergency stay to block the rules one day before they were scheduled to take effect, pending review (Ahrens 2003a; Labaton 2003; Stern and Krim 2003). And the rules were thrown into further doubt after the Senate Appropriations Committee added an amendment to a spending bill that would block funding to implement the rule changes (Ahrens 2003b). As I write, Republican leaders in Congress and the White House have announced a compromise agreement that would relax the audience cap to 39 percent. The deal would avert a threatened presidential veto of a measure that would have rolled back the FCC decision to loosen the ownership rules (Ahrens 2003c).

Another significant moment came in 1982 when the FCC eliminated the "anti-trafficking rule." The regulation had forbidden the sale of a broadcast property for three years after its purchase. The rule was designed to stop speculation in broadcast licences in order to promote community programming. But with its renewed market-driven approach, the FCC reasoned that any company that wished to purchase a broadcast property would be more interested in delivering a wide range of services than a company that wanted to sell (Fairchild 1999: 554). It could not have been more wrong. The anti-trafficking rule was rescinded during the recession of the early 1980s. The advertising market was tight, and there was mounting pressure for broadcasters to increase short-term profits. Once the rule was eliminated, speculation in broadcast properties began in earnest, increasing corporate consolidation. The 1980s saw ABC acquired by Capital Cities, and NBC purchased by General Electric. CBS was bought by entrepreneur Laurence Tisch. According to Robin Andersen, "speculators who had no interest or experience in the media bought and sold stations simply to make a profit. This practice set a trend for broadcasting that resulted in the devastation of news departments, increasing demands for low-cost programming, and the escalating competition of short-term profits" (Andersen 1995: 19). The radio industry was particularly affected. And, by 1996, with the passing of the U.S. Telecommunications Act, the general trend of consolidation was accelerated. Today, Clear Channel Communications, the largest owner of radio properties in the U.S., owns close to 1,200 stations. Together with Viacom's Infinity Broadcasting, the pair control one-third of all radio advertising in the United States (Boehlert: 2001).

In the past, news departments of the major U.S. networks were not seen merely as profit centers. News departments contributed to broadcasters' public-service requirements; and besides, they added prestige and conferred power upon owners interested in the prospect of influencing public policy. In the 1980s, the pressure to maximize short-term profits meant that newsrooms would be expected to contribute to the bottom line as well. The proscriptions of Taylorism reached all three U.S. networks as they began using time and motion studies in their newsrooms. And, in March 1987, CBS News, the "crown jewel" of the "Tiffany Network," had its budget slashed by $34 million; it laid off 200 people and closed two foreign bureaus (Wallis and Baran 1990: 21). Moreover, network news organizations, as well as newspapers in the U.S., Canada, and Britain—which had seen their circulation drop since the 1970s (Underwood 1993; Franklin 1997; Miller 1998)—began using increasingly sophisticated market surveys to tailor their newscasts and news sections to particular consumer lifestyles. Lifestyle sections began appearing in newspapers, while broadcasters created "Action News" formats and other stylized forms of news delivery to personalize news and heighten its intensity. Identity was used as a marketing tool and dramatic narratives with highly charged emotional appeal became more common. Newscasts and newspapers were massaged in order to appeal to audience members' sense of community, status concerns, or self-image. Stories providing consumer hints and news-you-can-use became popular, while CBS News revamped its news policy in search of dramatic "emotional moments."[3] Moreover, the new technical ability of broadcasters to "go live" had a dual function: first, it provided audiences with the opportunity to fulfill an apparent need to connect with others through a shared televisual experience; second, it allowed broadcasters "to create a connection between the masses and events (thereby reinforcing mass sentiments" (Bourdon 2000: 552). As W. Lance Bennett argues, news was being "integrated" with everyday life for the purposes of profit maximization, not merely to meet the varied interests and needs of public life (Bennett 1988: 7).

### New Media, Blurring Boundaries, and Audience Fragmentation

Thoughout the 1970s the market was regulating and competitive pressures were intensifying. The tension escalated in the early 1980s with the introduction of new technologies such as VCRs, satellites, and the burgeoning cable industry. Development of these technologies was being spurred on by the increased demand of global businesses for faster and more reliable forms of communication (Herman and McChesney 1997: 38). The introduction of the VCR and remote technologies gave audiences the ability to channel surf, tape, and fast forward through programs. Advertising avoidance was on the rise; and, advertisers began demanding more content that would be supportive of their "good-news" message (Andersen 1995: 20). For example, in the early 1990s the staff of CNN's Beltway-politics program *Capital Gang* obliged a group of advertisers by providing them with a live audition of a program (24). The editorial staff could not have been made more aware of the need to please advertisers. By

2000, the promotional integration of advertisements into current-affairs programming reached the point of brazen shamelessness. That is when ABC's talk show *The View* inked a contract with Campbell's Soup to turn eight shows into paid infomercials. In one episode, cohost Barbara Walters—a news and current-affairs professional with enormous brand strength—made good on a promise to Campbell's to insert a soup message into the show's on-air banter when she posed the question: "Didn't we grow up . . . eating Campbell's Soup?" Properly cued, her colleagues broke into a rousing chorus of the soup king's jingle "M'm! M'm! Good!" Officials at ABC deflected criticism of the Campbell's contract by insisting the show was part of the network's entertainment programming—a claim dismissed by Bob Steele, director of the ethics program at the Poynter Institute. "Even if the show is part of its entertainment division," says Steele, "the seeming erosion of independence by the producers, in allowing an advertiser this much influence, raises significant questions" (Branch 2000). And, one might add, the use of Barbara Walters belies any real adherence to a "church-and-state" separation between the news and entertainment divisions. Barbara Walters, by lending her presence as a well-known news brand to *The View*, was contributing to the integration of programming content and overt promotional strategies—a process already well underway. The new industry buzzword for the practice is "integrated advertising."

In one priceless quote published by the *Wall Street Journal*, Bill Geddie, Barbara Walters's coexecutive producer of *The View*, did his level best to blur the important distinction between promotion and programming independence. Geddie told the *Journal*, the deal was experimental. "'There's always a concern anytime we have a big sponsor that it might compromise the show,' he says. He adds that 'nobody controls our content. We're willing to plug shamelessly, but we have limits. The integrity of the show has to be maintained'" (Branch 2000).

Blurring lines between promotion and news has been made particularly enticing for cash-strapped broadcast-news organizations through the use of video news releases (VNR). Public-relations firms, and the pharmaceutical industry in particular, began in the 1980s to supply broadcasters with inexpensive generic footage that local anchors could read around, giving audiences the impression that the story had been produced by a legitimate news organization. Local network affiliates became particularly vulnerable. The result was that promotional plugs about the latest wonder drug were being passed off as disinterested news (Andersen 1995: 30).

Competitive pressures were ramped up further by the proliferation of satellite technology during the early 1980s. The use of satellites by network affiliates decreased the demand for specialty network news programming. Local affiliates now had the technical capability to cover more stories on their own and they had more access to different sources of news using video feeds provided by wire services such as Visnews (since renamed Reuters TV News), World Television News (WTN), the Newsfeed Network, and in Europe, the Eurovision News Exchange (EVN) cooperative. Local stations expanded, and in some cases doubled, their news coverage as they found they could attract relatively large audiences while stretching the fixed costs of news production over more hours. Local broadcasters were discovering that news programming could be extremely efficient and profitable (Wallis and Baran 1990: 23–24; Owen and Wildman 1992: 176). Satellite technology also gave them, for the first time, the ability to break big international stories before the networks. And, because the choice of footage tended towards the sensational (earthquakes, fires, floods, riots, and foreign sex scandals), the networks were challenged to match it.

The growth of cable and direct-broadcast satellite technology in the 1980s contributed to a growing fragmentation of audiences. The Cable News Network (CNN), the Entertainment and Sports Network (ESPN), and Music Television (MTV) were all launched during the 1980s to appeal to specific demographic segments; and all three went on to become successful global enterprises. In addition to helping new cable broadcasters, such as CNN, cable providers also supplied a lift to struggling UHF stations, which had suffered in the past from their weaker signal strength. With the larger potential audiences that cable offered, these stations became fertile ground for syndicated programming; they also made fledgling networks such as Fox, UPN, and WB financially viable (Budd, Craig, and Steinman 1999: 27). Correspondingly, the networks' share of the fragmenting audience shrunk drastically. In 1970, the big three U.S. networks controlled more than 90 percent of the total broadcast audience. By 1990, their slice of the pie had been trimmed to less than 60 percent (Owen and Wildman 1992: 198). And, by the 1997–1998 season, the networks attracted less than 50 percent of the average prime-time audience (Budd, Craig, and Steinman 1999: 26). As for the U.S. networks' overall news audience, Michael Gurevitch reports that by 1994, it had fallen "to an all-time low of slightly over 30 percent of the total television audience" (Gurevitch 1996: 219). In 1999, the Bureau of Broadcast Measurement (BBM) reported a similar decline in audience share for Canada's two private television networks, CTV and CanWest (Shecter 1999).[4] The trend accelerated in March and April 2003 during coverage of the U.S.-led invasion of Iraq (Carter 2003).

## *Dealing with Market Uncertainty*

By the late 1980s, the major U.S. networks were in a bind. Fixed costs associated with large-scale news production remained extremely high, while their audience was fragmenting. Local affiliates had become more independent and were expanding their newscasts, further siphoning off market share. CNN began broadcasting in 1980, and by 1983 it had launched a second 24-hour news service, CNN-2, later to be called CNN Headline News. Affiliates now had a fourth network provider of news feeds. In addition, by the end of the decade, syndicated tabloid news shows such as *First Edition* and *A Current Affair* were starting to draw larger audiences. In short, the rapid technological development and the re-regulated broadcast media environment of the

1980s had created significant economic uncertainties. The networks had to decide how best to meet the new economic challenges.

An early response to the increased news competition came from ABC and Westinghouse. In 1982, they started their own 24-hour news station, Satellite News Channel (SNC), only to end the experiment 16 months later after racking up US$60 million in losses (Owen and Wildman 1992: 174–175). CNN Headline News, which had been launched in direct response to SNC, had won the battle. All three major networks increased their news and current-affairs production in response to the mounting competitive challenges.[5] They, too, had become aware of the economic efficiencies to be gained from news and current-affairs programming. In the late 1980s, the networks began replacing entertainment programming with less expensive current-affairs shows such as *48 Hours, 20/20, Dateline, Nightline,* and *Primetime Live.* Newsmagazines attracted smaller audiences than sitcoms and other standard prime-time entertainment, but what made them attractive to networks was their "relatively low incremental costs." Each successive program built "on the fixed-cost investment of the news division" (Owen and Wildman 1992: 177). As Mike Budd, Steve Craig, and Clay Steinman explain, the networks adjusted their production strategies in order to limit their exposure to economic risk.

> The proliferation of new channels has heightened the demand for new television programs, but at the same time it has reduced the potential size for each show. The result has been both a scaling back of production budgets for traditional network series and a need for new shows that can be produced quickly and at lower costs than traditional prime-time sitcoms or dramas. As a result, the 1990s have seen major increases in sports programming, talk, and other "reality" shows, all relatively cheap to produce. (Budd, Craig, and Steinman 1999: 34)

Emphasis was being placed on cheaper, more flexible programming that could reduce the risk of capital accumulation. Newsmagazine programs that emphasized so-called softer and more entertaining stories were part of this strategy.

Two North American newsmagazine programs predate the trend described above. In 1966, CTV News launched *W-Five,* and two-years later CBS News premiered the venerable *60 Minutes.* Both programs were started, in part, to meet public-service commitments and were not created solely to increase profits. *60 Minutes,* in particular, was seen from its inception as a continuation of the public-service ethic embodied in the legendary figure of CBS newsman Edward R. Murrow—the man who is largely credited with taking on the rabidly anticommunist Senator Joseph McCarthy. That is not to say, however, that the program was not profitable. The 1999–2000 season marked the 23rd consecutive season the program had ranked in the top-ten highest rated prime-time programs. Over the years, starting perhaps with the introduction of Andy Rooney's populist commentary segment in 1978, the program began to stray from its original focus on investigative reporting. In 1998 CBS News decided to extend the *60 Minutes* brand through the creation of *60 Minutes II*. From the beginning, *60 Minutes II* was designed to amortize the fixed costs of its parent program. The midweek prime-time program also had a decidedly lighter news and current-affairs content.

The newsmagazines are an excellent example of what Todd Gitlin (1983) calls "recombinant" forms of popular culture. Recombinant forms of popular culture are born out of the need to maximize short-term profits while simultaneously reducing a company's exposure to economic risk. Relying on creative talent to divine the tastes of audiences is risky and unpredictable. Networks, argues Gitlin, are like any other modern organization—they "aspire to order, regularity, routine, which make for efficiency and control" (Gitlin 1983: 65). To achieve those goals they rely on proven past successes. Networks had long shown they could mix and recombine selective elements from successful programs to create new hits. Two fundamental strategies were employed: (1) develop characters people either loved or loathed, but whom they would faithfully tune in to watch every week; and (2) create episodic series. The lovable detective (James Garner's Jim Rockford, or Telly Savala's Kojak) or the scoundrel people loved to hate (J.R. Ewing of *Dallas*) are staple character types. Series with proven characters attract loyal audiences and regularize production; they are also, to use Andrew Wernick's language, commodity-signs—"In series," says Gitlin, "each episode is a billboard advertising the next" (66).

Newsmagazines not only enjoyed economies of scale—they could feed stories to the main network newscasts, and vice versa—but they could tap into recurring narrative forms which they could be reasonably sure would develop loyal audiences. This is the secret behind the success of *Entertainment Tonight, A Current Affair,* and *First Edition.* The so-called tabloid newsmagazines provided weekly or nightly episodes of continuing melodramas, often involving celebrities—stories of mayhem, disaster, personal tragedy, and personal triumph all flourished. The network newsmagazines soon followed suit with stories about the tragedies and triumphs of their favorite characters—Diana the troubled princess, bad-girl skater Tonya Harding, and the younger "other" woman Monica Lewinsky. In addition, news organizations began emphasizing the personalities of their star journalists.

Finally, the proliferation of newsmagazine shows was helped along by the regulatory ban on network ownership of most of their prime-time programs.[6] There is no such rule for news programming (Owen and Wildman 1992: 177). However, until 1987, there were important content rules that U.S. news organizations were obliged to honor.

### *All Is Fair in All-Talk Broadcasting*

In addition to the loosening of ownership limits, the second major prong in the influential re-regulation of broadcast media in the United States involved the re-regulation of content. The principal content regulation to be targeted for replacement by the FCC was the Fairness Doctrine. The doctrine was originally introduced by the FCC in 1949 as a means of enforcing the public-service requirement of broadcast licensees to broadcast all legitimate opposing views on controversial topics in their news and current-affairs programming. An unpublished primer written by FCC staff in 1981, before the push for regulatory change took hold, describes the purpose of the doctrine:

> The broadcaster need not give the same amount of time to each issue as he would in granting 'equal opportunities' to political candidates. All it need do is to encourage the presentation of, and provide reasonable opportunity for, different views on the issue in the overall programming of the station. (Goldoff 1996: 55)

The FCC and academic proponents of the doctrine argued that an advertiser-supported broadcast industry dominated by three networks would inevitably produce content of the lowest common denominator. It was also thought at the time that informational programming, such as news and current affairs, was less profitable than entertainment. Proponents concluded, therefore, that guidelines were required to ensure genuine diversity of opinion.

The doctrine's goal of content diversity was not terribly controversial on the surface. Few people would claim to be against diversity. And in the landmark 1969 decision *Red Lion Broadcasting v. FCC,* the Supreme Court of the United States ruled that the doctrine was constitutional and did not contravene the country's First Amendment right to free speech. Nevertheless, the doctrine caused much consternation among individuals and groups who were ideologically opposed to any form of government stewardship of media content. The widely held assumption among critics of the doctrine is that programming diversity can best be achieved through the unfettered workings of the market. In 1985, the FCC released its Fairness Report in which the commission concluded that the doctrine no longer served the public's interest in obtaining access to a diversity of controversial opinions. First, it rejected the long-held position that the doctrine was justified due to spectrum scarcity. It held that while there was a limit to spectrum space due to the laws of physics, the uses to which that space could be put and subdivided were almost limitless. Second, it said advancements in cable and satellite technologies had contributed to an increase in the number of broadcast choices available to the public. And finally, the commission argued the doctrine had a potential "chilling effect" on broadcasters who would minimize the presentation of controversial programming in order to avoid possible FCC sanctions and litigation costs (Lentz 1996: 281–285). In 1987, despite stiff resistance from Congress, the FCC placed its faith in the market and abolished the Fairness Doctrine.

The impact of the decision to scrap the Fairness Doctrine continues to be debated. Supporters (Cronauer 1994; Lentz 1996) argue that the beneficence of the market has proven itself, particularly in light of the technological improvements that have expanded the number of program providers. One study found that so-called informational programming, such as talk radio and television, increased significantly following the lifting of the content rules (Hazlett and Sosa 1997). At the same time, so-called tabloid-TV shows were gaining market share. For example, Fox's *A Current Affair,* the program credited with pioneering tabloid television, became nationally syndicated in 1988. Adrian Cronauer points to the proliferation of talk-radio formats, in particular, as evidence of the market's benevolence. Cronauer admits that some opinions—those he apparently considers of less importance—will not be represented. But this outcome is not a problem, as he sees it. "No *responsible viewpoint* is in danger of being stifled simply because it is denied access to a particular station—so long as there are other available stations. . . . Allowing the 'invisible hand' of market forces to operate in the marketplace of ideas accommodates *all viewpoints with enough proponents to warrant attention*" [my emphasis] (Cronauer 1994: 74–75). Cronauer's evangelical faith in the market blinds him to the essential flaw of his position—that the market itself has a disproportionate influence on which viewpoints warrant attention. As numerous critical media studies have indicated (McChesney 1997: 44–54; Bagdikian 2000; Hackett and Gruneau 2000: 47–73), affluent audiences are privileged over others. Moreover, when combined with established work routines and the professional code of objectivity, the views of government and the corporate elite are disproportionately represented in news discourse when compared to those of labor and various social-activist organizations (Bennett 1988: 117).

Market forces and organizational work routines influenced news content well before the Fairness Doctrine was eliminated in 1987. And, as W. Lance Bennett argues persuasively, news objectivity is itself ideological in its favoritism of official sources. Brian McNair adds that "political commentary" is a 20th-century phenomenon that has developed to secure "brand identification and consumer loyalty." It is a "consequence of the commodification of the public sphere, which made it necessary for news organizations to brand their output (give it exchange value in a marketplace containing many other superficially similar brands)" (McNair 2000: 64).

It can be argued, however, that the demise of the Fairness Doctrine, in concert with increasing fast-changing technological developments and competitive forces, helped usher in a shift in the style and form of news and current-affairs programming. Talk-television programs in which journalists interview politicians—such as *Meet the Press* in the U.S. and the influential and hard-hitting *This Hour Has Seven Days* in Canada—have been a part of broadcasting for decades. But following 1987 a more vox-pop version of the radio and TV talk-show format proliferated. It wasn't until the obligation to provide a balance of opinions was eliminated that formats featuring bombastic right-wing radio talk-show hosts mushroomed across North America. The most influential of these was Rush Limbaugh.

Howard Kurtz, media critic for the *Washington Post,* argues that Limbaugh "turned many money-losing [radio] stations into financial winners and cleared a path for the stampede of conservative hosts that followed in his wake" (Kurtz 1996: 231).[7] In 1988, ABC signed a national-syndication deal with Limbaugh, who used the national exposure and his ability to entertain to great advantage. Limbaugh routinely screens calls to ensure that like-minded people get on air. "The purpose of a call is to make me look good," he says. "There is no right to be boring on my show"(Kurtz 1996: 237). Targets of his vitriolic right-wing tirades have included gays and lesbians, racial minorities, and all forms of government welfare programs. By 1990, Limbaugh was carried by 200 stations. That number continued to grow and by 2001 his program could be heard on more than 600 stations, with a weekly audience of close to 20 million listeners. In July 2001, Limbaugh signed an eight-year contract with Clear Channel Communications Inc.'s Premiere Radio Networks rumored to be worth more than US$285 million (Weil 2001). The wind was taken out of his sails in October 2003 when Limbaugh checked himself into a drug-addiction program. The radio titan took a self-imposed exile after media reports suggested he had obtained painkillers without a prescription. The man who had previously claimed drug addicts should receive lengthy jail terms was much easier on himself when he returned to the air November 17 (Steinberg 2003).

Sensationally spun topics, snap judgments, and rapid-fire pacing have become the norm for talk-radio and talk-TV formats. PBS—itself, not completely insulated from market forces—is home to *The McLaughlin Group,* with its vociferous host, John McLaughlin; such programs are now standard. "The format brought out the worst in everybody," says former *McLaughlin Group* guest William Greider. "It made you more provocative and half-baked" (Kurtz 1996: 24). But the mixture of high-decibel chatter, outrageous comment, and partisan posturing has proven successful.

The ability to rant or pontificate in order to fill airtime is favored over reasoned judgments that include shades of gray. Well-researched news stories and documentaries cost money and tie up enormous resources. Whereas, instant faux-analysis is inexpensive, quick and easy to produce, entertaining and, above all, profitable. The talk shows want "fast thinkers," people capable of thinking on the fly in "clichés" and "received ideas" (Bourdieu 1998: 28–29). As Howard Kurtz quips, "Talk is cheap" (4), and one might add flexible. In the evolving environment of all-talk-all-the-time broadcasting, the dramatic fusion of politics, sex, morality, and ethics provided by the Monicagate scandal was almost too good to be true. Frank Ahrens, of the *Washington Post* writes that for Limbaugh and his colleagues the scandal "must have seemed like a gift from heaven. . . . Limbaugh ought to send Clinton a lavish thank-you gift upon his exit from the Oval Office" (Ahrens 2000).[8] The all-talk-all-the-time format found a welcome home on 24-hour cable news networks. CNBC's prime-time lineup during Monicagate included *Hardball* with Chris Mathews and *Rivera Live.* MSNBC used to rebroadcast *Hardball,* but is now the sole carrier of the program. It also broadcasts veteran radio-personality Don Imus every weekday morning. Unabashed conservative Bill O'Reilly heads up Fox's *The O'Reilly Factor.* CNN has *Crossfire;* and in 2000, the cable network added *The*

*Spin Room,* a program entirely devoted to the excessive punditry of its nominally liberal and conservative hosts along with added commentary from audience members. *Spin Room* has since been cancelled, and Geraldo Rivera has moved to Fox.

All-talk programs contributed to the intensity and scale of media spectacles such as Monicagate, Elián González and the Columbine High School massacre. It is in the all-talk-all-the-time format where full-throated force is given to mining the latent pathos of a story. Bill Clinton, one of the most polarizing figures in U.S. political history, became the perfect foil for these programs, and his departure from active political life frightened many producers. These programs needed a particular kind of story in order to maximize their economic efficiencies; and in lieu of the occasional Elián González–type story, what would they talk about in Clinton's absence? Their prayers were answered with the 2000 U.S. election dispute between Democrat Al Gore and Republican George W. Bush. "The election dispute," writes Bill Carter of the *New York Times,* "created the prospect of a presidency forever dogged by questions of legitimacy and that could give the political talk shows a new, richly partisan and potentially enduring subject to mine for the intensely heated conversation they aim to sell" (Carter 2000a). Carter goes on to quote Gail Evans, the executive vice-president of programming for CNN, as saying "I could come up with four months of shows off the nuances of this story right now. Whenever there isn't a hot story in the news, you can gin up something on this topic in some way" (Carter 2000a). This prediction foundered as questions of the political legitimacy evaporated from media discourse following the terror attacks of September 11, 2001, itself a spectacular media event that trumped all others.

Big spectacular media events are "never-ending" recombinant stories. The seemingly timeless nature of the moral and ethical questions posed by these dramatized narratives appear to give them the gloss of eternal or mythological status. Conversely, it is because these narratives involve interesting and existentially troubled characters that they hold commercial value as human-interest stories par excellence. What made the 2000 U.S. election dispute unique is that it actually involved a substantive political dispute—the outcome of a presidential election. The human-interest qualities at the heart of spectacular stories help make these narratives transposable. Moreover, it is this quality of transposability that makes Monicagate, and other stories like it, perfect hog fuel for the integrated media spectacle. And the organizations best positioned to take advantage of these efficiencies are the 24-hour news channels.

### The Integrated Efficiencies of 24-Hour News

CNN began broadcasting on June 1, 1980. At first, the quality of programming was shoddy. The mostly green staff made regular on-air mistakes and the fledgling round-the-clock network was dubbed Chicken Noodle News by reporters of the big-three

U.S. networks. CNN first raised eyebrows at the established networks in 1986 with its live broadcast of the Challenger space-shuttle explosion. CNN's exclusive video of the spectacular sky-high conflagration was transmitted via satellite around the globe. The power and potential of the live-satellite transmission of news had been dramatically demonstrated. CNN cameras also provided live coverage of the Tiananmen Square massacre and the revolutions in Eastern Europe in 1989. Many commentators began talking about the supposed "CNN effect" when discussing the role live-satellite broadcasts played in possibly altering the actions of both government officials and demonstrators (Gurevitch 1996: 214; MacGregor 1997: 4). News was being transmitted faster than ever before, and in a way that made the international news agencies of the 19th century look like horse-drawn carriages in comparison. In one much-repeated story, a CNN broadcast alerted the president of Turkey to a soon-to-be-placed phone call from U.S. President George Bush. Bush had used the call as an excuse to slip out of a live-televised news conference. Turgut Ozal, who had been watching CNN, walked from the television, lifted the ringing phone and said, "Hello, Mr. President" (Tracey 1995: 146, cited in MacGregor 1997: 4). But such anecdotal examples, with their focus on the novel use of new technology, overlook how news has long been an actor in politics and how various news actors have learned to adapt themselves to the work routines of reporters in order to gain access to the media spotlight (Gitlin 1980). The real importance of CNN lies in how it pioneered the economic efficiencies of 24-hour news. CNN proved that a low-budget integrated system of news production could make a profit in a highly competitive news environment characterized by economic uncertainty and fragmented audiences. The increased speed of news transmission contributed to these changes and became a factor in this historically unique commodification of news.

CNN owner Ted Turner poured more than US$70 million into the network until the mid-1980s. By then, however, CNN's ability to spread its fixed costs across multiple broadcast platforms while simultaneously expanding its audience began to pay off. "Cable," as Don Flournoy and Robert Stewart argue, "changed the formula for making money in broadcasting." The number of people watching any single CNN program was dwarfed by the audience for the nightly newscasts of the big-three networks. However, "the cumulative effect of small but multiple (and 24-hour) revenue streams could still generate operating profits." Plus, CNN was able to collect individual subscriber fees—a reliable second revenue stream. In 1985, the same year CNN International was launched, Turner's experiment in around-the-clock news started making money (Flournoy and Stewart 1997: 1–3). CNN continued to grow; today, the CNN News Group stands at six cable networks, three out-of-house private networks, including CNN Airport Network, two radio networks, four Web sites, and CNN Newsource, a syndicated news service.

Richard Parker argues that from the beginning, the CNN strategy was predicated on the integration of "three simple rules: computerize, economize, and piggyback."

CNN "took advantage of the latest computer and satellite technology that would allow the company to integrate newswires, the assignment desk, producers, graphics rundowns, tape lists, and anchor scripts." CNN became, says Parker, "television's first truly 'electronic newsroom'" (Parker 1995: 52). This kind of integration is now standard for all newsrooms at prominent media organizations.

Ted Turner also insisted that CNN be a strictly nonunion workplace. This policy saved CNN millions of dollars. Unlike the major U.S. networks, CNN did not have work rules restricting what jobs personnel could do. The extremely flexible working conditions meant that CNN staff could write stories, produce programs, and operate camera equipment, while at the same time working longer hours and being paid much less than their network colleagues. These efficiencies meant that CNN could produce its 24-hour news programming for close to "one-third of the budget required by the network news programmes" (MacGregor 1997: 143). Parker argues the cost efficiencies realized by CNN further contributed to the layoffs that swept the newsrooms of the U.S. networks in the 1980s (Parker 1995: 52). CNN's labor policy also can be held responsible for the initially high number of mistakes made by its inexperienced staff, many of whom were fresh out of college and willing to work cheap.

Finally, CNN saves enormous sums of money by "piggybacking." Instead of initially establishing the same number of foreign bureaus as the networks, CNN decided to *reuse* or *repurpose* material supplied by foreign broadcasters—saving millions. As part of this strategy, CNN created *World Report,* a program that broadcasts stories supplied by foreign broadcasters. What makes the program unique is that stories run unedited by CNN staff. The program is cited by CNN publicists and Flournoy and Stewart as an example of CNN's commitment to providing a broad diversity of opinions from around the globe. But there is no hiding the fact that it was part of a smart business strategy. The global market for goods and services was growing during the 1980s. The European Union was forging a large integrated economy that rivaled the United States in size, while in Asia countries such as India were seeing their middle class expand (estimated today at between 200 and 250 million). Increasingly, transnational corporations wanted to "skim the cream" from these countries by targeting their affluent English-speaking elites (Parker 1995: 65). As a result, advertisers were keen to reach and develop this burgeoning transnational clientele (Herman and McChesney 1997: 39).[9] In order to capitalize on the expanding global media market, Flournoy and Stewart suggest CNN "needed to build bridges to every country in the world to gain access to content and to market its products." *World Report* was a useful calling card in this project (Flournoy and Stewart 1997: 33).

CNN was helping to pioneer one of the defining elements of the integrated news environment: the development of partnership or "co-op strategies." This took the form of linking separate news organizations through news-footage sharing agreements, co-ownership, or through the integration of one company's many subsidiaries. European broadcasters began co-producing entertainment programs as part of their response to the continuing fragmentation of audiences during the 1980s. The former state-owned broadcast monopolies faced competition from private broadcasters and they were being forced to privatize in an effort to attract advertising revenue. Moreover, the integration of the European economies under the European Union was well underway. When the costs of production could be shared by the subsidiaries of different broadcasters, often from different countries, the risks of production were greatly reduced (Parker 1995: 40–41). The improved economies of scale realized through cooperative agreements applied to news production as well. So as part of its news-sharing strategy, CNN has struck partnerships with local broadcasters all over the world, such as Wharf Cable in Hong Kong, and more recently TVi in India.

The basic economics of the network television-news business are fairly simple. Extremely high fixed costs are incurred by large-scale news organizations in producing their first newscast. Beyond that first program, however, additional programming can be produced at progressively lower incremental cost. CNN's great advantage over other networks has been that it can repurpose its news content over an array of integrated networks, thus reducing costs even further. "The key to survival and success," say Flournoy and Stewart, "is simple: take any given news item and air it again and again in different ways on each of the company's networks" (Flournoy and Stewart 1997: 3). It is this *production imperative* that is at the heart of the intensity and scale of spectacular media events.

### The Attraction of the Big Story

The live-televised explosion of the Challenger Space Shuttle may have marked the first time that CNN caught the attention of the major U.S. networks, but the defining moment for the network came during the 1991 Persian Gulf War. CNN's *Crisis in the Gulf,* as its coverage was labeled, gave the all-news network the legitimacy, ratings, and advertising revenue that it craved. On January 16, CNN caught all major news organizations off guard when it broadcast live pictures announcing the allied bombing of Baghdad had begun. CNN's prime-time rating during the *Crisis in the Gulf* was 5, or 2.8 million U.S. households. It was an unprecedented ratings peak for the network, which settled back into its regular prewar audience of roughly 568,000 households following the end of the conflict (Walley 1992).[10] It also topped the big-three U.S. networks.

The *Crisis in the Gulf* gave CNN the Big Story it needed to take full advantage of its unique ability to provide blanket 24-hour coverage of an event. If one dominant story could be used to fuel programming over CNN's 24-hour schedule, the efficiency gains would be enormous. The *Crisis in the Gulf* marked the moment when the "constant flow" of rolling news made the big leagues.

> Night after night, CNN, and the other networks as well, broadcast an incessant flow of pictures of troops, airplanes, ships, tanks, and military equipment, with interview after interview of the troops and their military spokespeople. Footage of the U.S. military was frequently supplemented on CNN by footage from the British and other allies' military establishments, resulting in seemingly endless images of military hardware and personnel. (Kellner 1992: 87)

The Big Story of the Gulf War was tailor-made for CNN's need for endlessly repeatable and easily updated footage and storytelling. The 24-hour broadcast day was filled with the repetition of images of wholesome troops, Baghdad's surreal night sky lit by antiaircraft flashes, and F-15E fighter jets thrusting off Navy aircraft carriers. Perhaps the most memorable image left from the war is not the horror of dead bodies, but the antiseptic video-game briefings depicting so-called smart bombs destroying their targets. These images were supplemented by seemingly endless discussion among military experts and journalists about the tactical aspects of the war. But behind the vast majority of the coverage was the easily transposable and "episodic framing" (Iyengar and Simon 1994: 179) of an emotional confrontation between good and evil, personified in the characters of U.S. President George Bush and Iraqi President Saddam Hussein.

The story of the Gulf War was covered by CNN and other media organizations as a dramatic ritual. "Like all rituals," write Daniel Hallin and Todd Gitlin, "the war was treated as an affair of the 'heart' more than of the 'head': the emphasis was on people's feelings"(Hallin and Gitlin 1994: 160). The nonrational aspects of the Gulf War imagery appealed to a broad range of people and cut across demographic, racial, and gender lines. From this perspective, the war was less about the "purposive rational action" of U.S. and allied foreign policy than it was about "the drama of war" (152–153). At a basic level, war coverage was about the threat to family, friends, and community. The ritualized emotional intensity of the television coverage enabled CNN, and other networks, to "aestheticize the war" (155), and in the process appeal to people's desire to participate in the dramatic experience and show their support for the troops.

> The journalists mediated all of this, participated, indeed, in the process, and thereby supplied themselves with an ever-replenished stock of stories through which the conventions of journalism meshed with the viewers' ritual needs. . . . The war had a narrative logic full of suspense, crescendoes, and collective emotion. It was the stuff of high drama—valuable not only for high ratings but for high excitement in the community and the newsroom alike. (Hallin and Gitlin 1994: 161)

The spectacular media event of the Persian Gulf War was, as George Gerbner suggests, "an unprecedented motion picture spectacular" (Gerbner 1992: 246). But it was not a passive spectacle; media coverage of the war deeply engaged viewers. It can be read as a liminal moment in which the sacred values of a community are rehearsed and debated. This includes debates about the legitimacy of the military action. Although, as many media studies indicate, most U.S. media organizations, at the national and local level, quickly closed ranks behind the allied troops once the war started (Chomsky 1992; Kellner 1992; Hackett and Zhao 1994; Hallin and Gitlin 1994).

The participatory aspect of the war, viewed as an aspect of popular culture, also found expression in the sale of numerous retail items ranging from t-shirts and flag pins to Patriot watches and Operation Desert Storm collectors' cards (Hallin and Gitlin 1994:149). Many advertisers were leery about associating their products and services with the war. For example, The Gap, which expressed its opposition to the war, did not participate in any war-related promotions (War and Fahey 1991). Conversely, many other companies risked being labeled as war profiteers. Bulova Corp.—the makers of the Patriot watch—donated its profits to the USO, a veterans' service group. CEO Herbert Hofmann said the watches would demonstrate the company's support for the troops (Associated Press 1991). In this instance, tapping into the spectacle was less about making a quick profit than it was about associating one's company with the patriotic effort of the troops and the hopes and fears of the national community for their safe return. It was an exercise in branding.

The Gulf War put CNN on the map as a global provider of news and as a significant competitor to the major U.S. networks. Moreover, CNN's coverage of the Gulf War helped kindle an interest in Western commercial television among elite-urban populations in India and other "emerging markets" in Asia and the Middle East. In 1991, liberalization policies were introduced in India that opened the door for large global-media conglomerates. The introduction of cable and satellite technologies, plus the growing strength of the advertising market expanded the industry exponentially. India went in 1991 from having one state-controlled channel (Doordarshan) to nearly 70 cable and satellite channels in 1998. These included big transnational media organizations such as Hong Kong–based STAR (Satellite Television Asian Region), BBC, Discovery, Sony, Disney, CNBC, and, of course the already established CNN.[11]

Daya Kishan Thussu argues that the privatization of broadcasting in India has followed the global trend toward market forces dominating the broadcast agenda. The commodification of news and information in India means, as it has in other countries, that melodramatic narratives emphasizing basic character types are favored over the complexities of historical and economic context (Thussu 1999: 126–129). These more universal human-interest stories are far more transposable among various countries and disparate cultures than economic and political stories tied to the specificity of place.[12]

These stories are all the more important for global broadcasters, such as CNN, because research has shown that the majority of broadcast news coverage around the world is regional or local in focus. In 1991, research conducted by the International Institute of Communications examining television newscasts in 87 countries indicated an overwhelming preponderance of news stories were about local or regional issues. In Latin America, the local/regional share reached 92 percent. Seventy-eight percent of the stories broadcast in Japan were about that country, while in North America the proportion was 80 percent (InterMedia 1992, cited in Parker 1995: 78). In other words, cultural and national differences in news coverage remain an important aspect of the overall news environment (Cohen et al. 1996; Wallis and Baran 1990). In order to overcome the barriers of language, culture and place, the all-news satellite and cable networks must rely on stories that translate easily.[13] They rely on stories that are decontextualized and socially constructed to meet the needs of different media's promotional interests. The dramatic portrayal of *Crisis in the Gulf* fit the bill. The fact that the bloody conflict directly affected dozens of nations added value to the story, of course. But the direct interest that millions of people had in the war does not discount the need on the part of news organizations to aestheticize the war. Besides, as Erik Sorenson, former MSNBC president, says: "The big problem in cable is that nobody watches unless there's a big story" (Kurtz 2000c).

The next Big Story came June 17, 1994, when CNN broadcast live the police chase of former football star O.J. Simpson's white Ford Bronco along a Los Angeles freeway. Millions saw the police pursuit as CNN ran footage captured by local TV affiliates who followed the chase in helicopters. The subsequent trial and acquittal of Simpson on charges that he murdered his wife became a major media event covered by more than 1,000 journalists (MacGregor 1997: 38). The 1995 verdict was watched by an estimated 51 million American viewers. By the time it ended, the Simpson trial had provided nearly a full year of media fodder. And this time, unlike *Crisis in the Gulf,* CNN would have more difficulty justifying the global significance of the story. In 1997, the Big Story was the death and mourning of Princess Diana, followed in 1998 by the Monica Lewinsky scandal and U.S. President Bill Clinton's televised speech in which he admitted to having a relationship with the young intern. The collective broadcasts of the Clinton confession netted an estimated 68 million U.S. viewers (Bloomberg News 1998).

By 1997, the year of Princess Diana's death, CNN was facing rising competition for 24-hour news. NBC had launched its all-business news channel CNBC in 1989, but by 1996 it had joined forces with software giant Microsoft to form the 24-hour cable and Internet news service MSNBC. That same year the conservative-tilting 24-hour Fox News channel and its sister Fox News Web site were launched. The relatively small audience for 24-hour news was being carved up into tinier and tinier pieces as each network faced the recurring problem of significantly reduced audiences during gaps between big media events. The networks responded, as they had in the past, by striving to bring some semblance of rational order and control to the production of news. After all, production, not consumption, was the only thing they could control completely. The networks and other news organizations did this by reverting to the logic of recombinant culture—they produced more large-scale media events. Each news organization applied the same basic logic and thus contributed to the production of the same spectacular product, all the while, competing with each other using the superficial distinction of being the first newsroom to break the latest Big Story update. Speed of delivery was adding value to the news commodity—as had been the case since the early days of the news-wire services. In 1999, the year after the Monicagate scandal had run its course, we saw a proliferation of large-scale media spectacles. April 1999 saw the media invasion of Littleton, Colorado, followed in July of that year by the blanket coverage of the death by plane crash of JFK Jr. By Thanksgiving 1999, the politically drenched tug-of-war over young Elián González had assumed the role of the next "Big Thing."

The networks, of course, were not engaged in a massive conspiracy. They did not cause John F. Kennedy Jr.'s plane to crash, or Bill Clinton to be unfaithful to his wife. These media events were becoming more and more frequent, and they were given the "Gulf War treatment" because the increased competition and production imperatives of around-the-clock news demanded it. The networks were simply trying to minimize their exposure to risk while simultaneously maximizing their opportunities for capital accumulation. This basic economic imperative is what Debord means when he says, "the spectacle is simply the economic realm developing *for itself*" (Debord 1995: sec. 16). The Big Story approach to news was developed to meet the needs of capital accumulation in a fast-changing environment characterized by high levels of economic uncertainty and fast-paced technological change. The Big Story approach was not created to meet the needs of audiences for "primordial" or "eternal" stories (Lule 2001). However genuine those audience needs may be, the production of those stories is subject to the priorities of capital accumulation. Paul Richard of the *Washington Post,* writing at the peak of the Elián González frenzy, captures the imperative nicely: "We don't yet know the name of the next big story, but this is sure: It's stewing out there somewhere, and it is going to be huge. O.J. and Diana, Monica and John-John long ago went cold. Elián, the big story of the moment, is already losing heat. But there's another coming. Got to have it. For there's a core chore of the news business: You have to feed the goat" (Richard 2000).

As it turned out, the next "Big Thing" would be the mysterious disappearance of Washington political intern Chandra Levy and her alleged sexual relationship with congressional representative Gary Condit. Speculation and rumor about Condit's alleged involvement in her disappearance fed cable talk-TV for most of the summer of 2001. The Condit/Levy affair was eventually pushed aside by overheated reports of shark attacks off the Florida coast. Melodramatic stories have been popular for centuries, but their reappearance as large-scale media events has a particular historical context. As always, the needs of the producers and consumers are dialectically related, but not necessarily equal.

Frank Rich (2000b), of the *New York Times,* dubs the new "All-Calamity-All-the-Time" genre the "Mediathon." Rich acknowledges, correctly, that there have been other big media events. As we have seen, the feeding frenzy surrounding the 1935 kidnapping of the Lindbergh baby is one example. Moreover, there was the continuous coverage of the 1963 assassination of U.S. President John Kennedy and the 1979 Iranian Hostage crisis, which launched ABC's *Nightline*—not to mention the career of its host, Ted Koppel.

> But in "War in the Gulf," cable's first all-news network surpassed these forms by melding them, updating their primitive technology and bursting through their previous boundaries of time and space. The Gulf War was the first war to have its own logos, theme music and telegenic overnight stars (whether leading men like Colin Powell or Robert Duvall-esque character types like Peter Arnett). Most important, it played out in real time before a mass audience—the first instance history had been shaped (and spun, often by the military brass) on the spot into a dramatic 24/7 TV mini-series. (Rich 2000b)

The 1991 Gulf War was the moment when CNN forged a unique news format that packaged multiple promotional interests into a melodramatic narrative that could be recycled endlessly through newscasts and the newly thriving talk shows. Again, Frank Rich captures the essence of the format.

> But unlike Hollywood's cast of thousands—who had to be paid—the armchair generals, preening academics and Washington bloviators who endlessly sliced and diced each day's dramatic action were so eager for TV celebrity that they played their roles and improvised their scripts gratis. So much so that they were capable of vamping for hours on end, pumping artificial respiration into a story that otherwise had no fresh information to sustain it. (Rich 2000b)[14]

The scenario was reenacted with chilling sameness following the horrific September 11, 2001, terrorist attacks on New York City's World Trade Center and the Pentagon in Washington, D.C. Audiences for the all-news cable channels were once again offered a parade of retired generals and "security experts" who provided endless speculation about the tactics used by the suspected perpetrators of the attacks.

The Manichean logic of good versus evil quickly became the frame within which most mainstream news organizations structured their stories. "This will be a monumental struggle of good versus evil, but good will prevail," President George W. Bush announced the day following the suicide attacks. He literally pronounced Osama bin Laden, the wealthy Saudi developer and leader of the Al Qaeda terrorist network, as the number-one suspect on America's most-wanted list. He was, said Bush, mimicking the dialogue of cheap Hollywood westerns, "wanted dead or alive." The logo adopted by most American news organizations for this conflict, "America Under Attack," eventually morphed into "America Strikes Back." Various Americans were praised for their selfless rescue efforts, from New York's fire and police officers to Mayor Rudolph Gulliani—hailed for his stoic leadership during a time of national crisis. They were offered as the nation's heroes. As with the "War in the Gulf," the episodic good-versus-evil framing of most mainstream news coverage fit well with President Bush's almost daily reference to "evildoers." It invited audience members to participate in a dramatic ritual in which they could show their support and grief for the families of the more than 3,000 people murdered in the suicide-hijacking attacks. It also allowed people to share very real and legitimate fears about their own personal security.

Again, as in the "War in the Gulf," the emotional intensity of the coverage enabled news organizations to aestheticize the so-called war on terrorism in a way that both encouraged audience involvement across gender, class, and racial demographics, and contributed to a steady stream of stories that meshed with conventional norms of storytelling. The attacks and the response to them can be read as a liminal moment in which the sacred values of a community are rehearsed in mythic form. The *New York Times,* as part of its coverage, ran a series of stories called "Portraits of Grief" about the lives of people killed and injured by the disaster. One story went further to examine the "new context" of grief for those mourning the passing of people unrelated to the events of September 11. "As thousands of families who lost someone at the World Trade Center have mourned in the glare of history," wrote Shaila Dewan, "thousands more who lost someone to sickness, old age or accident have mourned in its shadow" (Dewan 2001).

Jack Lule, however, provides a useful caution in his study of mythical narratives in the editorial pages of the *New York Times* following the attack. The myth of a city and nation in crisis, Lule says, "can also be seen as ideological, limiting and channelling interpretations of events, defending social order and legitimating the response of authorities" (Lule 2002). The ritual of public mourning was itself shadowed by a jingoistic backlash against dissent and a call for national unity at all costs (Carter and Barringer 2001; Houpt 2001; Waisbord 2003). A consortium of news organizations had been planning to publish the results of a recount of the Florida presidential ballots. After September 11, the project was temporarily shelved. *New York Times* reporter Richard Berke would write that the project designed to determine who is the legitimate president of the United States "now seems utterly irrelevant" (Berke 2001).[15] An issue that on September 10 would have been *the* story covered by all major media organizations had been summarily spiked. Consortium members eventually published the results November 12, 2001.[16] According to Erik Sorenson, former president of MSNBC, there simply was not enough dissent to warrant coverage. "Most of the dissent we've had on the air is the opposite," Sorenson told the *New York Times, "*—conservatives like John McCain and Bill Bennet saying we should bomb more or attack

Iraq" (Stanley 2001a). CNN chairman Walter Isaacson ordered his staff to "balance" images and stories about civilian casualties and destruction in Afghanistan with reminders that the Taliban government had harbored terrorists thought responsible for the September 11 attacks. The Manichean narrative of good versus evil clearly played a role in structuring news coverage, but the political ramifications of this framing were not front and center. "No one remarked, to my knowledge," commented Douglas Kellner, "that [Bush's] position was a resurrection of National Socialist theorist Carl Schmitt's doctrine of 'friend' and 'enemy,' that defined politics as coalitions against enemies and with friends" (Kellner 2002).

Coverage of U.S. forces bombing Afghanistan was enormously expensive, especially at a time when broadcast and print news organizations were suffering from depressed advertising revenue and rising newsprint costs. To be sure, economic interest was not the sole factor driving coverage. The spectacular terrorist attacks of September 11, and the events flowing from them were of undeniable news value and importance. If these events do not justify 24-hour coverage, what does? The WTC, itself a symbol of America's leading role in global capitalism, was chosen for destruction in order to create a global media spectacle. It was a form of "mass-mediated terrorism" designed to attract media interest (Nacos 2002). At the same time, "America Strikes Back" was also a promotional fulcrum point of enormous proportions for the all-news networks. "This is costing a fortune to sit and wait," one CNN employee told the *Globe and Mail* prior to the American-led bombing campaign on Afghanistan. "The suits in Atlanta are worried about the profit margins. But there's no question this has been good for our ratings. We're still at the top of our game" (Cernetig 2001). Predictably, the ratings for 24-hour cable news skyrocketed to levels seen in 1991 during the Gulf War (Kempner 2001). However, this time CNN was not the lone 24-hour cable channel with exclusive pictures. Qatar-based Al Jazeera quickly became the main source of pictures from the Afghani war zone.

CNN used its advantage in foreign bureaus to reestablish its ratings dominance over rivals MSNBC and Fox during the first couple of weeks following September 11. Eventually, MSNBC and Fox gained ground. Both networks saw an opportunity in the conflict to expand their international news presence. Fox was most aggressive. The network hired Steve Harrigan—one of the first Western TV reporters to enter Afghanistan—away from CNN. Harrigan was snapped up by Fox after its chief rival failed to renew his contract. Then in a promotional coup, Fox lured Geraldo Rivera away from his popular prime-time talk show on CNBC. Rivera, whose checkered career includes working as a foreign correspondent, searching Al Capone's vault and having his nose broken by a chair in a brawl with white supremacists, joined Harrigan as a war correspondent in Afghanistan. "I'm feeling more patriotic than at any time in my life," Rivera tells the Associated Press, "itching for justice, or maybe just revenge" (Bauder 2001). So much for professional objectivity. Reporters and talk-show personalities steeped in patriotic fervor are now hot wartime commodities.

Meanwhile, Fox allowed dozens of cable and satellite channels around the world free access to its network feed. *New York Times* reporter Jim Rutenberg sums up the strategy: "Fox News Channel executives clearly hope that it can become for its parent company, the News Corporation, what CNN is for AOL Time Warner—a global news brand with an international reach (and ad sales power)" (Rutenberg 2001b).

The growing Arab-language news market being developed by Al Jazeera did not pass unnoticed by MSNBC. The company signed a deal in May 2001 with an Egyptian partner, www.gn4me.com, to run an Arabic-language version of the MSNBC Web site (www.gn4msnbc.com). But the company chose to announce the venture in October during the U.S.-led air strikes in Afghanistan. "Certainly there's an interest in that region in American culture and business," Michael Salata, MSNBC's business development manager, told *Wired* magazine, "as well as other stories in the living and travel sections" (Manjoo 2001). CNN announced in August of that year its own plans to operate www.cnnarabic.com. MSNBC and Fox, like all-news cable pioneer CNN in 1991, were tapping into the spectacle of a massive war effort in an attempt to expand their international brand strength and market presence. Web traffic to online news sites saw a corresponding spike after the attacks of September 11 (Warner 2001).

In the newspaper world, the *Chicago Tribune* used the headline "When evil struck America: a time capsule of 10 historic days," to promote its commemorative September 11 CD-ROM. The CD—inserted into copies of the paper's Sunday, September 8, 2002, edition—marked the one-year anniversary of the disaster. Sales for the Sunday edition of the paper spiked by about 100,000 copies. It sold separately for $5.95, including shipping and handling. Proceeds went to charity (Fitzgerald 2002).

The rolling-news format is now standard practice for all so-called 24/7 networks. Often efforts to sustain a story stretch the limits of credibility. For nearly an hour and a half during the final hours of the 2000 U.S. presidential campaign, MSNBC fed the gaping maw of their 24-hour news hole with live coverage of Al Gore's campaign office in Little Rock, Arkansas. President Clinton had popped in unexpectedly and so MSNBC kept a camera trained on a dumpster at the back of the office where they expected Clinton to emerge. While waiting for the president, MSNBC filled the airtime with small talk between anchor Gregg Jarrett and NBC soundman Leonard Chamble. After finally getting a chance to shout a question at Clinton as he left the building, Chamble was asked by Jarrett how it felt to interview the president. Chamble replied simply: "It's good there's [*sic*] people like you who can talk like this for hours" (Marks 2000).

## *Market Regulation and the Perceived Safety of Convergence*

On June 1, 2000, CNN publicly celebrated the cable network's 20th anniversary. In private, however, worried executives huddled to discuss the drop in the cable network's ratings. Evidence of the slide had been trickling in since 1997 as MSNBC and Fox "cannibalized" the already small all-news audience (Rust 1997; Heyboer 2000a; Rutenberg 2000a). CNN still attracted more U.S. viewers, but the pair were gaining ground. By June 2000, MSNBC had moved into the red. Fox News started making a profit in 2001, its fifth broadcasting year, and by January 2002 the opinion-driven cable network pulled ahead of CNN to become the undisputed ratings leader among cable news networks. MSNBC remained stalled in third place (Sella 2001; Hickey 2003). Fox's and MSNBC's success has been predicated on the approach first utilized by CNN—repetition and repurposing of content. In MSNBC's case, heavy reliance is placed on the news resources of its parent NBC and the profitable *Nightly News With Tom Brokaw* (Lafayette 2000).

The cutthroat competition among the cable-news networks had created unsettled waters; by 2000, all three networks were starting to rethink their business strategies. Despite the success of NBC's flagship nightly newscast, executives at MSNBC began to question their staple of "All-Monica-All-the-Time." MSNBC had continued to push the story hard, long after the public appetite for the scandal had started to wear thin. Some analysts suggest the obsession contributed to Fox's success in overtaking MSNBC in the prime-time ratings in 1999 (Heyboer 2000a). Meanwhile, CNN found itself licking a self-inflicted wound caused by the flop of its newsmagazine program *Newsstand*. The program, a synergistic collaboration with *Time* magazine, had failed to establish a loyal audience after it was forced to retract an exclusive story from its debut episode alleging the U.S. military had used nerve gas during the Vietnam War.[17] The person responsible for *Newsstand,* former CNN executive Richard Kaplan, says the program could have been more successful if it had been advertised more. "I think our problem is that, in an age when people are promoting the hell out of everything they do, for CNN to still do absolutely no promotion is wrong, and is debilitating" (Rutenberg 2000b).

The increased competition, slumping advertising revenue, and depressed stock prices were forcing AOL Time Warner and CNN executives to ponder the company's future with renewed urgency. Predictably, CNN's initial response was to apply the logic of integration more vigorously. In January 2001, CNN announced it would lay off close to 400 people—roughly 10 percent of its workforce. One of the people to lose his job was Kaplan. CNN brass then announced that in the future journalists would be expected to produce separate reports for its television, radio, and Internet networks. Generally, in the past journalists had written one report for each network, which was picked up and reworked by staff at sister networks. A month later, executives gave word that business channel CNNfn would be renamed CNN Money. The financial channel had fared badly against its chief rival, CNBC. CNN Money's Web site was to be given prominent placement on the AOL and Netscape Internet services. As well, more content and resources would be shared between AOL Time Warner properties such as *Time, Money,* and *Fortune.* These magazines would also supply

CNN Money with additional promotional support. And, with some coaxing, CNN successfully wooed back Lou Dobbs to refill the anchor chair on *Moneyline,* renamed *Lou Dobbs Moneyline* and eventually *Lou Dobbs Tonight.* The program had trailed CNBC's *Business Center* in the ratings ever since Dobbs resigned as host. These measures were seen in the business press as part of a corporate-wide business strategy for AOL Time Warner. So was a controversial decision to hire Andrea Thompson, a former actress on ABC's *N.Y.P.D. Blue* with a brief stint in an Italian erotic film, as a *Headline News* anchor—an effort by CNN to match MSNBC's relative success in attracting a younger news audience. By July 2001 ratings at the original all-news network began to stabilize (Rutenberg 2001c, 2001d, 2001e).

The shake-up at CNN is part of a general trend at major media organizations struggling to find a safe haven in a new media environment characterized by the uncertainty of increased competition and technological upheaval. Shortly after receiving regulatory approval for their merger, AOL Time Warner announced, on top of the CNN layoffs, that it would eliminate more than 2,000 jobs. The copartnerships and merger mania of the 1990s can be attributed, in part, to this desire to insulate businesses from each other and the unknown. Rupert Murdoch of News Corporation sums up the situation: "We can join forces now, or we can kill each other and then join forces" (Dwyer 1996, cited in Herman and McChesney 1997: 57). AOL founder Steve Case agreed. Speaking weeks after the merger, Case predicted that no single corporation would be able to dominate on its own, particularly once the promise of wireless Internet delivery becomes widespread. "It's a new world, and it requires a new spirit of partnership," says Case. "Any company that thinks they can do it alone is making a huge mistake" (Hamilton 2000).

The big media players believed that in order to ride out the uncertainty of a rapidly changing media environment, they needed to become more flexible and adapt themselves to the changing market conditions brought about by the fast pace of technological development. Explaining the elimination of 2,000 jobs, AOL Time Warner executive Robert W. Pittman said: "It is really about getting the company ready to take the next step, which means it was two separate companies and we want to get the redundancy out. . . . We are going to move at a pace that we think no other company of our size moves on. We are going to adopt 'quick, nimble, fast' as a corporate culture" (Schiesel and Rutenberg 2001). One way to preserve that flexibility, while simultaneously providing economic security, says Robert McChesney, is "to establish joint ventures with prospective competitors, to reduce potential competition and risk" (McChesney 1999: 140).

Fear began to take hold in the traditional-media world of newspapers when publishers realized their lifeblood of classified advertisements was under threat from online classified ad sites such as Autobytel.com, and Monster.com. These sites offered quick, easy and free access to searchable databases that allow people to pinpoint exactly what they are looking for, whether it be cars, apartments, or antiques. Online auction sites such as eBay.com pose a similar threat; and some television stations have also started up their own online classified pages in an attempt to slice off a portion of the $15 billion annual market for classified advertising in the United States (Schiller 1999: 98). Because classified advertising accounts for anywhere between 25 to 50 percent of a newspaper's revenue, newspaper companies were forced to respond with their own online classifieds. In December 1997, the Washington Post Co. joined a consortium of newspapers to form Classified Ventures, a group of interlinked Web sites that offer searchable listings. By 2003 its corporate partners included Tribune, Belo, Gannett, Knight Ridder Inc., and The McClatchy Company. In 2000 Tribune also joined the online classified service careerpath.com, which later merged with careerbuilder.com. Its corporate partners include Knight Ridder Inc., Gannett, Microsoft MSN and America Online. Meanwhile, the number of newspapers online grew from 20 to 4,925 worldwide between 1994 and 1999. Of those sites, 2,799 were in the United States (Brown 1999: 54–56). Worried publishers were giving serious consideration to the emerging business model of multimedia convergence.

Corporate consolidation in the U.S. continued, particularly in the wake of the monumental 1996 Telecommunications Act. In the early 1980s, the majority of information and entertainment programming was controlled by a mere 50 large firms. By 2000, Ben Bagdikian would report that six firms dominated all American mass media. They are General Electric (NBC, MSNBC, CNBC), Disney (ABC), Viacom (CBS), Bertelsmann, AOL Time Warner (CNN), and News Corporation (Fox News). Howard Stringer, chairman and CEO of Sony Corporation of America, captured the pathological mood of the late 1990s while commenting on Viacom Inc.'s then-record purchase of CBS for US$37 million, in September 1999. "After a deal like this, the urge to merge becomes feverish. And right now the temperatures are soaring all over the city" (Weinraub 1999).

Merger mania also hit Canada. The watershed AOL Time Warner announcement that they would form a cross-media powerhouse struck fear in Canadian boardrooms. Executives felt that to compete in the new "converged" media environment, they too had to be big and integrated. CanWest Global Communications, Canada's second-largest private broadcaster, announced in July 2000 that it was buying the major Canadian newspaper titles of Hollinger Inc. And by December of that year, the CRTC had already given its blessing to the merger of BCE Inc. and CTV Television Inc., Canada's largest telecommunications company and the country's largest private broadcaster respectively. The month of September saw BCE swallow the *Globe and Mail,* Canada's leading national daily newspaper. CTV and the *Globe* were then bundled together with BCE's Internet portal Sympatico/Lycos to form Bell Globemedia. "We did this to be the preeminent collection of media brands in the country and to leverage all of that expertise for better quality and to provide better marketing opportunities for our clients," said Bell Globemedia CEO Ivan Fecan. "That's the real nub of the story" (Damsell 2001a). The Bell Globemedia announcement came exactly a year to the day after the AOL Time Warner deal was made public. By April 2001, Leonard Asper, president and CEO of CanWest, bragged that his company's efforts at convergence had trimmed close to C$10 million in annual costs and generated nearly C$5 million in additional revenue (Damsell 2001b). The process would prove to be much more complicated.

More than ever, in the wake of the mega-media mergers of the 1990s, news is subject to regulation by market forces. Eleanor Fox, an antitrust scholar at the New York University Law School, sums up the prevailing commonsense wisdom among industry insiders:

> The perception is that markets are more open than earlier times and that barriers are lower. In any of these markets, firms are more under the gun to survive growing competition. And of course, the philosophy of regulation has changed. It used to be there was a lot of socio-economic concern for the concentration of power in a few hands. The concentration of power used to be seen in a dark light. Now, the concern is that businesses be free from regulation in order to compete in the global marketplace. (Labaton 1999)

Lost in this perspective, as Fox admits, is the belief that communication media have any social, moral, or political obligations beyond profit maximization. "Mergers of this size," argues Bagdikian, "further dwarfs news as merely another industrial by-product." Bagdikian goes on to say that "the new mergers deepen the dangers of more deterioration of news as a handmaiden of its owners' corporate ambitions, endangering the future of the independent and diverse public information on which democracy depends" (Bagdikian 2000: xi). The much-ballyhooed "synergies" that result from these massive mergers "don't constitute social efficiencies," says Edward Herman, "they are merely privileged tie-ins that make it possible to get business without competing for it or to more effectively target the customers advertisers want" (Herman 2000).

The implications of the neoliberal policies implemented in the United States by the FCC during the 1980s and 1990s are far reaching; and, they contributed enormously to the fast pace of media mergers that have swept the communication industries and to the proliferation of talk-TV and tabloid formats. As Armand Mattelart suggests, the discourse of market self-regulation continues to play "the role of a veritable Trojan horse in the privatization of the public sphere" (Mattelart 1996: 307). The Reagan administration's scrapping of the FCC's Fairness Doctrine helped lay the groundwork for the growth of spectacular forms of news media—it propelled the growth in aggressive personality-driven talk-radio programming and the globally syndicated tabloid-TV programs such as *Inside Edition,* and *A Current Affair.*

The re-regulation of U.S. broadcast industries was conducted in the name of public interest, but clearly it was driven by the demands and interests of media conglom-

erates. Charles Fairchild argues that the "fundamental transformation of the regulatory code. . . had the ultimate effect of greatly reducing the number of voices available
on radio and television and stifled almost all serious attempts at fostering diversity of
ownership and information within the broadcasting industry" (Fairchild 1999: 557). It
is the proliferation of these types of programs that, over time, began to shift the culture of journalism towards some of the professional excesses that occurred during the
Monicagate scandal.

# CHAPTER FOUR

# Convergence and the Myth of Variety

*With a hundred modern improvements there is*
*an illusion about them; there is not always a positive advance.*
HENRY DAVID THOREAU

## The Unity of Abundance and the Abundance of Unity

Since the mid-20th century, media conglomerates have made an implicit deal with the public and government regulators (in the case of broadcasting): the deal is that the professional standards of journalism will more than compensate for the increasing concentration of corporate ownership. Despite lingering questions about its ideological nature, the "regime of objectivity" (Hackett and Zhao 1998) remains the guarantor of journalism's legitimacy. The problem is that in practice the promotional logic of the spectacle can and does come into conflict with the seemingly eternal promise of media abundance and diversity. The conflict is difficult to resolve because the culture of journalism, from which the promise of diversity flows, has its own semi-independent existence. It can be tampered with, but it cannot be eliminated.[1] All mainstream news organizations, at least in North America, are united in their public commitment to the fair and balanced presentation of diverse views and opinion.

The phenomenal development of communication technologies during the course of the 20th century, and in particular, over the last 30 years—from satellites to the Internet—has been shadowed by a host of promotional discourses. These discourses—in tandem with the free-market discourse of market regulation—suggest improvements in communication technologies have ushered in a brand-new era characterized by the proliferation of choice and democratic freedom. "As proof," Armand Mattelart argues, "one need only point out the kinship between the messianic discourses on the networks of steam and electricity in the nineteenth century, and those that in the twentieth accompany the policies of economic and social recovery through information high tech" (Mattelart 1996: xvi).

Some 19th-century thinkers believed the telegraph would liberate citizens by giving them the ability to communicate across long distances. In the 1920s, radio, with its ability to broadcast directly into people's homes for free, was hyped by some as a great leap forward in democratic communication. Similar claims have been made of television. Moses Znaimer, Canadian TV maven and aging erstwhile hipster, insists in his McLuhanesque documentary *TV TV: The Television Revolution,* that "Print created illiteracy." Whereas, "TV is democratic. Everybody gets it." In 1992, U.S. cable mogul John Malone coined the phrase "500-channel universe" and boldly predicted that digital compression would create a pay-per-view cable industry that is sensitive to the needs and tastes of individuals. "Our ultimate goal here is to give our customers control of their TV service. That means giving them hundreds and hundreds of options, letting them control what they want to see and what they pay for it" (Fraser 1999: 15). Then, of course, came the explosion of popular excitement surrounding the Internet and the World Wide Web in 1994. John Perry Barlow and other Internet gurus tell us that the Internet obliterates top-down hierarchical structures and encourages the horizontal flow of one-to-one and one-to-many communication. Any kid with a computer and an Internet connection, we are told, can create a Web site with the same potential audience as CNN or any other major broadcast network. "As a result," says journalism scholar John Pavlik, "literally millions of citizens in the United States and around the world are active participants in the communication process online" (Pavlik 2000: 236).

The truth is that the technologies of communication media are not inherently democratic any more than they are inherently antidemocratic. To assess the democratic potential of media, one must look at how they are structured and used, how they are used in practice. Once again, we find that the promotional logic of spectacle plays an important role. "Technology," according to Kevin Robins and Frank Webster, "is presented as a spectacle, as something which can evoke only a gee-whiz, awed response (Robins and Webster 1999: 68). We find ready examples of this phenomenon in the comments of corporate boosters of technological, media, and corporate convergence. "I don't think there is as much a policy concern about media concentration right now as everybody makes it out to be," CanWest Global president and CEO Leonard Asper told the Canadian Press following CanWest's buyout of Hollinger's Canadian newspaper assets. "There are more services today than there have ever been in the history of the world—and of Canada. And there is more diversity today than there ever was" (Thorne 2000).

Promotional discourses celebrating the democratic potential of new technologies are a part of the integrated spectacular system of commodity production. "The spectacle," Debord says, "manifests itself as an enormous positivity, out of reach and beyond dispute. All it says is: 'Everything that appears is good; whatever is good will appear'" (Debord 1995: sec. 12). The promise of endless choice and total consumption is the necessary guarantee for the spectacle's continued development and reification of journalistic professional life. It is the carrot that justifies the institution of journalism placing itself under the rule of the integrated spectacle's logic.

In order for the integrated news spectacle to expand, a promise of endless choice and diversity of information and opinion must be present; conversely, in order for the public to be offered endless diversity of information and opinion, we are told that news organizations must become more integrated. Corporate consolidation and the convergence of formerly distinct media—print, broadcast, and the Internet—is justified on the basis that news organizations must develop economies of scope (a broad array of well-known brands and services) and scale (vertically integrated channels of production and distribution) if they are to be able to compete with other similarly integrated media conglomerates in the global-media marketplace. "If you don't have scale and lots of outlets on a global stage, it will make it more difficult to survive," said Barry Diller, the former head of the USA Network, speaking in 2000. "Anyone who is a second-tier player in the media industry has to be concerned right now" (Pearlstein 2000).

In September 2000, Tribune Co., a corporate pioneer in multimedia convergence, asked the FCC to allow its Miami TV station WBZL to use reporting from the Tribune's Fort Lauderdale newspaper in its newscasts. The FCC had approved Tribune's ownership of both the *Sun-Sentinel* and WBZL on the condition that the two news organizations be run separately. In a stunning piece of logic, Tribune argued that the FCC's requirement was actually stifling competition in the market because WBZL, a WB affiliate, carries a prepackaged newscast produced by NBC's Miami station, WTVJ. Tribune said that it would prefer WBZL to produce its own news, but was forced into the partnership due to "sobering facts in the Miami market." The company went on to argue that if it could merge its print and broadcast resources, the Miami station would be able "to produce a fresh, new, local television newscast for South Florida viewers" (Associated Press 2000b). What were the "sobering facts in the Miami market"? That other news organizations in Miami already were integrated though resource-sharing partnerships.[2] The concentration of economic power—already in existence through the NBC partnership with WBZL and others—becomes the guarantee of diversity, while the promise of endless diversity legitimates the concentration of economic and promotional power in the hands of fewer and fewer corporate media giants. Danny Schechter, a veteran TV-news producer, has dubbed the phenomenon "competition through consolidation" (Schechter 2001a). The FCC granted Tribune a temporary waiver of its cross-ownership rule.

Following Debord we might say that, within the logic of the integrated news spectacle, journalistic diversity is "the indispensable packaging for things produced . . . as a general gloss on the rationality" of an integrated system of production, distribution and exchange (Debord 1995: sec. 15). To understand the convergence of formerly distinct news media organizations, we must understand how the logic of the spectacle manifests itself as an objective social force within convergence. The logic of the spectacle is a constitutive element of the reconfiguration of the news media industry.

### Dreams of Digital Transcendence and Material Constraints

In recent years, the technical and corporate convergence of Internet, broadcasting, and print media has been heralded as a new milestone on the road to cultural abundance. Self-styled techno-prophet George Gilder provides perhaps the best example of how neoliberal ideology has become fused with a breed of techno-libertarianism. In Gilder's religiously tinged vision of techno-utopia, all individuals become entrepreneurs whose only limits are their own imagination and the technical boundaries of bandwidth. But even this antediluvian encumbrance will soon be overcome, giving birth to a new age of nearly infinite information flow. "After the floods of bandwidth," asks Gilder, "who will greet the dawn and the dove?" (Rothstein 2000).[3] Dreams of bodily transcendence through digitization aside, at the core of this promotional discourse rests the simple belief in the individual's ability to conquer the endless spaces created by the Internet. According to John Perry Barlow, "the cool thing about the Internet is that it never runs out of room. No one is being crowded out" (Harris 2000). The digital economy, we are told, is based on abundance, not scarcity. Because of this, the market is inevitably driven by demand and not supply. As Korinna Patelis says, in the minds of the techno-libertarians "a distinction between production and consumption on-line can be made, but it is insignificant since the power relationship between the two has been subverted by the perfect market" (Patelis 2000: 88).

The belief that the Internet and the World Wide Web have opened a new world of democratic communication is not limited to Internet gurus. It is also prevalent in some corners of the academic community. Sylvia M. Chan-Olmsted argues, correctly, that the digital convergence of previously distinct communication sectors is "amplifying the strategic importance of the Internet." It is also "blurring traditional market boundaries and fostering competition between firms that did not previously compete with one another"—e.g., newspapers, magazines, broadcasting, telecommunications, and the Internet (Chan-Olmsted 2000: 95). She argues further, however, that: "In the Internet age, the premise of scale economics of mass production or mass distribution is no longer relevant" (97). This is because of the Internet's heralded capacity for horizontal one-to-one and one-to-many communication. Consumers on the World Wide Web do not sit passively while content is pushed to them, as is the case in broadcasting.

Instead, Chan-Olmsted says, they actively select and "personalize" content to suit their individual needs. Most news organizations allow visitors to create an online "profile" that cues the site to present preselected information categories. A site called CRAYON (create your own newspaper) was an early experiment with this technology.

Having made the case for how old hierarchical relationships have been overturned by the Web's empowerment of consumers, Chan-Olmsted proceeds, without apparently realizing it, to undermine her own argument. She advises media organizations to reassert themselves by leveraging their brand identities through the promotional integration of their multimedia platforms (111). In other words, media organizations should counter the level playing field of the Internet by reasserting their advantages in economies of scale and scope, advantages that Chan-Olmsted believes no longer exist.

The belief that time and space constraints, market imperfections, and socio-economic disparities have been eliminated by new media—as I've indicated above—is a recurring theme. This "techno-orthodoxy," says Marjorie Ferguson, is difficult to dismiss because of the many instances in which everyday perceptions and uses of time and space have shifted with the introduction of new electronic media, from the telegraph through to the Internet. However, that does not mean that these technologies remain free of the specific economic, social and cultural contexts in which they are situated. The telegraph, for example, was used to extend "economic (and political) domination over time and space" (Ferguson 1990: 154). It also contributed to the news media's vast expansion of the commodification of time and space. Early media events such as the Lindbergh baby kidnapping were component parts of a much larger process in which public space and the time spent with media were made phantasmagoric. Time and space became detached from place as the production, distribution, and exchange of news became progressively more subject to the exigencies of capital accumulation. The drive to aestheticize news through the use of dramatic storytelling became more and more refined and integrated into news production; today's spectacular media events are a part of this progression.

Ferguson suggests that we rework Durkheim's theory that the social constructs of time and space are culturally specific. Drawing upon Anthony Giddens's discussion of "world time," Ferguson encourages us to place time and space within a broader context of "'world time-space' in order to infer the interconnection between the growth of the capitalist world market and shifting temporal and spatial horizons" (Ferguson 1990: 161). Once again, we must turn our attention towards how the logic of the integrated spectacle has been employed by capital to rationalize and control the use of time and space. The common technical platform of the Internet is being used by corporations to merge "formerly differentiated distribution systems"—newspapers' use of cars and trucks, magazines, and mail delivery, television and radio through airborne broadcast signals. And just like the telegraph before it, says Dan Schiller, the Internet has created a new "avenue to market power" by giving corporations new ways to "exclude would-be competitors" (Schiller 1999: 97).

*Protecting Discrete Revenue Streams*

While it is certainly true that the exponential growth of the Internet during the 1990s has encouraged a corresponding increase in the number of information providers (that is, for those people with Internet access), this fact is often confused with ideological diversity and the absence of power relationships in practice.[4] It is relatively inexpensive to create a Web site, but the resources required to promote the site in order to be competitive with the likes of AOL Time Warner are enormous. In other words, the Internet does not create a level playing field upon which social, economic, and political advantages are totally curbed. Internet pioneer Stewart Brand is famous for saying that "Information wants to be free." The phrase has become synonymous with discourses heralding high-tech democracy. Brand admits making the statement. "But," he says, "nobody remembers the second line, which is 'information wants to be expensive.' That's the paradox that drives this thing" (Garreau and Weeks 2000). John Haile, editor of the *Orlando Sentinel,* and a proponent of multimedia convergence, clarifies the situation for his newspaper: "The idea that you can get the newspaper for free is one we are going to challenge. . . . The newspaper itself continues to be the real engine that drives all this, and we're saying let's not undermine that unnecessarily" (Weaver, J. 2000: 24–25).

Dan Schiller frames the issue by asking: "How, in this emerging common context, will formerly disparate media products retain their discrete revenue streams?" (Schiller 1999: 98). Telecommunication companies such as Nortel and Cisco have responded to the challenge at the base level by starting to alter the open network architecture of their own high-speed digital networks. As Dwayne Winseck points out, this is being done to exert greater control over their networks.

> Consequently, open network architectures are yielding to network designs that enhance network providers' ability to allocate resources, bandwidth, and speed to varying types of information and services based on their relation to the network owner, revenue potential, class of user served, and judgements regarding the quality of content, i.e., "objectionable content" such as pornography, hate literature, and so on, but also political dissent where that is objectionable. (Winseck 2001: 11)

These "netscapes of power," argues Winseck, are being used to "hardwire" gatekeeping functions "into network architectures as part of the communications industries' strategies to cultivate and control markets" (12).

As mentioned in Chapter Three, newspapers and television broadcasters have created additional revenue streams by launching Web sites that tap into the burgeoning market for online classifieds. In addition, companies have turned to the creation of proprietary content. One of the ways in which AOL has maintained the value of its fabled "walled garden" of proprietary services is by imposing contractual obligations on content providers designed to reduce the chance that users will venture beyond AOL. Under a contract signed in 1997, for example, Disney's ABC News unit agreed to limit or remove hyperlinks to other sites. The contract could be cancelled if more than 25 percent of the traffic leapt over AOL's garden wall (Klein 2000).[5]

In addition, the entry points to the Internet for most people remain Web portals such as Google, AOL, Netscape, Yahoo, MSN, and Alta Vista. These sites aggregate information for users and include search engines that allow people to locate specific content. These so-called on-ramps to the information highway have a huge strategic importance, which is why both Netscape and Microsoft waged a war for control of the startup screen on individual desktop computers, in the late 1990s (Schiller 1999: 120). Both companies were taking steps to corral audiences as they take their first steps onto the Internet.

Web portals also are becoming increasingly commercialized. With banner advertisements not selling very well, many companies have begun to accept payments in exchange for priority placement in their search-engine results. For a fee, Web sites also can reduce by months the waiting period to be added to a search engine's database. The problem, of course, is that important information carried by nonprofit organizations and other groups that cannot afford fees for "paid inclusion" in search engines may not be as easy to find as those who can (Introna and Nissenbaum 2000; Weise 2000; Lohse 2001). The growth in paid-search advertising sales has been linked to the rise in online advertising revenue in 2003 (Mack 2003).

Surveys released by Media Metrix, an online audience-measurement firm, indicate that Web sites associated with multinational brands dominate worldwide.[6] In January 2001, sites operated by AOL Time Warner, Microsoft, and Yahoo were ranked number one, two, and three among sites visited by Americans. Surveys that followed indicated a similar pattern of use. Significantly, *one-third* of all time spent online by Americans that month was spent at AOL Time Warner properties. Sites owned by AOL's main competitors Yahoo and Microsoft claimed 7 and 6 percent of total time online respectively. Moreover, 72 percent of American users visited an AOL Time Warner site—which includes CNN.com and CNNSI.com, among others—at least once during the period of time surveyed (Walker 2001a). While AOL's 27 million American subscribers may have spent only 10 percent of their total time online within AOL's "walled garden" (Walker 2001b),[7] it would appear that AOL Time Warner's stable of multinational brands, backed by the company's hefty promotional muscle, has contributed to the company's strong online presence. U.S. audience numbers at both CNN.com (No. 2 ranked online news site) and Time.com sites rose after AOL began to heavily promote its online ventures—a trend that has been duplicated at other online news sites such as MSNBC.com (No. 1). In fact, as the online audience for news and information grows (14.7 percent from July 2000 to July 2001), the main beneficiaries are those sites operated by established news organizations. In the United States as of May 2003, following MSNBC.com and CNN.com in popularity were

Yahoo News (which aggregates top news brands, at No. 3), AOL News (No. 4), and NYTimes.com (No. 5). The Web sites of Gannett, Knight Ridder, and Tribune newspaper chains came in sixth, seventh, and eighth spot, respectively. Washington-post.com, ABC News and Fox News placed ninth, tenth, and eleventh overall (Editor and Publisher Online 2003).

Scale is just as important as ever. "The economic reality is that you need more and more capital to play in integrated businesses," says market analyst Roger Kay. "The anarchy of the high seas of the old Internet was a great place for entrepreneurs to float their little boats. A lot of that opportunity will be cut off, or at least taxed, by these big companies" (Streitfeld 2000). In 1999 and early 2000, small independent Internet start-ups surfed the promotional wave of Internet hype and attracted millions of dollars in start-up money from eager venture capitalists. That money dried up when the dot-com stock-market bubble burst in March 2000 and the value of the NASDAQ stock exchange began its precipitous slide downward. Now, more than ever, commercial success for Internet businesses requires deep financial pockets and the heft that comes with economies of scope and scale. In June, 2001 two long-running online magazines, *Feed* and *Suck*, suspended publication and laid off their staff. *Feed* co-founder and coeditor Stefanie Syman spoke of the online magazine's strong brand and loyal readership, but concluded that the magazine "just didn't have the scale to pull it off" (Harmon 2001).

Finally, the principal strategy employed by companies to protect their revenue streams in the new common delivery platform created by the Internet was summarized by Conrad Black, former chairman of Hollinger International, which publishes the *Telegraph* in London, the *Chicago Sun-Times*, and the *Jerusalem Post*. Writing in 2000, before the dot-com collapse, Black remained bullish on the future of newspapers in spite of slipping circulation (overall circulation in the United States is down roughly 10 percent from the late 1980s) and increased competition from online publications. As Black explains, his optimism is predicated on the belief that the promotional brawn of major media brands can be leveraged effectively. He is worth quoting at length on this point.

> Anyone will be able to set up on the Internet and compete directly with telecasters and established Internet sites. In this era of overwhelming choice, the central question is: Who can attract the proverbial eyeballs? As the profusion of dot-com advertising in the *Wall Street Journal* demonstrates, there is no better platform for launching, promoting, co-branding and joint selling with Internet sites than an authoritative newspaper.
>
> Serious newspapers will offer their loyal readers a range of Internet services as varied as their content. Those that can bridge the newspaper and Internet cultures will have their full share in the rise of the Internet. They will retain a base of goodwill and brand loyalty that other media will rival only with great persistence and difficulty. (Black 2000)

Black has summarized the strategies employed by major media organizations designed to harness the promotional potential of the integrated news spectacle. Promote and extend your news organization's brand by repurposing content, cross-promotion, and the creation of new synergistic business opportunities. In essence, Black has outlined the strategy employed by media conglomerates to transfer loyal audiences from one media property to another. It has become the principal way in which media conglomerates hope to protect their revenue streams while dealing with the added competition created by the common delivery platform of the Internet. Once broadcaster CanWest Global purchased Black's Canadian Southam newspaper chain, Global wasted no time in announcing its intension to promotionally integrate its newly acquired print titles with its national broadcast network.

Black's decision to sell off his top Canadian newspaper titles can also be seen as a response to market uncertainty. The purchase of the Canadian Southam newspaper chain had saddled Hollinger Inc. with an enormous debt load and it had not been able to live up to its promise that share prices would rise. There was, therefore, considerable pressure from unhappy shareholders to increase the value of their investment.

### Branding from the Inside Out

The first step in the convergence of multimedia properties is not about reconciling different media technologies such as print, broadcasting, and the Internet in order to produce a daily interactive Webcast. Nor is it about providing a wide array of information and opinion. The potential benefits of new technology for democratic communication are secondary. "The primary goal of the Webcasters who see the Internet as a nascent media platform," says Dan Schiller, "is to concentrate and stabilize relations between program services and audiences" (Schiller 1999: 115).

According to the managers of media convergence, the first step on the road to convergence is to formalize a company's or partnership's brand image. George Bell, president and CEO of Excite@Home Corp. emphasized this point in March 2000 at the peak of the dot-com stock market frenzy. Speaking in Toronto at the launch of his company's now-defunct Canadian Web portal, *Excite.ca,* Bell suggested that the strategic value of content is overrated because most sites provide similar information and services.[8] In order to differentiate oneself from the competition, he argued, a company needs to establish its brand identity. "We're in a distribution war, we're in a branding war," said Bell. "In the later stages we will move beyond those areas to content and broadband [services]" (Evans 2000).

The strategy outlined by Conrad Black, and implicitly endorsed by George Bell, has become so standardized within media circles that the American Society of Newspaper Editors released a collection of essays in 2000 under the title *Extending the*

*Brand: A Newspaper Editor's Guide to Partnerships and Diversification in a Converging Media World*. The ASNE report provides a duffers' guide to the logic of the integrated news spectacle and how it became the driving force within converged news organizations, such as Tribune. The goal of branding is to associate certain values, emotions, and personality traits with a particular news organization and its partners. Branding is about more than pitching a news product; it is about matching the "personality" of a news organization with the hopes and desires of audiences.[9]

As part of its branding strategy, the *Seattle Times* newspaper created a team of "brand stewards" to study and oversee the creation and implementation of the newspaper's brand identity. The brand stewards were taken from all sectors of the company, including editorial, advertising, marketing, circulation, and the paper's new-media division. From the beginning, the goal of the brand stewards would be extremely ambitious. It would not be enough to sell readers on the company's brand image. Management wanted to *brand the newspaper* "from the inside out." What this means in practice is that all employees are expected to take responsibility for the paper's brand. "We would take the most ambitious view of brand management," says Cyndi Nash, the *Times* associate managing editor, "and set as a goal when we were done that every employee would understand and be an ambassador for the *Seattle Times* brand" (Fancher 2000: 9). It is not enough for employees to understand and accept the branding of the newspaper; they are expected to live it in their professional capacity as reporters and editors. They are, in a sense, expected to assume the brand's personality and values. Branding is to be a total experience on the part of both readers and employees as they develop a mutual relationship mediated through the brand image. The brand, according to this view, is meant to guide all aspects of the newspaper production, distribution, and consumption.

The "brand stewards" at the *Times* are following the advice of former Nike-brand guru Scott Bedbury: "The goal for any company," says Bedbury, "is to build a brand that weaves itself into the fabric of life" (Bock 2000: 17). Bedbury wants companies to use their brands to create distinct personalities that have their own dramatic stories and experiences to relate. "Bedbury believes *brands organize society*" [emphasis added], says Paula Bock, of the *Times*'s *Pacific Northwest Magazine:* "they help us know what to expect, whether we're buying a car or cellular service or life insurance," or, one might add, newspapers (18). Lee Jacobson, a Toronto-based consultant on branding and design, puts it this way: "At a time when products and services are becoming commodities, a strong brand is capable of making decisions simpler for customers—or any audience. It allows for *one-thought shopping*" [emphasis added] (Jacobson 2000). For example, readers want to know what to expect when they pick up a copy of the *National Enquirer* or the *New York Times;* and their respective brand slogans: "Inquiring minds want to know," and "All the news that's fit to print," contribute to the certainty of each paper's respective brand identity. So, whereas Bedbury created

Nike's brand slogan "Just Do It" as an emotional bridge for people's desire for physical fitness, the *Seattle Times*—many focus groups later—settled on the slogan "Serving your need to know" as a way of forming an emotional bond with readers based on their desire to be informed about their community.

The *Seattle Times*'s "brand vision" is a variation on the standard journalistic theme of fairness, accuracy, and balance. The same can be said of the *Orlando Sentinel*'s brand slogan: "If it says Sentinel, I trust it," or the "We report, you decide" branding of Fox News. The *Orlando Sentinel*'s theme was the result of a series of "brand labs" it conducted in preparation for the 1997 launch of Central Florida News 13 (CFN 13)—a 24-hour regional-news channel jointly owned by Time Warner and the *Sentinel*'s parent, Tribune. The *Sentinel* also operates a Web site devoted to online news and has a partnership agreement with six Orlando radio stations owned by Clear Channel Communications, the largest owner of radio stations in the United States. The branding labs were conducted as part of the two companies' efforts to build a shared commitment among journalists in the print, broadcast and Internet newsrooms. Mainstream news organizations like the *Sentinel* and the *Seattle Times* have no choice but to present themselves as fair and balanced. As a result, news brands are variations on a familiar theme. As Janet Weaver, executive editor of the *Sarasota Herald-Tribune*, says, "While the methodology may be cutting edge, the message—that the *Sentinel*, in all its forms, is a deep, reliable source of local news and information—is universal to newspaper journalists" (Weaver, J. 2000: 23).

But while news brands communicate the same basic message of trust and reliability they also have another strategic importance. In addition to distinguishing a news organization from the competition, brands are used to form a bond among media partners. In 1992, a partnership between the *Sentinel* and the Orlando ABC TV affiliate hit troubled waters. According to *Sentinel* editor John Haile, the clash of cultures between the television and print newsrooms was at the root of the problem. With the launch of Channel 13, both Time Warner and the Tribune Company wanted to form shared bonds of allegiance among what in the past (that is, preconvergence) would have been considered competing news organizations with distinctly different news cultures and agendas—newsrooms with different personalities. Journalists are asked to set aside the traditional feelings of competition—and in some cases, disdain—that exist between print and broadcast journalists.[10] Some reporters resisted, claiming that going on television would put their integrity into question; and, they ended up leaving the paper as a result. Other journalists report they enjoy the extra duties of filing several updates a day for the online edition and being interviewed on television. One of those reporters, Debra Salamone Wickham, says the added exposure she receives being on television has increased her profile and credibility with sources. "If you have to get on television to get them interested in newspapers, that's what you have to do" (Schneider 2000).

What is important here is that the promotional benefit referred to by Wickham is the result of the practical steps taken by managers to rationally organize and extend the company's brand. Reporters are not paid more for their extra work. Instead, they receive nonmonetary rewards and incentives such as an enhanced public profile. Moreover, reporters' sincere and deeply held beliefs in their duty to inform the public—a constitutive component of news branding—help to legitimate the repurposing of labor in integrated newsrooms. "My job is to inform the public and I will use any means possible to do that," says Michael Griffin, *Orlando Sentinel* political editor. "I consider this another part of the newspaper" (Schneider 2000). Terrie Mitchell, who led the *Sentinel's* branding strategy, says if the staff does not believe in the brand, neither will the public. "We've told the community and the market about our vision for ourselves, but we need employees to believe it as strongly," says Mitchell. "The question was, how do we make the brand live inside the company?" As part of their efforts, the company provided employees with a branding package. It explained the brand strategy, the values they want to reinforce, and the kind of culture they wanted to foster (Weaver, J. 2000: 24–25).

To extend its brand message, the *Sentinel* increased its advertising budget fivefold. And it appears to have worked: a 1998 survey indicated a 43-percent market awareness for the *Sentinel*. In addition, the number of respondents who viewed the *Sentinel* as a trusted source of information for the community was bumped up 10 percent (24).

Brands are used to subject newsrooms to rational organization and control. The brand personalities of news organizations are reified so as to solicit the loyalty and trust of audiences and employees. They are used for strategic promotional purposes to signify unity or difference, depending on the needs of the organization. None of this questions the commitment of individual journalists to provide quality journalism that serves the needs of the public. Quite to the contrary. The values of journalistic professionalism and the forms of subjectivity that reporters and editors establish through them have roots outside of the *business* of news media. The problem is that these professional identities have become constitutive elements of economic competition and rational organization; they have become objects of rational and strategic action by commercial interests and institutions. It is in this sense that the professional autonomy of journalism is under threat. The more the logic of the integrated spectacle is extended, the more journalism is conducted according to *its* rules, not the values of public service. And, while the proponents of newsroom branding, such as Janet Weaver, argue that brands derive from deeply held journalistic values, that does not mean that the newsroom always is guided by those principles. The purpose of branding has less to do with producing quality journalism than it does with appearing to produce quality journalism. It is a promotional tool required to facilitate marketing and advertising strategies. As proof we need only see what Cyndi Nash, the associate managing editor of the *Seattle Times,* lists as the *accomplishments* of branding:

- A basis for guiding new product development, particularly the use of our name on these products.
- A consistent way of answering telephones, and talking to customers about the role the *Seattle Times* plays in representing its JOA [joint operating agreement] partner, the *Seattle Post-Intelligencer*.
- A redesigned logo and nameplate, as well as clearer guidelines for using it.
- An entirely new look to all our marketing materials and in-paper advertising that is carried out on our newspaper boxes, trucks, subscriber bills, and business stationery.
- A set of newspaper differentiation guidelines that help circulation and marketing talk about the differences between the two newspapers in the JOA.
- A new and growing understanding between departments about exactly what the newspaper stands for in the minds of consumers.
- A nomenclature system to guide usage of the brand as it relates to core products, subsidiaries, and alliances.
- A clearer understanding of what undermines our brand, and a stronger commitment to avoiding actions that do. (Fancher 2000: 13–14)

Nowhere in Nash's list is the word *journalism* mentioned. Instead, she refers to products and their relationship to marketing and advertising. While the values of the brand are said to guide staff in their efforts to serve the community with quality journalism, the actual net gains listed by Nash relate to the economic benefits of promotion and improved efficiency.

### *Reaggregating Fragmented Audiences*

A news organization's use of its brand identity to channel loyal audiences from one media property to another is a response to a fundamental shift in the mediascape—the fragmentation of audiences. The fragmentation of audiences sped up in the 1980s with the expansion of cable, and it has continued apace with the development of the Internet. The new mediascape has put a premium on the creation of brands as destinations in themselves—brands attract proverbial eyeballs while simultaneously helping in their redistribution. According to the logic of the emerging business model, commercial advantage will be given to those companies with the best unified collection of top brands, or those companies that can best extend one trusted brand to their converged media properties.

When the Tribune announced March 13, 2000, that it would acquire the Times Mirror Co. of Los Angeles, it created a multimedia powerhouse that would be tailored for the specifications of convergence. The combined company now owns 12 daily newspapers, including the flagship *Chicago Tribune, Newsday* in New York, and the *Los Angeles Times* in California, 26 television stations, one Chicago radio station, all-news cable channels in Chicago and Miami, a magazine-publishing arm, a

22-percent stake in Time Warner's WB network, and a network of Internet sites across the United States. It also owns the Chicago Cubs baseball team. As Neil Hickey writes in the *Columbia Journalism Review,* "Tribune is hardly the only multimedia practitioner but it is surely one of the most devoted" (Hickey 2000: 19).

Tribune invested in AOL in 1991. It has since invested in such online operations as online grocer Peapod, and iVillage.com, a portal geared to women. Tribune also was one of the first news companies to have its reporters multitask—delivering reports to its print, broadcast, and Internet operations. Its newsrooms are models of convergence with a central command desk at which sit editors from online, graphics, TV, cable, and radio departments. Their close proximity allows for easy coordination of stories throughout what is now a 24-hour news cycle. Star Trek afficionados in the Orlando newsroom have dubbed their central editorial desk "the bridge."

The newsroom experiments are all part of Tribune's plan to become a multimedia conglomerate that combines disparate media properties in a way that offers marketers and advertisers enticing regional and national cross-media packages. It is about providing advertisers with one-stop shopping for their media buys in local markets such as Miami; but more importantly, it provides an opportunity for the company to tap into the lucrative national advertising market now that it has properties in New York, Chicago and Los Angeles—the three largest media markets in the United States. Jack Fuller, president of Tribune Publishing, explains the strategy:

> Having television and newspapers in three major markets in the country is a powerful position to be in a changing environment. So whether it's getting national advertising into our newspapers, or staking out a position on the Internet, or moving toward a broadband environment in which print, video, and audio all will be elements—having that position in the strong spine of a network in the major cities of the country looked to us to be strategically an important move. (Hickey 2000: 19)

And to keep all of the pieces of their multimedia network working in sync, Tribune relies on the strength of its brand identity. Journalist Ken Auletta conducted extensive interviews with management and staff at the *Chicago Tribune,* prior to the Times Mirror buyout, and concluded that the company has been quite successful in fostering a belief in the brand identity among employees. "Executives—and editors, too—go on about *synergy* and *brand extension,* about how their individual companies are not mere newspapers, broadcast stations or Web sites, but *partners* and *information providers.*" In Auletta's view, Tribune has "lowered the wall between news and business. Here, journalism is *content*" (Auletta 1998: 20).

The contradiction between journalism's expressed commitment to the values of public service and the logic of integration is at the heart of news-media convergence. The values of public service do not require convergence, but the promotional project of convergence *does* require that lip service be paid to the values of public service and the promise of diversity. Top managers at MSNBC were stung by the All-Monica-All-the-Time label that became attached to the network precisely because it sullied their brand. Journalists do not want to be thought of as lascivious hacks preoccupied with catching politicians literally with their pants down. The proponents of news-media convergence implicitly understand this situation. They know that convergence must be sold by appealing to journalists' belief in a higher calling. "I still believe the reason most people become journalists is to discover things about people, places and events, and then share that discovery through good story telling," says Dan Bradley, news director of NBC-affiliate WFLA-TV in Tampa Bay. Bradley is among a group of senior editors steering the convergence of his TV newsroom with the *Tampa Tribune* newspaper and Tampa Bay Online. "Stories get new life and affect our customers in different ways when told or delivered on different platforms," says Bradley. "We need to constantly remind our folks that this is about telling stories, not filling newspapers or newscasts" (Gentry 2000: 35). Once again, the values of public service along with good story telling are appealed to in order to justify the convergence of disparate newsroom resources and the repackaging of stories.

Nevertheless, the top editors at Tribune newspapers understand very well what the primary purpose of branding and the convergence of news media organizations is about. Howard Tyner, editor of the *Chicago Tribune,* spells out in plain language why the newspaper's WGN ("World's Greatest Newspaper") brand was extended to Tribune's other Chicago-area media holdings, including WGN-TV, ChicagoLand TV (CLTV, a 24-hour news channel), WGN-AM radio, chicagotribune.com and the Chicago Cubs baseball team:

> Because we have a media information world that is fragmenting moment by moment. People have trouble navigating through the environment, and they are looking for a brand they know and trust.
>
> On the advertising side, a big name brand or a collection of big name brands under the same tent gives you opportunities with advertisers that wouldn't exist or would exist to a lesser extent when a newspaper is operating individually.
>
> The act of naming WGN ("World's Greatest Newspaper") was a brand extension. The fact that today our reporters or critics on CLTV (ChicagoLand TV) are always identified with a *Chicago Tribune* logo, as they are on WGN TV or anywhere else, is an attempt to push that brand out further. (Dedinsky 2000: 43)

Here the WGN brand is used to organize audience expectations about the quality of the news product. "The idea," says Tyner, "is to develop relationships so you can extend your reach to as many eyeballs as possible in a particularly fertile area, such as local television news" (44). It is also designed to build a sense of allegiance among the employees of the co-owned or partnered media outlets. "I am not the editor of a newspaper," Tyner tells Auletta. "I am the manager of a content company. That's what I do. I don't do newspapers alone. We gather content" (Auletta 1998: 22).

Tribune is not the only media company adopting the strategy of media integration. In June 2000, Gannett, the owner of a large chain of newspapers including the flagship *USA Today,* released a report to its publishers outlining the company's new business plan (Currie 2000). "The aim of all of our steps is to build readership," wrote Phil Currie, senior vice president of news. "But the definition of readership is expanded beyond the people we draw to the newspapers. It now includes the people we can bring to our online sites and related products as well." Currie stressed the importance of Gannett's "core values: upholding First Amendment responsibilities; reflecting and serving diverse readers; achieving high-quality journalistic standards; and ensuring credibility in content and integrity in newsgathering," so as to distinguish the company's newspapers from competing media. But these values were set against the company's primary goal of reaching particular reader segments—a goal not always easy to square with the commitment to serve diverse readers. Of special interest to Gannett are 25- to 34-year-olds. This is the market segment most highly prized by advertisers because of the willingness among young affluent people to spend disposable income on leisure products and services. The demographic group makes up less than a third of the total population in both Canada and the United States, according to data published online by the Canadian and U.S. Census Bureaus.[11] Polls indicate, however, that young affluent people interested in financial information are turning to the Web more frequently (Associated Press 2000c), a trend news producers have noticed with much satisfaction (see below). So much for diversity.

A similar, but slightly broader demographic (25- to 54-year-olds), is being chased by MSNBC, whose MSNBC.com is the most visited news site on the Web. The online side of the all-news multimedia giant has attracted as many as three million unique users on days when big stories are breaking, such as the plane crash of John F. Kennedy Jr. (Heyboer 2000b). And for former MSNBC president Erik Sorenson, the younger the better. "When we're applying our decision-making apparatus to the flow of all the news that's coming across the transom every day, we're thinking of it from a 25- to 54-year-old point of view, and we don't make any bones about that," says Sorensen. The implications for news values are clear. "To an 18-year-old, news might be that *Erin Brockovich* is No. 1 at the box office. News might be that 'N Sync has the hottest album at Tower Records. News might be that there's a cool new Web site that allows you as an Internet consumer to download an MP3 to your hard drive" (Heyboer 2000a). Sorensen's list of news values as seen through the eyes of his prototypical 18-year-old provides a fairly accurate portrayal of how audiences are conceived primarily as consumers, not citizens.

That news media are interested in young affluent audiences should not come as a surprise. As Andrew Wernick (1991) argues, promotion has long been constitutive of the production process itself. From the beginning of ad-supported media, advertiser interest in attracting affluent audiences has contributed to the type of news stories produced and their style of presentation. Editorial content has always been the honey that attracts the bee for commercial news media. What is significant about integrated newsrooms is that the dividing line between editorial and promotional interests has been blurred irrevocably. In the past, news media sold mass audiences to advertisers who were given the opportunity to place their advertisements in front of the delivered eyeballs. News media simply attracted the eyeballs. They were not involved in producing the advertisement, or in cajoling audiences into making a purchase, beyond providing a "buying mood" with the appropriate programming. In integrated newsrooms, however, the goal is to use editorial content to steer audiences toward preferred nodes on a company's or group of companies proprietary network of multimedia outlets. These nodes may be ad-supported media (TV, radio, newspapers, magazines) or they may be retail sites that sell goods and services. In either case, news outlets often have a direct interest in seeing the transaction completed, either because they own the integrated commercial site or because they have entered into a cross-promotion or profit-sharing agreement. The situation is rife for potential conflicts of interest to develop between the public-service commitments of news organizations and their particular commercial interests.

Steve Outing, columnist for *Editor and Publisher,* a widely read news-industry trade journal, offers the following advice: "One of the content site's goals should be to turn more of those browsers into buyers—by offering high-value content that helps them make buying decisions when they are in the position to buy, and facilitating the actual purchase with e-commerce relationships" (Outing 2000). This might mean partnering with companies that distribute and produce such movies as *Erin Brockovich,* or that sell downloads of MP3 audio files. This is exactly what MSNBC.com has done. A Shop@MSNBC hyperlink placed on the site's omnipresent menu bar takes users to an online shopping mall where users can buy a CD from amazon.com, a book from Barnes & Noble or a bouquet of flowers from JustFlowers.com. Other industry executives have been listening to this kind of advice. The *Washington Post* has set up a mini-mall in conjunction with other retailers as part of its Web site. The *New York Times* online site also contains links to book-giant Barnes & Noble. Under the arrangement, the *Times* receives a cut of any sale that is finalized through a link on the nytimes.com site.

Bell Globemedia is the holding company for the *Globe and Mail,* CTV News network, and the Sympatico Web portal, until it was folded back into its parent, Bell Canada. CEO Ivan Fecan wants to "figure out how we can be more effective on these multiple platforms: print, broadcast, specialty and the Internet." Fecan wants to use Globemedia's distribution network, still in its infancy, to offer advertisers "custom-built advertising solutions" (Olive 2001). The *Globe and Mail*'s Web pages have a number of integrated links that direct users to proprietary services. These include globeinvestor.com, a site devoted to stock information; globefund.com, an on-line mutual-funds site; globebooks.com, where users can purchase the latest best-selling novel from the Chapters book chain; workopolis.com, a classified-ad site jointly operated with the *Toronto Star* newspaper; and globemegawheels.com, where users can either place a classified ad indicating they want to buy or sell a vehicle or search for vehicles online.

The *Globe*'s Web site extends its brand by using editorial content to attract users who are presented with banner-type advertising and opportunities to purchase various goods and services. At globeinvestor.com, for example, users can read repurposed stories from the paper's "Report on Business" section along with breaking stories from the wire. They also can link to a live Webcast repurposed from the *Globe*'s all-business-news cable channel *ROB-TV*. They can sign up with a choice of affiliated brokerage houses to trade online. The site has also experimented with online investment games, such as InvestorRally in which players build simulated portfolios. No real money was at stake; instead, the game was billed as a way for novice investors to learn how to research and play the stock market. The winners—those with the highest portfolio returns—were offered a car, cash, or in some cases rink-side seats for Toronto Maple Leaf hockey games. The site was sponsored by the brokerage firm TD Waterhouse, which collected personal information about the players through the game's registration page. The information could be used to build investor profiles. In this way, the Web site's interactivity—the design function net-libertarians most often point to as evidence of the Internet's inherently liberating qualities—is used explicitly to corral audiences in an effort to sell them an assortment of goods and services. "We have identified key market opportunities and developed specific online products that dominate those categories," explains Lib Gibson, president and CEO of Globe Interactive in an April 13, 2000, press release. "We targeted North American stock information with globeinvestor.com, Canadian mutual funds with globefund.com, and careers with workopolis.com. As a result, we are able to attract and hold user audiences to our sites, building loyalty and making them very appealing to advertisers." In this way, value is added to editorial content. It is, to use Steve Outing's phrase, "monetized."

AOL Time Warner tried to take the strategy even further. Early in 2001, AOL's Netscape browser tools were integrated into AOL Time Warner Web sites. A Netscape-branded navigational menu bar offering access to Netscape's search engine, an online personal calendar, and AOL's popular Instant Messaging service was placed above the masthead at CNN.com, Time.com, People.com, and Money.com Web sites. As Frank Houston writes: "The idea [was] to begin integrating online habits—in these cases chatting, Web searching, and to-do lists—with news consuming." The top editors at Time Inc. also hope that the audience measurement and target marketing available through the Web sites will, in the future, create opportunities for new magazine titles (Houston 2001: 23–24). "We're looking to monetize the audience that we bring in place, to get them to transact even more, to buy more online," said Netscape president Jim Bankoff. One idea floated by Bankoff involved using Netscape software to create a message board for the film *The Lord of the Rings*. The film is produced by Time Warner's New Line Cinema. According to Bankoff, the "Lord of the

Rings" message board could be used as a "launchpad" to drive traffic back to Netscape and other integrated sites (Klein 2001). Eventually, an online Lord of the Rings gift shop was integrated into the Netscape menu bar, as were other AOL Time Warner properties such as the Harry Potter Wizard's Shop. AOL's cross-promotional strategy scored an early victory: by July 2001, AOL had used its online service to sell more than a million new subscriptions to its Time Inc. magazines, at a rate of 100,000 per month (Houston 2001: 24).

Hopes were high. But the universally integrated Netscape menu bar was eventually abandoned. A wide-ranging settlement announced in May 2003 saw AOL Time Warner drop antitrust litigation against Microsoft—part of their long-standing browser feud—in return for a $750-million payment. The deal also included a seven-year royalty-free license of Microsoft's Internet Explorer browser for use by AOL customers. In essence, frustrated AOL Timer Warner executives decided to cut their losses and concede the browser market to Microsoft. It would not be the only promotional strategy to fall on hard times.

### *Convergence and Market Uncertainty*

There are a number of business models being considered by news-media organizations that attempt to integrate editorial content with the need to generate new and reliable revenue streams—the *Globe and Mail*'s assortment of online business sites is one, the e-commerce shopping mall adopted by MSNBC.com is another. That is not to say, however, that it has been smooth sailing for online news providers. Banner advertisements, for example, have proven to be a big bust with click-through rates, in March 2001, hovering at around 0.25 percent overall (White 2001). One avenue that has interested media executives and advertisers is the ability to use digital networks to engage in one-on-one marketing. Internet marketing firms such as DoubleClick offer advertisers the ability to track the movement and behavior of audiences. DoubleClick builds demographic profiles of Internet users in conjunction with close to 11,000 affiliated Web sites by placing "cookie" files on users' computers. The company then collects three types of data. GIF tags are used to track the movement of users through a Web site. GET data tells companies what specific information users requested, for example business, sports, or lifestyle stories. And thirdly, DoubleClick records POST information. This is data that users must enter when using many interactive features such as discussion groups, Web polls, or games like the one offered by the *Globe and Mail* (Kaplan 2001). Once a user profile is compiled, Web sites can display advertising that is targeted at individual users—male drivers of Volvos who are interested in hockey and the stock market, for instance. The hope is that advertisers will be willing to pay a premium for access to these kinds of customized audiences with whom they can develop more stable relationships. Here too, advertisers have expressed regret that the "holy grail" of data mining has not yet proven it can turn all Web sites into reliable profit centers (Hansell 2000). However, the pursuit of the grail continues.

Aggressive advertisers have more ambitious plans. They want to merge the ability to use television to speak to people's emotions (a form of brand marketing successful on TV) with the opportunities for direct selling and e-commerce that interactive digital platforms make possible (Chan-Olmsted 2000: 101). Successful ad agencies will be those that take "a much more integrated view of marketing," predicted Chris Charron, research director at Forrester Research in Cambridge, MA. Some advertisers hope to resume the role they once played as coproducers of radio and TV programming in the 1930s, '40s and '50s. "The convergence we should be thinking of," says Keith Reinhard, chairman and CEO at DDB Worldwide Communications Group in New York, "is the convergence of entertainment, information and interactive one-on-one selling as inter-tainment" (Elliott 1999).

It is still relatively early days in the convergence of formerly distinct media organizations. Tribune is far ahead of others in trying to integrate its entire body of media holdings, while giant AOL Time Warner has struggled with its integration plans. Faced with slumping stock values, and shouldering a mammoth debt load, some critics in the business press have called for the dismantling of the merger.

Canada's converged media companies have moved to downplay expectations of any forthcoming environment of media abundance. Exciting rhetoric about the information riches associated with convergence is less important now that BCE and CanWest have received federal approval for their merger plans. Moreover, Canada's federal regulator, the CRTC, has signaled that it intends to limit its regulation of the Internet and appears poised to waive further ownership restrictions to allow more distributors to own content companies. Accordingly, Leonard Asper, president and CEO of CanWest Global Communications Corp., has warned customers, advertisers and investors, that it may take "five, 10 or 15 years" before the benefits of multimedia convergence are reaped (Damsell 2001b).

News organizations have yet to settle on exactly how they will exploit the new technologies at their disposal, while the steep decline in the value of dot-com stocks in 2000–2001 has taken the wind out of many high-flying online journalism sites (Richtel 2000). Following the dot-com stock collapse of April 2000, many highly touted journalism Web sites fell on hard times as investors started demanding that they make money. APB-News.com, an award-winning crime-news site, filed for bankruptcy protection in July 2000 after it fired 140 people. Salon.com, the popular webzine acclaimed for its irreverent writing, slashed its workforce by 20 percent in December 2000, citing the need to cut expenses and move toward a profitable business plan. The cash-strapped company later announced it would again start charging an annual fee for a premium service, without advertisements and including content not available on the ad-supported site (Bloomberg News 2000; Associated Press 2001). In December 2002, AOL announced its exclusive access to premium content from CNN and *People* magazine sites.

Some of the more successful Web efforts have been those that are closely aligned with broadcast programming. ESPN.com has benefited from the heavy cross-promotion given by its broadcast and cable cousins ABC and ESPN (Hansell 2000b). But, despite these examples and the financial success of Tribune Co., many big media players have had trouble turning their established brands, expertise, and promotional clout into successful moneymaking businesses in the online world. In January 2001, Disney chose to abandon plans to make its Go.com site a dominant one-stop Web portal. The change in strategy came in the face of stiff competition from AOL Time Warner sites, Yahoo, and Microsoft's MSN—consistently some of the most visited sites on the Web (Hansell 2001). After initially announcing it would scrap the once-hyped portal, Disney eventually decided to keep Go.com alive at minimal cost and without advertising. It now restricts itself to cross-promoting top Disney-owned properties, such as ABCNews.com, ESPN.com, and Disney.com (Chipman 2001). In April 2001, NBC followed suit and announced it would partially close its money-losing NBCi Web portal (Gaither 2001). Both Disney and NBC cited the steep downturn in online advertising caused by the slumping U.S. economy as the reason. According to the Internet Advertising Bureau, most online advertising—71 percent of American dot-com advertising revenues—is placed with the top-ten sites. The bureau further reports that the share of U.S. advertising for the top-25 dot-com firms is 83 percent, and 91 percent for the top 50 (Tomkins 2000).

In 2000, the *New York Times,* NBC News, CBS News, News Corp., and CNN all announced layoffs at their online newsrooms. The *Times* bailed out of its partnership with the respected online financial-news service TheStreet.com. And Quebecor Inc., announced it would restructure its Internet properties and chop 65 jobs, nearly one-third of its online workforce. The Montreal-based multimedia company, which owns the Sun Media newspaper chain and the *Canoe* Web portal, says the cuts were necessary to reduce operating costs (Sinclair 2000). Even the *Wall Street Journal*'s vaunted subscriber-based online-news site, WSJ.com, announced layoffs in 2001 (Wan and Britt 2001). "What the mania and hysteria and over-optimism did was make people forget how hard it is to build a brand," says Kurt Andersen, cofounder of Inside.com. "It takes years. Coming back to earth is the realization that for all the power, magic and novelty of this medium, certain facts of life haven't changed" (Kurtz 2001). The layoffs were part of an industry-wide dot-com shakeout in which overhyped stock prices were deflated. Even digital-titan America Online—a company well positioned on the top of the dot-com food chain—has seen the value of its stock suffer. When the AOL Time–Warner merger was announced, AOL's net stock value was US$164 billion. By late October 2000, AOL was worth $108 billion (Swisher 2000). Two years after the merger, the value of AOL Time Warner stock had slipped 80 percent. Shareholders were not happy.

Merger talks between AOL Time Warner and Disney aimed at integrating CNN and ABC News were pursued vigorously during the fall and winter of 2002–2003.

The discussions were called off in mid-February 2003 amid uncertainty over the poor performance of the America Online division and increasingly public bickering among AOL Timer Warner's top executives over how to bolster sliding stock values and stagnant profits. The windfall of promotional synergy had failed to materialize. The company was also under a cloud of suspicion as American accounting watchdogs investigated allegations that executives misled investors about the company's prospects by falsely inflating advertising revenue (Kirkpatrick 2003).

The weight of these combined pressures proved too much for Steve Case. The AOL founder was forced to resign as chairman of the media giant. Gerald Levin, the other chairman behind the original deal, also stepped down, while CNN founder Ted Turner resigned as AOL Timer Warner vice chairman, complaining about his decreased clout in the company and his eroding financial stake. Turner, the company's largest shareholder, watched the value of his holdings plummet from $9 billion to about $2 billion (Kirkpatrick and Rutenberg 2003). The situation had become so dire for the AOL Time Warner brand that company executives decided to drop AOL from the parent company's name altogether (Ahrens and Klein 2003).

Shareholder anger forced Jean-Marie Messier to resign as chief executive of Vivendi Universal. In July 2002, the company stood on the edge of bankruptcy after Messier had transformed the former French water and sewage utility into a multimedia giant with the $41-billion purchase of Seagram Co., the owner of Universal music and film operations. Messier's wild acquisition binge, made at the top of the stock-market bubble, had saddled the company with an unmanageable debt load. And with Vivendi shares slumping 70 percent, the board of directors were pressured to take action (McKenna 2002).

These considerable problems notwithstanding, it remains premature to dismiss the logic of corporate and media integration as a fleeting business fad. The financial difficulties faced by AOL Time Warner, Vivendi, CanWest Global, and other media organizations strapped with high debt loads can be traced to a number of factors, not the least of which is the fact that they bought into the merger mania at the top of the stock-market bubble of 2000, combined with an overall economic downturn that hammered advertising revenues. Despite the problems, corporate interest in cross-media mergers and acquisitions continues to exist, as evidenced by the intense lobbying conducted on behalf of these same media giants to ensure the FCC would revamp its regulatory policy and raise the cap on radio and television cross-ownership.

Instead of a wholesale abandonment of corporate and promotional integration, the largest media conglomerates began to sell off so-called noncore assets to ease their financial burdens. AOL Time Warner sold its share of satellite company Hughes Electronics for a fraction of what it originally paid. It then unloaded its 50 percent stake in cable network Comedy Central to media competitor Viacom. In Canada, CanWest Global sold off many of its newspaper titles in small markets. For its part, Disney indicated it might have to part with its professional hockey and baseball franchises. Stuck with a crippling debt, Vivendi attracted a number of corporate suitors for the sale of its American entertainment assets, and eventually entered into exclusive negotiations with General Electric for the merger of Vivendi Universal and NBC, in September 2003. Belief in vertical integration was not dead.

With news-media convergence in its infancy, it may be difficult to assess the full impact of how corporations will eventually utilize the logic of the integrated spectacle. Most media companies are struggling to find a stable and profitable business model for their converged multimedia businesses. Many companies want to be certain which delivery system (cable, DSL, satellite, wireless, or—more likely—some combination of those four) becomes dominant in the marketplace.[12] What is clear is that market forces are regulating and shaping multimedia news organizations. The three strategies of multimedia convergence—*repurposing resources, cross-promotion,* and the *creation of new synergistic business opportunities*—are still very much in play. Companies have become wary of taking on unnecessary debt through costly mergers; but less risky strategic partnerships remain popular as companies gird themselves for uncertain market conditions.

In 2003, AOL Time Warner and Microsoft announced they would partner with the online job site CareerBuilder.com. An advertising partnership was announced between MediaNews Group Inc. of Denver and Knight Ridder Digital's Real Cities Network (Editor and Publisher 2003). Bell Canada and Microsoft announced a five-year deal to combine the Sympatico.ca and MSN.ca Web sites by 2004 (Ebner 2003). Increasing numbers of newspapers and broadcasters are forming strategic alliances and partnerships. It is estimated that "52 newspapers have partnered with TV stations" in the United States (Dotinga 2003). The *San Francisco Chronicle* joined forces with KPIX-TV, CBS's owned-and-operated station, and radio station KCBS-AM in a three-way partnership for "news projects, polls, events, cross-promotion." Similar deals have been formed in Oklahoma City and Sarasota, Florida (Brunelli 2003). The *Toronto Star* struck a deal to allow its print reporters to appear on Craig Media's Toronto One TV news program. The companies also agreed to combine forces to cover Toronto's municipal elections and to cooperate on promotional and advertising campaigns (Blackwell 2003). Moreover, since the dot-com fallout, four of North America's largest newspaper chains, owned by Belo, Knight Ridder, Tribune, and CanWest Global, have recommitted themselves to online convergence strategies by investing in large-scale and fully integrated news Web sites and newsrooms (Lasica 2002). And while the majority of newspaper Web sites lose money, news sites with strong brands have begun to show signs of financial success. By October 2002, close to 664,000 people had signed up to pay for the online version of the *Wall Street Journal,* and the company reported an online advertising increase of 24 percent (Martinson 2001; Buffalo News 2002). That same year, New York Times Digital reported increasing revenue flow at boston.com and nytimes.com, with a slim operating profit of $200,000

(Gipson 2002). With the help of the promotional muscle of the MSN Network, Microsoft's online magazine *Slate* reported positive cash flow during the first quarter of 2003, a milestone for Web-based magazine publishing (Carr 2003).

Despite increased skepticism, convergence strategies are still seen as a way to stabilize businesses amid a sea of technological upheaval and market uncertainty. Moreover, media companies must keep an eye to the future. News organizations that have been profitable for years may find themselves in the red down the road if they do not enjoy the same economies of scale and scope as their converged competitors.

### Benefits of Repurposing News Resources

The repackaging or repurposing of resources can take different forms. It refers most often to the reuse of stories or story components, but it can also mean the imposition of flexible work routines through such practices as multitasking and the repackaging of audience-viewing and consumption patterns.

First, it must be said that repackaging or repurposing news-media resources is not necessarily a bad thing. Web sites such as commondreams.org, alternet.org, mediachannel.org, guerrillanews.com, and rabble.ca reaggregate independent and mainstream news stories that provide a diverse selection of news and opinion. And there are many other examples of how the practice can enhance a news file. John V. Pavlik and Steven S. Ross argue that the common delivery platform of the Internet frees journalists from some of the old technical limitations associated with print, television, and radio. Perhaps the most important of these is that the time and space available for the overall news file has the potential to be greatly expanded. The GlobeandMail.com, for example, created links to press releases from the Canadian Alliance Party, the country's official opposition, that were partially quoted by the paper. One release denounced a story by the newspaper as grossly misleading. The story claimed the Alliance had hired a paid former U.S. federal undercover agent to investigate and "get the goods" on Canadian Prime Minister Jean Chrétien's Liberal government. Repurposing of primary source material—information that is available to journalists but that cannot be placed inside a print or broadcast story due to time and space limitations—"is important," say Pavlik and Ross, "because it helps to place stories in better context and can hold journalists accountable for their reporting by enabling the audience to compare a journalist's report with the actual primary source material he or she is reporting about" (Pavlik and Ross 2000: 120). Both the *New York Times* and the *Washington Post,* among other news organizations, made good use of the technology when they posted the full-text transcription of the U.S. Supreme Court's final decision ending the 2000 presidential election. The *Times* also made available audio files of the oral arguments made by both Republican and Democratic lawyers to the U.S. high court.[13] Here we have examples of newspapers using their online operations to add value to their printed news files that is potentially useful to people as citizens, not consumers.

William Thorsell, former editor-in-chief of the *Globe and Mail,* and Kirk La-Pointe, former senior vice-president of news at CTV Inc., both believe that in the future, quality journalism will require that news organizations add value to previously existing content. Thorsell argues that newspapers are not in the business of selling papers; they are in the "business of buying time" from time-pressed customers. Newspapers that can provide the best "proprietary value" for their intended customers will be successful in the end. (Thorsell 1998). As for LaPointe, he believes the key will be to add value by providing context to stories. "As time goes on," wrote La-Pointe, "and as more and more of the things we present in all of our media are commodities, the only loyalty will be to those who can add new value, and help people recognize the meaning of something." To that end, he suggests TV news will be called upon to get people talking to one another by delivering "talking points" for discussion (Posner 2001a).

### *Repurposing News 24/7 and Big News Stories*

The sanguine assessment provided by Thorsell and LaPointe changes, however, when news organizations add proprietary value by repurposing resources based primarily on commercial considerations. The commercial and promotional integration of the *Globe and Mail*'s Web site is one obvious example. Despite Thorsell's belief that the market will provide all, there is enough substantive evidence to suggest the underlying logic of promotional integration—that is, the push for increased efficiencies and synergistic promotional benefits—runs contrary to the goal of public service—that is, serving the individual and collective needs of citizens, not consumers.

First, the economic incentives that encouraged CNN, Fox, and MSNBC to apply the "All-Monica-All-the-Time" approach to news remain as potent as ever. There are enormous savings to be gained if news organizations can reuse stories and spread their fixed productions costs throughout a 24-hour news cycle, or across a number of integrated media platforms. The Internet simply extends the business model proven successful by CNN. Integrated multimedia systems continue to grow in both number and size with major media players, such as the *New York Times,* CNN, CTV, and CBC, starting to deliver headline-news services via wireless cell phones and e-mail (Barringer 2000; Sorkin 2000). And with recent regulatory approval of multimedia mergers in Canada and the United States, the established all-news channels face even more competition from integrated newsrooms than was the case during the Diana and Lewinsky media spectacles.

CNN demonstrated that Big News stories, while they last, make good business sense. Moreover, top managers involved in administering a cluster of integrated news organizations in Dallas agree that "convergence happens easiest on the biggest stories." Doug Weaver, an editor with the *Kansas City Star,* reports that managers at Texas Cable News (TXCN) and dallasnews.com say the "single-minded focus" and "urgency" that Big Stories provide, "help solidify the reporting and heighten cooperation." Their lament is that vestiges of independence remain among their integrated newsrooms. Consequently, Weaver would write in 2000 that "such cooperation and story-sharing is not yet routine" (Weaver, D. 2000: 28).

It did not take long for the Big News stories to find a home online. Frank Houston spent two years working as an editor at Fox News Online and wrote an account of his experiences for the *Columbia Journalism Review* (Houston 1999). Houston says he was attracted to the job because of his desire to experiment with novel approaches to storytelling that online media made possible. Houston says he and other editors took pride in crafting layered online features that combined elements of text, graphics, audio, and video. He says one feature on artificial intelligence alone involved the fulltime efforts of five staff employees and a freelance video crew for several weeks. However, it soon became apparent to Houston that these efforts could not continue to be justified as cost efficient. Audience measurements indicate that most visitors to the Fox site spent only a few seconds per Web page. It became clear, says Houston, that their "sprawling and eclectic stories" would not "be the site's bread and butter." Instead, the defining moments for online news, like their all-news TV cousins, became the death of Diana and Monicagate. The ability of online news organizations to produce "rolling news," complete with multiple updates of the latest developments in the Lewinsky scandal, soon came to typify the work routines at Fox News Online. Users of online news sites were gravitating toward Big News headlines and breaking news. "Each new development—Monica's immunity deal with Ken Starr, the DNA test, and so on—corresponds to a boost, or 'spike,' in traffic," wrote Houston (Houston 1999: 36). The same pattern was being played out at MSNBC.com, CNN.com and ABCNews.com.

"An online news site," writes columnist Steve Outing, "is more akin to a wire service than a printed publication, because it can (and should) publish news on a round-the-clock basis. While the notion of 'editions' still prevails at many news sites, the trend is more toward a constant publishing cycle, where news is published whenever it breaks" (Outing 2000). The trend toward online news sites relying on wire copy continues today, although to a lesser extent.[14]

The digital convergence of formerly distinct delivery platforms has put pressure on network TV newsrooms and newspapers, in particular, to match the new competition by publishing Big Stories and their various updates online before they are seen on the parent newscast or printed edition of the newspaper. The 24-hour news cycle now affects all major media outlets. The economic incentive to push stories harder than what might otherwise be justified, combined with lightning-speed deadlines and cut-throat competition from cross-media competitors, are responsible for many of the journalistic excesses of the Monicagate scandal. Coverage of the scandal was noteworthy for its intensity, scale, and frequency, but also because it marked a moment when basic journalistic standards were conspicuously absent. "I believe that we're all going to be doing a lot of soul-searching for a long time to come about the way we did that," says Peter Mansbridge, CBC-TV's top anchor, ". . . stuff was getting on the air which shouldn't have got on the air, because it simply wasn't sourced enough" (McKay 1998). Clear and credible attribution of sources and fact checking were missing from many stories about the presidential sex scandal produced by the mainstream media. "There were journalists standing on the White House lawn that never left the White House lawn but were relaying information that was being gathered in some cases in a questionable manner," Mansbridge told about 300 delegates at the Canadian Association of Journalists' annual convention in 1998 (McKay 1998).

The most infamous of these unsourced leaks came in a January 23, 1998, report aired by ABC News. Correspondent Jackie Judd's story cited an unnamed source who told her Lewinsky had saved a semen-stained dress as a souvenir of the president. The Judd story sparked a flurry of wild hearsay and speculation about the dress from both mainstream and tabloid news organizations. Because at the time there was only "One" story of significance to the U.S. national media, unsourced leaks spread like wildfire as media outlets engaged in a first-past-the-post frenzy of competition.[15]

For the most part, the mainstream media did not accept blame for the drop in journalistic standards. Instead, a convenient scapegoat was created in Matt Drudge. The first hint of the scandal was published on the Internet gossip columnist's Web site when Drudge poached *Newsweek*'s spiked story about the former White House intern's liaisons with President Clinton. The magazine's editors had held the story saying they were not yet comfortable with it. Following the Drudge leak, there was much hand-wringing from industry observers who pointed to the Internet as "the source" of declining journalistic standards. It was the Internet, many said, that allowed untrained hacks like Drudge to become instant publishers. Online journalists with established media companies, such as Rich Jaroslovsky, managing editor of the *Wall Street Journal Interactive Edition,* were so worried by the aspersions cast upon online journalism that they formed their own professional association, the Online News Association (ONA), to encourage "the highest possible standards in this new medium" (Stein 1999). Jodie Allen, Washington editor for the Microsoft-owned Webzine *Slate,* went so far as to label Drudge "the troll under the bridge of Internet journalism" (Witcover 1998: 20).

Jules Witcover has wryly observed those who would blame Matt Drudge for the drop in professional standards among many first-tier news media organizations covering the Lewinksy scandal ignore the fact that *Newsweek*—a major weekly newsmagazine—already had the story. It also assumes "that had Drudge not reported that

*Newsweek* had the story, the newsmagazine never would have printed it the next week, and therefore the Internet could take credit for 'forcing' the story on the main-stream news media" (20). It also ignores the fact that mainstream news organizations such as ABC News were breaking stories that Drudge did not have. And besides, both ABC and America Online gave implicit approval of Drudge's ethical behavior by em-ploying him as a talk-show host.

A more plausible explanation for the drop in standards is that mainstream news outlets were succumbing to the pressure of intense competition brought about by the reconfiguration of the news-media industry. Competitive pressure to scoop the com-petition, combined with the ability to file stories almost immediately, has strained tra-ditional sourcing and fact-checking routines. Indeed, a survey of 203 editors by Janna Anderson, a journalism instructor at Elon (N.C.) College and David Arant of the University of Memphis found widespread concern among newspaper editors. The survey found that 47 percent of respondents "agreed the ability to publish informa-tion immediately online has led to an erosion of the standards of verification." Among online editors, the survey found that 37 percent said it would be easier to uphold tra-ditional ethical standards if they had larger staffs (Kornblum 2000).

Michael Getler of the *Washington Post* asks whether the flexible work routines of integrated newsrooms will harm reporting. "Will newspaper reporters who interrupt their news gathering, interviewing, thinking, research or writing to do that 'quick update' for TV or the Web ultimately do less reporting?" (Getler 2000). It is reason-able to assume that the emphasis placed on flexible work routines in integrated news-rooms may have an impact on the quality of news produced. The more time report-ers are required to multitask—that is, file stories to their print, broadcast, and Internet arms—the less time they have to do the job of reporting. And, as journalist Nat Hentoff notes, while a reporter may not be "forced to multiply himself" some news outlets already consider a reporter's willingness to participate when making job evaluations. Resistance to multitasking may harm a person's career. Furthermore, asks Hentoff, invoking a quip by A.J. Liebling, "when would I have time to think?" (Hentoff 2000).

### *Repurposing News: The Threat to Independent Newsgathering*

A second major negative outcome of the reconfiguration brought about by the forces of media integration is the threat it poses to the diversity of media voices. One of the conundrums of the early stages of media convergence is that at the same time that competitive pressures among large media corporations are on the rise (the result of newfound cross-media competitors), there also is a substitution of cooperation for competition among integrated multimedia partners. The logic of convergence encourages the sharing of information and stories among partnered newsrooms. It follows that as the sharing of resources and stories increases among formerly competitive news outlets, fewer independently produced stories will be produced.

This view has been challenged successfully in Canada by the country's two largest private television networks. In August 2001, Canada's broadcast regulator ruled that CTV and CanWest Global Communications must maintain separate news management for their broadcast and newspaper outlets. However, the CRTC's decision did not preclude the companies from merging their newsgathering activities. In essence, the CRTC granted the companies the right to delegate multitasking to their reporters, share news resources, and cross-promote their affiliated news organizations. Despite voicing its concern that editorial diversity could decline as a result of corporate convergence, the regulator accepted the companies' assurances that editorial independence and diversity could be maintained alongside synergistic strategies of cross-promotion and repurposing news resources. The guarantee came in the form of a *Statement of Principles and Practices* written by CTV and CanWest and approved by the CRTC as a condition of the broadcasters' seven-year license renewal. As part of their condition of license, the two broadcasters each agreed to appoint three-person monitoring committees. The purpose of the committees is to accept complaints from the public and journalists as to the broadcasters' compliance with the *Statement of Principles.* The persons appointed to these so-called neutral bodies serve at the pleasure of CanWest and CTV and report to their respective boards of directors (Canadian Radio-Television and Telecommunications Commission 2001a; CRTC 2001b). Not surprisingly, the Newspaper Guild of Canada decried the decision, saying it would allow the companies to assign a single reporter to cover both broadcast and print stories. "It will clearly cut down on diversity of voices and coverage," said TNG spokesperson Jan Ravensbergen. "We believe it also goes against the public interest because it does not encourage more voices, more perspectives, more debate, more information for all Canadians. Instead, it encourages less" (Canada NewsWire 2001).

Some journalists, such as Doug Anderson, assignment editor for General Media's WFLA-TV in Tampa Bay, FL, argue that the sharing of newsroom resources only improves the quality of journalism. Anderson says his newsroom's partnership with the *Tampa Tribune* newspaper has given his newsroom a considerable edge on the competition.

> The best thing is research, when we'll be working some, you know, fatal train accident, and they'll quietly come up and say, do you know that there's [*sic*] been three fatal accidents at this intersection since 1996? And we're like, oh, my God, it's a huge story now, it's not just a VO bite. We are so far ahead of our competition with the way we're set up now that it's going to take them a long time to catch up, if they ever can. (Smith 2000)

While, arguably, WFLA-TV's research may be improved by its partnership with the *Tribune,* Anderson's enthusiastic endorsement of convergence avoids its most obvious outcome: that newsrooms that used to operate independently, no longer do so. The repurposing of stories among formerly independent newsrooms poses a threat to editorial diversity. "My fear is that it's [convergence] is going to end up being bad for journalism," says Bob Haiman, a fellow at the Freedom Forum's First Amendment Center and the former executive editor of the *St. Petersburg Times.*

> You don't have to get very far beyond Political Science 101 to know that a multiplicity of voices always best serves a democracy and an informed public, and these converged companies may intend, they may swear an oath to try to maintain separate, independent reporting energies in the market, but inevitably, I think that's going to be corroded. And it's going to be one operation doing work for all of the various outlets and platforms. That can't be a winner for good journalism. (Smith 2000)

There is plenty of reason to take Haiman's warning seriously.

As mentioned above, most news Web sites rely heavily on news wires, such as Associated Press, Canadian Press, and Reuters for breaking news bulletins. Moreover, many major news organizations have entered into partnership agreements that commit newsrooms to share resources. These arrangements are made easier on certain kinds of stories where broadcasters, for example, all want the same footage. CTV, CBC, Radio Canada, and Global all pooled their resources and pictures for coverage of the death of former Canadian prime minister Pierre Trudeau. Deals to share polling costs have been commonplace among cross-media news outlets for years. All five U.S. television networks and the Associated Press created Voter News Service (VNS) to provide low-cost election polling data.[16] In an effort to save costs, ABC News has entered an editorial-sharing agreement with BBC News and Japan's NHK. And in December 1999, CBS, ABC, and Fox affiliated themselves by creating Network News Service (NNS). The jointly owned cooperative news service shares generic and breaking news-video footage with affiliates of all three networks. And, in fact, deals to swap technical resources in exchange for footage during the first-run news cycle have been commonplace among national broadcast networks for years. What is different about more recent partnerships is that they are as much about cross-promotion as they are about cost-sharing (Flint 1999; Jones 1999).

The vertical-integration strategy pursued by Time Warner has prompted CNN and *Time* magazine to cross-promote each other and share editorial content. In Canada, multimedia mergers have produced tentative steps towards cross-promotion and the sharing of news resources. For the most part, cross-promotion has been limited to newscasters on CTV News and CanWest television stations directing viewers to their respective newspapers and Web sites for additional information and stories. Sometimes CanWest newspaper reporters are debriefed on air during newscasts. The *Globe and Mail* sometimes publishes stories written by CTV News reporters, and regularly cites reports from its sister network in its own stories.

Newsroom integration has taken a further step in Vancouver, where CanWest now owns top-rated BCTV along with both of the city's major daily newspapers, the *Vancouver Sun* and the tabloid *Province*. On March 14, 2001, Keith Baldrey, Victoria bureau chief for BCTV, received a leaked document containing detailed information about a provincial budget that was to be tabled in the British Columbia legislature the next day by the New Democratic Party government. Baldrey immediately shared the information with his sister newsrooms. The story ran on BCTV's evening newscast, and the next day it appeared above the fold on the front pages of both the *Vancouver Sun* and CanWest's national daily, the *National Post*. Prior to the merger of CanWest and the Southam newspaper chain, the *Sun* and the *Post* would have been forced to pursue the story on their own. In April 2001, CanWest utilized the promotional value of the British Columbia provincial election to launch www.bcvotes2001.com. The Web site aggregated stories from three CanWest newspapers: the *Vancouver Sun,* the tabloid *Province* and Victoria's *Times Colonist*. The trial site also provided streaming video and repurposed copy from BCTV and CanWest's Victoria station CHEK-TV. The *Sun* and BCTV also have run a series of lifestyle-related stories that have cross-promoted the newspaper's community *Sun Run* and BCTV. Each week leading up to the April 2001 run both BCTV and the *Sun* ran stories tracking the training regime of BCTV anchor Pamela Martin—touted by the *Sun* as a "celebrity" runner. The *Sun*'s health section, in which the stories appeared, included other health tips, and on one occasion, a story about a trendy warm-rock-massage service available at a local hotel spa. The health section was full of health-related advertising. Finally, on August 16, 2001, the *Sun* ran a piece about upcoming personnel changes at BCTV that read more like a press release than a news story. It included photos of the station's repositioned news anchors and quoted company employees. This editorial gem from news director Steve Wyatt: "We are responding to the needs of the audience, because lives change, lifestyles change, schedules change, so now we deliver news at a whole bunch of different times during the day to meet the demands" (Hanson 2001). By 2003, CanWest had extended its corporate brand throughout the company's holdings. The company integrated newspaper editorial operations by creating a news hub, known as the Canada News Desk, responsible for coordinating national editorial copy. The 126-year-old Southam News Service, which served CanWest's 11 major Canadian dailies, was renamed CanWest News. In a particularly opportunistic move, the CanWest Global brand was even extended to stories about disaster-relief assistance that was organized in part by the company to help families displaced by summer forest fires in British Columbia (O'Brian 2003).

Instead of vertically integrating themselves through the purchase of other news outlets, some companies have opted for the more flexible strategy of copartnerships.

These agreements involve even public-sector corporations, such as the Canadian Broadcasting Corporation. The CBC has alliances with the *Toronto Star* newspaper and *Maclean's* magazine in which they jointly produce editorial content. On one occasion, the CBC and the *Star* teamed up to produce a pair of special features on retirement (Posner 2001b).

The *New York Times* and ABC News struck a deal in January 2000 that saw the two news operations share news coverage delivered on both the Internet and television. Under the deal, the *Times* agreed to coproduce reports for two programs—the *20/20* newsmagazine and ABC's morning show, *Good Morning America*. The contract had the *Times* deliver four to six reports to *20/20* and as many as 16 reports to *Good Morning America* (Carter 2000b).

Another outcome of this agreement was *Political Points,* a daily 15-minute Webcast delivered on both organizations' Web sites. *Political Points* was an experiment that focused coverage on the 2000 U.S. presidential election. It used the single Big Story of the election to both promote the convergence experiment and help ease the cooperation between the two newsrooms. The experiment ended following the conclusion of the electoral race. Although the Webcast was a new program, unlike *20/20* and *Good Morning America,* it did not produce original reporting. Instead, reporters from both ABC News and the *Times,* already assigned to cover various aspects along the campaign trail, were debriefed by the program's "moderator." The moderator's chair alternated between Michael Oreskes, then Washington bureau chief of the *Times,* and Mark Halpern, political director for ABC News. The program conducted live two-way interviews with various political newsmakers and rebroadcast news clips from ABC News.

The program had an interactive component that allowed users to e-mail questions to be asked by the moderator. The Webcast also allowed users to view archived news stories from the *Times* and previous installments of *Political Points.* Links to background information about candidates were incorporated into the site's resource section. Eventually, the site contained links to streaming video of political advertisements produced for the Democrats and Republicans. Subscribers to the program's e-mail service received daily messages outlining that day's program along with news headlines with hyperlinks to stories at both the ABC News and *New York Times* Web sites. So, while the convergence experiment had some beneficial aspects, its overall focus was to extend each organization's brand to an expanded audience by cross-promoting the partnered news organizations and repurposing preexisting material and resources. The program was sponsored by FamilyWonder.com, a child-oriented Web site that has a partnership agreement with Disney and ABC News.

The *New York Times* has another partnership agreement with PBS's news documentary program *Frontline,* as does ABC News. A documentary about the Clinton presidency that included an introduction by ABC's *Nightline* host Ted Koppel was broadcast on *Frontline* in January 2001. However, most of the footage and interviews in the two-hour special were shown a week earlier during a five-night series on *Nightline*. The *Frontline* program came about because staff at ABC News needed to control escalating production costs while simultaneously expanding *Nightline*'s shrinking audience at a time of reduced advertising revenue. The idea for the joint partnership stemmed from a request made in 1998 by ABC's parent corporation, Disney, to find new efficiencies in the news division. *Nightline* staff approached and sold *Frontline* on the idea. Under the contract, *Frontline* paid *Nightline* to report and produce the program. As *New York Times* reporter Jim Rutenberg writes, in essence "a group of news producers have become video entrepreneurs hawking their particular brand of journalism to competitors, for a fee" (Rutenberg 2000d). Two programs that once produced separate documentaries about U.S. politics were repeating the same footage, the same sources and voices, in an effort to pinch pennies and extend their brands. *Frontline* subsidizes a five-part series on *Nightline* while ABC extends the Ted Koppel brand to a potentially broader and well-heeled PBS audience.

The online version of the *New York Times* also has formed a cross-Atlantic partnership with the *Financial Times* of London. Starting in August 2001, the nytimes.com and FT.com began exchanging up to ten articles each business day on topics of business, technology and international affairs. Both nytimes.com and cnn.com share stories by maintaining links to their sites. The online version of the *Times* also has a cross-promotional deal with cnn.com that sees stories from both organizations repurposed on their respective sites.

An important and wide-ranging agreement was announced November 17, 1999, between the *Washington Post* and NBC News. The venture bundled together some of the most powerful and respected news organizations in the United States: a top broadcaster (NBC), the Web's most popular news site (MSNBC.com), America's No. 2 weekly newsmagazine (*Newsweek*), one of the most respected and influential newspapers in the U.S (*Washington Post*), and a 24-hour all-news cable channel (MSNBC).

The strategic alliance commits the organizations to share news material and technological and promotional resources. It also created the first major media partnership that delivers news via print, broadcast, cable and Internet multimedia platforms. Since the deal, journalists from the *Washington Post* and *Newsweek* magazine have appeared on NBC News and MSNBC, including regular segments on *The News with Brian Williams*. MSNBC.com also gained access to editorial content from *Newsweek* and the *Washington Post*. The online version of *Newsweek* is fully integrated into MSNBC.com. The site's home page includes the MSNBC menu bar that integrates the site with all editorial and commercial material connected to the MSNBC.com network. CNBC, NBC's other cable network, already has a deal with the *Wall Street Journal* to share business news.[17]

A good example of the promotional synergies being strived for by the partnership came March 12, 2001. That day washingtonpost.com posted a link to some streaming video of a repurposed interview that first appeared on NBC's morning program, *The Today Show*. The video clip featured an interview with David von Drehle, a *Washington Post* reporter. Drehle was on the show to promote a book written by the political staff of the *Washington Post* entitled *Deadlock: The Inside Story of America's Closest Election,* published by PublicAffairs. The book is a reworking of the newspaper's reporting during and after the 2000 presidential-election standoff. During the course of the interview, Drehle managed to work in a cross-promotional anecdote involving NBC's late-night comedy program *Saturday Night Live*.[18]

The audacity of the interview is striking. Here we have a repurposed broadcast interview with a reporter from a partnered newspaper that has been cross-posted to the newspaper's Web site. The interview is promoting a book that is the result of efforts to repurpose the daily reporting of the *Washington Post* into book form: an instant book of political history that is published in February 2001, only weeks after the end of one of the largest mediated political spectacles in U.S. history. And during all this, Drehle manages to work in a plug for the partnered broadcaster's entertainment programming.

### Integrated News and Conflicting Journalistic Interests

As multimedia partnerships increase in number and scale, so does the potential for trouble. The more it is that journalists are integrated into the goals of promotion, the more likely it becomes that their work will be used to serve the narrow commercial interests of their employer as opposed to the broader interests of public service. "News is no longer just selling itself with sensation," says Danny Schechter, a veteran TV news producer now writing for mediachannel.org, a nonprofit media-watchdog group, "it's selling the network's other programming. . . becoming barely more than a hype machine" (Schechter 2001b).

Schechter's hype machine has two sides: events that receive coverage and are promoted, and events that are ignored. Horizontal business relationships that tie media companies to nonmedia interests are growing in scale. General Electric, for example, now enjoys a corporate-media reach well beyond NBC. General Electric, a corporate behemoth with interests in military equipment, nuclear technology, and medical systems, among many others, is linked with Dow Jones & Company. This is because of CNBC's alliance with the *Wall Street Journal*. General Electric also is linked to computer software giant Microsoft due to its co-ownership of MSNBC. And, of course, there is the alliance between NBC and the Washington Post Co. These corporate relationships cast a long shadow over news coverage of Microsoft's federal antitrust case by any newsroom caught in this tangled promotional web. At the very least there is the lingering perception of a conflict of interest. *Los Angeles Times* TV-columnist Howard Rosenberg cut to the chase immediately following Tribune's purchase of his newspaper. Rosenberg's news beat now includes many companies, KTLA-TV for example, that his new employer has a commercial stake in. "If I praise Tribune properties," Rosenberg asks, "will it be because we're family, and I have my own financial stake at heart?" (Rosenberg 2000). The same could be asked of CNN or *Time* reporters if they were assigned to cover unionizing efforts at Wal-Mart. The so-called bricks-and-mortar retailer has a partnership with CNN parent America Online to promote its online service. Microsoft, the co-owner of MSNBC, has a similar alliance with low-brow retailer Best Buy and Radio Shack. Yahoo, which has a content-sharing deal with the *New York Times* and other major media outlets, is partnered with Kmart Corp. (Eunjung Cha 1999). The *New York Times* also enjoys a promotional alliance with retail coffee-king Starbucks.

Corporate executives swear up and down that the alliances and co-ownership agreements will not affect coverage. And yet we have evidence to the contrary. Media companies have taken steps on many occasions to protect their interests, including editorial intervention. American broadcasters lobbied long and hard to have a segment of the national airwaves set aside for digital services. Instead of being auctioned off to the highest bidder, the spectrum space, estimated to be worth US$70 billion, was given away free under the sweeping 1996 U.S. Telecommunications Act. The story was virtually ignored by the national broadcast media (Alger 1998: 109). There was a similar paucity of news coverage about the FCC's proposed changes to cross-ownership rules. "Although the media usually like to speculate about government intent," says Schechter, "this official comment period on cross-ownership has gone largely uncommented upon on TV or in the press, perhaps because many newspapers also own television stations" (Schechter 2001a). FCC chair Michael Powell was already on the record supporting changes that could free networks to buy up more stations.[19]

Fox News's editorial policy toward China has been under a cloud since 1994. In that year Fox's parent, News Corporation, removed BBC newscasts from its Hong Kong–based satellite station, Star TV. The decision was widely seen as an attempt to curry favor with the Chinese leadership after the BBC had run stories critical of the Chinese government. Harper Collins, News Corporation's publishing arm, also cancelled a book contract with former Hong Kong governor Chris Patten. Then in March 2001, Murdoch's 28-year-old son, James, criticized Western news media for what he said was their harsh coverage of China's policy toward Falun Gong, a religious group banned by the Chinese government (Carter 2001). China is viewed by News Corp. as a largely untapped market for future expansion.

*Brill's Content,* the self-proclaimed media watchdog magazine that suspended publication in October 2001, gave a thumbs down to a number of questionable synergistic arrangements. In October 1998, Michael Eisner, chairman of ABC parent, Disney, gave an interview to National Public Radio in which he made the following comment: "I would prefer ABC not cover Disney. . . . I think it's inappropriate for Disney to be covered by Disney. . . . [B]y and large, the way you avoid conflict of interest is to, as best you can, not cover yourself." As Rifka Rosenwein reports, the comments were made only days before ABC News killed a story about the employment of convicted pedophiles at Disney's Magic Kingdom in Florida (Rosenwein 2000: 94).

As the pace of corporate mergers increases along with the trend toward corporate partnerships, fewer and fewer media organizations are in a position to report independently on the affairs of their former competitors and their affiliated interests. On the other hand, there is more room for the promotional use of news resources. On numerous occasions, NBC's top anchor Tom Brokaw used his high-profile position at the peacock network to promote his book entitled *The Greatest Generation*. Brokaw appeared on NBC's *Today* four times in the six weeks after the book's publication in December 1998. *Dateline NBC*, the network's weeknight newsmagazine devoted an entire program to the book. It was later revealed that NBC owns nearly 25 percent of the book's profits (Rosenwein 2000: 93).

In 1999, NBC joined forces with Lou Dobbs, the creator of CNN's *Moneyline News Hour*, to produce a syndicated radio program hosted by Dobbs, and a monthly newsletter on the financial markets. As part of the alliance, NBC announced in a press release that Dobbs would make occasional appearances as a guest on NBC news programs to promote the co-branded products. In one such interview on NBC's Today, Dobbs responded to a question from host Matt Lauer by making his best stab to extend his personal brand: "We're, together, going to create a newsletter on markets, finance—the political economy, if you will—provide some monthly insight for folks," said Dobbs. Later in the interview, Dobbs continued with his theme of political economy. "This is all about creating a new product to add to the many platforms that NBC is leading in, whether it's interactive television, cable, broadcast. We think it's an important extension. And we'll have terrific reception." What is so astounding about the arrangement, as Eric Effron correctly observes, is that "we've come so far down the slope of news as promotion that media companies no longer feel compelled to be even a bit subtle about using their journalistic resources in this manner" (Effron 2000: 51–52).

Even Effron's employer, *Brill's Content,* a magazine that originally billed itself as "The Independent Voice of the Information Age," eventually succumbed to temptation in an ultimately failed attempt to save the financially troubled consumer title. The magazine's owner, New York–based Brill Media Holdings, embraced the logic of promotional integration as a partial response to poor financial results when it started the now-defunct Web site Contentville.com, in July 2000. The short-lived Web site—an online clearinghouse for books, magazine articles and academic manuscripts—was jointly owned by CBS, NBC, Primedia, Ingram Book Group, and EBSCO (a company that provides magazine databases and subscription services). Brill Media Holdings was for a short time 49 percent owned by Primedia, which, through its Media Central venture, is the publisher of more than 170 media-related magazines and Web sites.

The alliances formed through its ownership ties to Primedia made *Brill's Content* a partner with many of the companies it reported on—a direct conflict. The *Brill* synergy reports cited above were published prior to the magazine's integration with the other media divisions. At the time of its launch, Steven Brill insisted that Contentville would provide independent reviews of books and magazines. And, when the new e-commerce venture was announced, Brill promised the magazine and Web site would remain separate. The online version of *Brill's Content,* however, eventually contained multiple links to Contentville; and, not coincidentally, the media-watchdog magazine dropped any reference to being an independent voice from its masthead. Brill Media's haphazard integration strategy did not end there. The company gained control of rival Inside.com (a sassy online media-industry publication) through its acquisition of Powerful Media (Kuczynski 2000; Kirkpatrick 2001; Li 2001). A Media Central–branded menu bar eventually graced the top of both *Brill's Content* and Inside.com Web sites. The self-proclaimed watchdog of media integration had morphed into an enthusiastic practitioner before eventually closing its doors.[20]

There have been other experiments. Innx, a San Diego–based TV production company, further blurred the line between news reporting and advertising with its advertising service that integrates TV newscasts with advertiser Web sites. Innx's first major client, Proctor and Gamble, signed a deal that allowed P&G to "use plugs in television-news stories to market P&G brands more effectively over the Internet." Innx's plan modified the already widespread practice of supplying broadcasters with free Video News Releases that are inserted into newscasts. Under the contract, P&G agreed to sponsor 90-second features produced by Innx on various topics such as parenting, health care, and nutrition. At the end of each segment a narrator or anchor reads a script referring viewers to one of P&G's Web sites for more information about one of the manufacturing giant's many products—Pampers, for example. P&G made it clear it will only sponsor features that dovetail with its product line (White 2001). Innx also has a broadcast services and content agreement with Yahoo Inc.

The pressure to squeeze profits out of integrated media properties is enormous, and very real. AOL Time Warner set extremely aggressive financial goals for 2001, including increasing cash flow by 30 percent. According to the *Wall Street Journal,* staff felt pressure to make all the pieces of the integrated media puzzle fit seamlessly together. On one occasion, reports the *Journal,* editors at People.com, the online version of *People* magazine, a Time Inc. title, were asked to tamper with editorial copy. The request was an effort to improve the synergistic fit between an article written by People.com and an AOL online-chat session with actor Keanu Reeves. The offensive line that AOL wanted removed suggested that Reeves was not yet "Oscar material." People.com staff refused, and the story was not linked to the AOL chat session. A spokesperson for the news-media giant, reaffirmed the company's dedication to "journalistic integrity"; and yet, the *Journal* reports that AOL chairman Steve Case issued the tough earnings targets so that "[t]he pressure would force people to abandon old ways of thinking and forge new relationships across its various units" (Angwin and Rose 2001).

Because of the pressure to utilize "promotional resources," media observers such as Mike Hoyt of the *Columbia Journalism Review* have questions about the extent to which "joint promotion" will "affect editorial judgement" (Hoyt 2000). As an example, Hoyt cites the Tailwind debacle. The blockbuster promotional story was supposed to successfully launch *Newstand*—a newsmagazine program jointly produced by CNN and *Time* magazine. Instead, the erroneous story alleging the U.S. military had used nerve gas during Vietnam War nearly sunk the newsmagazine on its maiden program. The story is often cited by critics who argue promotional synergies can harm news judgment.

### Promotional Events and Questionable News Judgment

The logic of promotion is so pervasive that it is commonplace to see cross-promotional references made by anchors during newscasts. All network newscasts refer viewers to their affiliated Web sites or newspapers. But according to Sylvia Chan-Olmsted, the efficacy of cross-promotional campaigns improves significantly when a popular media event is integrated into a "promotional loop" between TV and the Web site. NBC made particularly good use of this strategy in 1996 during its coverage of the Summer Olympics. NBC, which owned the broadcast rights to the Olympic Games, made the "Olympics its most frequently covered story of the year, with nearly 20 percent more coverage than that of its second most-covered story." At the other U.S. networks, the Olympics did not even make the top-ten list of most covered stories (Herman and McChesney 1997: 63). NBC anchors continuously cross-promoted their new MSNBC Web site with the result that it quickly became the second-most-popular destination among American users of news, information, and entertainment sites (Tedesco 1996, cited in Chan-Olmsted 2000: 107). Cross-promotion had shown it could generate significant increases in traffic. "Furthermore," says Chan-Olmsted, "33 percent of online users surveyed said they had visited a sports-related [W]eb site while simultaneously watching sports on television" (Chan-Olmsted 2000: 107)—an impressive figure.

The example of how "promotional loops" can increase the size of broadcast audiences and Web traffic has not been lost on the newsrooms of major U.S. networks. Broadcast newsrooms routinely tap into spectacular media events, such as Monicagate, in cross-promotional efforts to hold on to and boost drifting audiences. Newsrooms also utilize media events of a lesser scale. One annual media event that traditionally has attracted a lot of attention from viewers is the Academy Awards ceremony. Hollywood's spring love-in has long been used by the movie industry as a promotional fulcrum point. Agents lobby to have their star clients seen at the event, which has become a spring-rite promotional display, while distributors flog their nominated films. Moreover, newspapers and TV newsrooms routinely run special Oscar features discussing who the likely winners and losers will be. Nothing new there. But the week before the 2001 awards show, ABC News did something unique that called into question its news judgment. *Nightline* ran a five-part series about drug trafficking inspired by the Steven Soderbergh film *Traffic*—a movie that eventually won four Oscars including best director. Billed as "the reality behind the movie *Traffic*," the *Nightline* series explored various themes that emerged from the movie. And while there is no question that drug trafficking is a legitimate news story, it seems equally legitimate to ask whether the news division got the idea for the series from the entertainment arm of ABC, which was broadcasting the Academy Awards. As it turned out, the ratings for the ABC Oscars broadcast that year were disappointingly low.

A more notorious example is the relentless use of newsroom resources by CBS News to promote the network's hit "reality program," *Survivor*, and by extension other CBS properties. Traffic to CBS's Web site soared during the opening week of the second edition of the series set in the Australian outback. The CBS Web site had 2.14 million unique visitors for the week ending February 3, 2001—212 percent from the previous week. On the final night of the first installment of *Survivor* traffic to the program's Web site jumped 115 percent from the previous day (Mariano 2000; 2001). The program features a cast of people stranded in a remote location (the first series was filmed on an island). Each week, after competing in a staged competition, someone is voted off the show by the other players. The last person remaining wins.

The program's mostly young viewers are coveted by the network, which has had trouble in recent years attracting the more advertiser-friendly under-35 demographic. In an effort to attract younger viewers CBS promoted *Survivor* on the Internet and advertised on MTV and rock radio stations (Carter and Fass 2000). But the network also used many media outlets under the umbrella of its Viacom parent besides MTV—from Paramount's *Entertainment Tonight* to CBS's revamped morning-news program, *The Early Show*—to breathlessly chronicle every small development in the program. The *Vancouver Sun,* a daily publication of CanWest Global, the television network that simulcasts *Survivor* in Canada, also ran a weekly column in its main news section informing readers of the identity of the unlucky person to be voted "out of the tribe."

The news department at CBS's Los Angeles station, KCBS, hired *Survivor I* alumnus Gervase Peterson, as a special "news" correspondent for *Survivor II*. One night KCBS devoted six minutes of its 11 p.m. newscast to a *Survivor II* story and tie-in. According to Scott Rosenberg of the *Los Angeles Times,* the KCBS newscast "failed to mention the [US]$1.6-trillion tax-cut proposal President Bush had sent to Congress that day or that former President Clinton had been savaged by Democrats and Republicans in Day One of congressional hearings on his last-minute pardon to fugitive oil broker Marc Rich" (Rosenberg 2001).

Each week, *The Early Show* carried features and interviews related to *Survivor*. On April 18, 2001, the *Early Show* Web site included a link to a feature that promised to reveal *Survivor* participant Alicia Calaway's fitness secrets. Once there, users found further links to an "Early Show Survivor Guide," that allowed users to e-mail questions to castaways, a CBSNews.com "Special Report"on *Survivor,* and the CBS.com official *Survivor* Web site. The Calaway fitness feature was repurposed onto CBS HealthWatch, one of the network's dozen CBS-branded, but independently operated specialized Web services. The site contained diagnoses for four Australian-outback–related maladies, including what to do if a wild pig severs an artery. Users could also link to the "CBS MarketWatch *Survivor* Contest," part of the CBS-branded online financial news service's Web site. As with the globeinvestor.com game, the team with the best stock portfolio is crowned the winner. The contest Web site included stories detailing the game's week-by-week progress. The *Survivor*-branded game was also a weekly live segment on the *Early Show*. There was even a weekly trivia challenge in which contestants could win $1,000 by correctly answering questions about each week's *Survivor* episode. And, of course, there was an online *Survivor* souvenir shop.

One reason the *Early Show* put so much energy into integrating the *Survivor* program with its other CBS properties is that it wants to hold on to its newfound young audience. The effort is also related to the intense competition among the network morning-news programs. "The morning," writes Jim Rutenberg, a business reporter with the *New York Times,* "is the only time when the audience for network news is actually growing" (Rutenberg 2000e).

The successful use of *Survivor* to attract a young audience and cross-promote other CBS properties is part of a growing belief among network executives that their Web strategies may work best when attached to popular broadcast events, be they sports or reality-TV (Hansell 2000b). The key is to create an appointment program that is also thought to be a noteworthy event. The strategy, however, does not always work. CBS tried a similar scheme with its reality program *Big Brother,* which turned out to be a ratings flop compared to *Survivor.* Fox's *Who Wants to Marry a Multimillionaire?* became a public-relations disaster for the network after it was discovered that would-be groom Rick Rockwell had a restraining order placed on him. What was a disaster for Fox soon became a media bonanza for the competing networks, whose news divisions practically tripped over each other in their dogged efforts to advance the story. Darva Conger, the game-show bride who later rejected her instant husband, revealed her motivation for joining the program during an interview on ABC's *Good Morning America,* as did Rockwell. Conger went on to pose for *Playboy.* And an unknown news Web site called The SmokingGun.com gained instant notoriety after it revealed Rockwell's tainted past.

Nonetheless, tapping into spectacular media events and the news coverage they generate remains a viable promotional strategy for many media and nonmedia companies. It is the future of independent public-service journalism that is at risk.

## CHAPTER FIVE

# Performance of Politics and the Politics of Performance

*Rational—and irrational—people may differ over the merits of Bill Clinton's presidency, but few can dispute that he was without peer as our entertainer in chief. He turned the whole citizenry, regardless of ideology or demographic, into drama fiends.*
FRANK RICH, COLUMNIST, *New York Times*

This chapter explores the unique ways in which politics has become aestheticized by the workings of the integrated news spectacle—a broad social process characterized by the reification of social actors, labor, and narrative forms within high-volume production systems involving flexible forms of management, labor performance, and increased intensity in the speed of production and turnover time (Harvey 1989; Castells 2000a). Political performances and spectacular media events—such as the Lewinsky-Clinton sex scandal—are moments along the circuit of production, distribution, and consumption. To understand the performance of politics, we must understand how symbolic commodities such as news narratives and political actors circulate through these integrated moments of capital accumulation. As Guy Debord suggests: "The spectacle is not a collection of images; rather, it is a social relationship between people that is mediated by images" (Debord 1995: sec. 4). In other words, to understand the performance of politics we must first grasp the politics of performance. We must understand how the promotional logic of the spectacle manifests itself within mediated political performance as an objective social force.

The chapter begins by critiquing Debord's understanding of political representation and his subsequent renunciation of all forms of political mediation. I argue that forms of political representation and mediation are problematic, but required in modern large-scale societies; in making my argument, the chapter explores questions of how best to judge the legitimacy of political representation. It then examines the performance of politics and asks who is better capable of taking advantage of the integrated news spectacle to further particular social and political interests. In making this assessment, I utilize Pierre Bourdieu's related concepts of "habitus" and "fields" of social interaction (Bourdieu 1990, 1991).

Habitus refers to a system of durable and "transposable dispositions" through which individuals and groups perceive, appreciate, and express themselves in the world. These learned, and mostly unconscious, dispositions are formed out of the complex practical encounters people have with social conditions of existence (economy, race, gender, class, etc.). Out of these experiences, people internalize the possibilities and constraints of social life. It is at the level of habitus that actors have a sense of *how* to act in any given social context or situation. Thus, habitus is both *structured* by given social contexts and *structuring,* in the sense that it helps to reproduce and incrementally change the social order by giving social actors a *practical* sense of how to act—i.e., a feel for the game.

Secondly, actors occupy positions within fields of social interaction that constitute the various spheres of life (art, politics, economy, etc.). Social fields are structured spaces of position. The position of individuals or groups within a field is determined by the amount of resources available to them, specific to each field. These resources, or capital, are constituted in various forms: economic (financial and material assets), cultural (skills and knowledge) and symbolic (titles, trusts, and prestige). Consequently, the position social actors occupy within a field is closely connected to the ability, or power, they possess to appropriate the particular profits emanating from each specific field, and thus preserve or overturn the status quo (Bourdieu 1991: 172; Thompson 1995: 12).

Social fields, suggests Bourdieu, impose their own internal rules of organization. Those actors who enter a field are, therefore, obliged to play by its particular rules of the game.

> The feel for the political game, which enables politicians to predict the stances of other politicians, is also what makes them predictable for other politicians: predictable and thus responsible, in other words, competent, serious, trustworthy—in short, ready to play, with consistency and without arousing surprise or disappointing people's expectations, the role assigned to them by the structure of the space of the game. (Bourdieu 1991: 179)

Moreover, political actors may have different interests. But they all share an investment in the game of politics. This imperative means learning the rules of political practice and performance. Importantly, the symbolic power of political actors—the ability to use symbolic forms to marshall public support for their policies, along with the ability to see those policies enacted—is not simply given by the social and material context of the political field. Symbolic power is dependent upon the *relation* between the actor or group's habitus and the political field. Political success depends, in part, on their compatibility with each other (200). There is no direct causal relationship. We must remember that we are talking of tendencies and not absolutes. It is the job of the researcher to *tease out* the dialectical relation between the practical activity of social actors and the broader context of their fields of social interaction.

I argue that the promotional logic of spectacle, intermingled with the complex historical progress of modernity, has increasingly become constitutive of various types of social fields—everyday life, the economy, the professional culture of journalism, and politics—and the habitus associated with them. The promotional logic of spectacle is constitutive of personal, economic, journalistic, and political fields of interaction. This promotional logic constitutes, in part, the rules of the game that contribute to the reification of political practice.

## Appearance, Politics, and Popular Culture

Since ancient Athens, the practice of politics has involved proficiency in the craft of performance. Expertise in the skills of rhetoric and oration have long been prerequisites for entering political life. However, the skills of debate associated with the ancient republican tradition were not needed in Monarchic societies where the "divine right" of kings was embodied in the display of the ruler's body. Eventually, as Hénaff and Strong (2001) remind us, the power of religious faith to confer political authority waned, due to the profane indiscretions of various popes and kings (17). This reduction of ecclesiastic authority created a vacuum of political legitimacy—a vacuum filled with secular forms of political power. It is with Machiavelli that Western society first learns how to *produce the appearance* of political authority by controlling the representation of political power. For Machiavelli's Prince, wielding power was related to the development of two skills: the power of observation and perspective, "because seeing amounted to controlling action" (19). But the Prince had to comply with a double logic. He had to control the representation of power, while at the same time offer himself to the gaze of others. Following the logic of perspective, one needed to calculate and alter representations in order that a true representation of reality could be rendered. The so-called accurate representation of reality and political authority, therefore, required "the use of artifice" (21). It also produced an enduring tension between political performance and public opinion.

> The Machiavellian formulation of political space as a strategy of appearances meant that power could no longer be separated from the display of its legitimacy. The paradoxical consequence was that power was all the more dependent on those for whom its show

was designed. The self-staging of power was an admission that power was subject to judgement, toward an evaluation by public opinion, the support of which was important to secure. Theatrical qualities of power lead necessarily in a politically democratic direction. (23)

During the 20th century, with the development of mass media, the performance of politics, and the skills and resources necessary for its organization, has become far more professionalized. This professionalization has further drawn out the tension between political representation and public opinion.

In the United States and other Western nations, the craft of public relations has become a constitutive element of political practice (Franklin 1994; Ewen 1996; Rutherford 2000). Moreover, the history of public relations has, from its beginnings in the 1920s and 1930s, been linked to government and corporate interests. Americans Walter Lippmann, Ivy Lee, and Edward Bernays, the founders of the U.S. public-relations industry, dedicated themselves to the task of using modern public-relations techniques to control what they believed to be the volatile moods of the public. They wished, in Lippmann's words, to "manufacture consent" (Ewen 1996).[1]

The marketing and promotion of politicians is a long-established trend.[2] George Gallup developed and used the first political-opinion polls in the 1930s; and, by the 1960s marketing surveys had become standard issue for most U.S. politicians. As Joe McGinness (1969) told us more than thirty years ago in his famous book *The Selling of the President*, politicians are being sold as if they were any other product. Professional consultants skilled in the crafts of marketing, media, and public-opinion management are intimately connected to the process of "packaging politics" (Franklin 1994), and have been for decades.

To maintain a career in business or politics, one must differentiate oneself by promoting one's personality. In constructing one's personal self-image, individuals and politicians alike become increasingly dependent upon the aestheticized symbolic resources provided by mediated forms of consumer culture. No longer dependent on traditional social roles as models of behavior, these "flexible personalities" (Castells 2000b: 380) engage in an endless remaking of the self.

The fast and steady stream of information produced by news (particularly television) in conjunction with the recycling of images and identities encouraged by the fashion industry and consumer culture, have helped foster a Zeitgeist of constant adaptation and change—particularly with respect to issues of identity. These changes have helped legitimize intimacy and personality in public life. It is in this postmodern environment that tabloid forms of journalism have flourished. Added to the mix are the positive gains of the feminist movement (Van Zoonen 1991; Hallin 1996: 252) in which the personal became political. According to W. Lance Bennett, "personal identity is replacing collective identity as the basis for contemporary political engagement" (Bennett 1998: 755).

Social identities, mediated through marketing and promotional strategies, become essential to economic and political competition; as such, they are subject to rational and strategic action by political, social and commercial interests, and institutions. This is particularly true in Western liberal democracies, where there are fewer and fewer ideological differences between political parties. Under these circumstances, the symbolic capital of personal character becomes a prime resource to be contested and struggled over (Thompson 2000: 113). Moreover, when increasing numbers of people are cynical about politics, the authenticity of a politician's character is a truly valuable symbolic resource.

In 1981, Americans elected a former movie actor, Ronald Reagan, who was equally praised for his vaunted ability as the "great communicator"—a grandfatherly figure for a nation—as he was mocked for his thin grasp of domestic and foreign policy. The latter did not matter. And by 1992, when Bill Clinton blew his saxophone on Arsenio Hall's talk show during his first successful run for the U.S. presidency, all barriers between popular culture and politics appeared to have evaporated. We had entered the seemingly perfected realm of image politics. The craft's consummate performer had taken center stage. Clinton loved detailed discussions of public policy, but what he chose to emphasize in his political performances was the charm of his personality. Clinton gave the impression that he felt your pain.

Bill Clinton was, in many ways, the consummate political performer. He was a smart, gifted orator with a firm grasp of the machinery of modern politics, from the minutia of economic policy to the importance of using polling and focus groups to target particular demographic voting segments. Most importantly, he could empathize on cue. This was the man who, in 1992 during a campaign TV debate, asked a woman to explain how she was being affected by the downturn in the economy. He was the president who cried when U.S. servicemen returned home in coffins. He was the president who confessed on MTV that he preferred briefs to boxer shorts. And in 1998, at the height of congressional impeachment hearings involving his sexual indiscretions with a young intern, Clinton was the president for whom many Americans felt empathy in return. His presidential approval rating rose following the initial revelations of the scandal, much to the bafflement and dismay of his political opponents (Zaller 2001).

In an era in which the popular and political realms are to some extent transposable, details of Clinton's personal life are both political assets and liabilities. Professionals in the crafts of political communications and public relations took notice; and in the 2000 U.S. presidential-election campaign, both Al Gore and George W. Bush practically bent over backwards to insert themselves within the entertainment industry's circuit of late-night talk shows. Being "dissed" is now viewed as potentially beneficial. Allowing oneself to be the butt of jokes portrays the human side of politicians; the secret is to be seen as the good sport who can take a little ribbing. Both presidential hopefuls also appeared in self-deprecating performances on the comedy show *Saturday*

*Night Live.* In Canada, Prime Minister Jean Chretien and other politicians routinely make appearances on CBC's satirical news program *This Hour Has 22 Minutes.* The mediascape is now economically, symbolically, and politically integrated in ways that make an appearance on *Late Show With David Letterman* coextensive with CBS News's venerable *Face the Nation.* That is not to say that the use of popular culture in the appeal for political support is new. As Michael Schudson (1992) argues, the haloed mid-19th century Lincoln-Douglas debates were not necessarily the benchmark for rational-political discussion that others (Postman 1985) have claimed.

> Political campaigns were, in a sense, more religious revivals and popular entertainments than the settings for rational-critical discussion. It is true that the voters who attended or read of the Lincoln-Douglas debates in their party newspapers were literate. It is true that they attended, but it is not at all apparent what in those debates they attended to. It is true that they participated, but it is not clear that they were interested in issues of transcendent importance. (Schudson 1992: 145)

Once we understand that the melding of popular and political cultures has a long history, we can pose the question of how this integration has changed and how it manifests itself today. We need to explain the increased scale and intensity of this integration.

### Representation, Politics, and Modernity

Liberal democratic politics is about the competition for political power using the scarce resources of economic, cultural, social, and symbolic capital to represent differentiated political and social interests. Paraphrasing Guy Debord, we might say that Bill Clinton is the political representative par excellence—the politician as commodified image whose gestures stand in for those of the public. According to Debord, political life is not directly experienced. It is something external to everyday life, and yet, as spectacular representation, a daily part of it. Politics in the society of the spectacle, argues Debord, is a realm of total self-alienation experienced as passive consumption. "The spectator's alienation from and submission to the contemplated object (which is the outcome of his unthinking activity) works like this: the more he recognizes his own needs in the images of need proposed by the dominant system, the less he understands his own existence and his own desires" (Debord 1995: sec. 30).

But how useful is Debord's assessment of political representation? As David Lloyd and Paul Thomas suggest, "Debord regards the inescapability in the postmodern era of 'being represented' as an index of disempowering alienation" (Lloyd and Thomas 1998: 33). Debord follows the young Marx in his critique of the bourgeois political subject who is bifurcated into an isolated and egoistic member of civil society on the one hand, and abstract citizen on the other (Marx 1963 [1844]: 31). The separation is justified by liberal theorists as the basis of ethical public life. It is only the "disinterested spectator" who is capable of judging the ends of public policy—that is to say the general interest. The conflicting interests of situated individuals are resolved by the state through the use of the regulative ideal of the divided subject. "For if at one level what is represented to the state are the competing claims of antagonistic interests, at another, ethically superior level, what the state in its turn represents is the universal, spectating human subject" (Lloyd and Thomas 1998: 33). Conversely, Debord argues, as did Marx before him, that human emancipation can only result from the unification of situated and abstract subjects. Only through direct action, direct communication, and participation with others can people organize their own social powers and avoid having them represented back to them in alienated form as political power. Consequently, all forms of mediated politics are suspect and must be rejected—especially the thought of a politician representing one's pain back to them. Populist movements today on both the right and left hold this view in partial form. Explaining their positions, Benjamin Barber writes that: "Representation is incompatible with freedom because it delegates and thus alienates political will at the cost of genuine self-government and autonomy" (Barber 1984, cited in Dalton 1996: 240).

It is certainly true that political life for most individuals is limited to the periodic ritual of casting a ballot—a ritual that fewer and fewer people in Western democracies participate in at the national level (Dalton 1996: 44). And there is a lot of truth in the cliché that political journalism reduces the complexities of political campaigns (to take one prominent example) to a horse race in which situated particular interests and the ends of public policy are occluded by the unfolding spectacle of the "theater" of politics as performed by political elites and their professional specialists. I will argue that the representation and performance of politics is constitutively linked to issues of social relations of power; but before doing so, I want to propose some criticisms of Debord's understanding of political representation before I elaborate on the concept of the "integrated spectacle" and how it can, with modification, help us construct a more precise critique of mediated political life.

First, Debord's theory of the spectacle assumes incorrectly that individuals passively consume the meanings conveyed in symbolic forms. It is true that the project of self-development in modernity is dependent upon individual appropriation of commercially produced and mediated symbolic forms. Nonetheless, this is an active project in which individuals construct meanings that are contingent upon their particular life histories and experiences and the multiplicity of symbolic forms available for appropriation (Thompson 1995: 210).

Second, mediated politics is the result of a long and complex historical process involving the development of new technology, the process of capital accumulation, state regulation, and competing social interests. Mediated forms of social relationships that have developed as a result of the rise of print, radio, television, and now the

Internet have fundamentally altered our experience of time and space. Public events are experienced discontinuously, and for the most part in privatized locales (private homes), by large numbers of people. The speed and frequency of these symbolic experiences has increased sharply. And for the vast majority of individuals, public life is experienced at a distance through mediated forms of representation (Thompson 1995). Manuel Castells refers to this experience as the "real culture of virtuality" (Castells 2000a: 403). In such a mediated environment, politics cannot be predicated on active, direct, face-to-face communication. Accordingly, John Thompson's critique of Jürgen Habermas's (1989) model of face-to-face communication applies equally to Debord. Using face-to-face direct communication as the index for political communication deprives one "of the means of understanding the new forms of publicness created by the media" (Thompson 1995: 132). Mediated visibility is an unavoidable element of modern political life (138). Inquiry into democratic communication in modern large-scale societies must focus on the extent to which the process of political mediation meets the diverse needs and interests of society.

Third, as part of his proposal to overcome political alienation, Debord believes that the elimination of political representation through the use of workers councils will allow for "that active direct communication which marks the end of all specialization, all hierarchy, and all separation" (Debord 1995: sec. 116). While Debord directs our attention, correctly, to the separation of professional political practice from political will formation in modern society, his theorization evokes a kind Rousseauian utopianism. It is true that control over the means of political representation has been used as a method of social domination by elite factions. And it would be preferable for citizens to have unmediated access to the political realm. However, the scale of modern societies is such that it is impractical to predicate emancipatory politics on the eradication of the division of political labor. We cannot wish a return to a kind of mythical Rousseauian political covenant under which no individual would be represented by another. Rousseau's "recuperative ideal" is predicated on a small-scale city-state that could, by the nature of its size, limit the social division of labor. To enforce small-scale direct action and communication on a complex large-scale modern society, as Debord suggests, would be to court disaster. The many intricate systems used to organize the production and distribution of public goods and services—from information flows to scientific and technical research and development—require some level of professional expertise. That is not to say that new forms of direct citizen participation cannot be fostered or encouraged (e.g., public forums, town-hall meetings). It does mean that they must accommodate some form of mediation and political representation. Modern democratic societies require political representatives charged with the responsibility of overseeing the management of these complex systems to ensure that they meet the diverse needs of the public.

The division of political labor under representative forms of government poses a problem to the extent that there is a *disconnect* between the actions of political representatives and the needs and interests of those whom they represent. According to Bourdieu, "the political discourses produced by professionals are always," in this sense, "doubly determined." Political professionals must play the game of politics using the internal rules of the political field. At the same time, they must mobilize the segments of the public through external appeals and actions that resonate with particular social interests (Bourdieu 1991: 183). The principal democratic issue concerns how those needs and interests are determined, communicated, and acted upon. To what extent are the rules, practices, and conventions of political life reified as natural, immutable, and beyond the control of both political professionals and the citizens they represent? To what extent are public representatives working according to the instrumental rules of an objectified system of organization and control as opposed to meeting the variable and contingent needs of those they represent? And finally, do the actions and interests of these political professionals favor particular situated interests?

Bourdieu argues that individuals can only come into being as a political group capable of representing its interests once that group selects a spokesperson or representative. "One must always risk political alienation in order to escape from political alienation." The only people who can escape this conundrum are members of the dominant elite. According to Bourdieu "the dominated exist only if they mobilize or avail themselves of instruments of representation" (Bourdieu 1991: 204). Similarly, Sylviane Agacinski writes that it is impossible for democracy to "abolish all relations of power" (Agacinski 2001: 136). Agacinski suggests that "democracy is never direct, . . . . that between the fiction of sovereignty and the reality of power, there are nothing other than representations." In other words, particular political communities cannot exist outside of the social constructions used to represent them. The challenge is to regulate the distance between people and power "in such a way that the people in its concrete reality remain, as much as possible, the organ within which a political 'will' is formed" (133). We can, in this way, reconcile with the early Marx (Marx 1963[1844]: 128) to say there is a necessary objectification of the political subject. Political subjectivity is only alienated to the extent that it becomes a means for others and not an expression of one's own interests and needs.

The difficult, and some would say rarely successful, balancing act forced upon would-be practitioners of democratic communication is to triangulate the basic values of freedom, equality, and solidarity. This sometimes contradictory troika of values is always at stake in debates about democratic communication (McQuail 1996: 70–76). The freedom to communicate, the equality of communicative opportunities, and the social concord required to pursue free and equal communicative experiences are all essential. The question is whether the media system through which political representation occurs can allow for the counterbalancing of these democratic values without any one value being hypostatized and privileged to the benefit of particular situated interests. That is to say, in a modern large-scale society distinguished by some form of political representation—accountable to citizens via the procedure of elections—avenues of expression must be open to individuals and social groups to communicate their interests and values to the political representatives and technical specialists charged with the responsibility of coordinating necessarily complex social activities—from welfare reform to immigration policy. Large-scale societies require social norms to reproduce themselves over time without constant recourse to coercive forms of power (military and police violence). Which values and norms (expressed in symbolic form) are chosen and used to guide and/or justify the actions of political and technical specialists is the stuff of politics, as is the ability to express one's opposition to those choices and actions. Nicholas Garnham clarifies the situation: "In essence modern democracy is about how we handle the relationship between individual freedom and moral agency on the one hand and the necessary and unavoidable social norms and structures within which alone such freedom can be exercised on the other" (Garnham 2000: 178). *It is the communication process through which those norms are determined, mediated, and acted upon that is the index of democratic life.* Moreover, the practices and institutions affecting the production, distribution, and exchange of symbolic forms contribute to the legitimacy of political power.

### *Legitimation, Rationality, and Judging Dramatic Representation*

Tension among the values of freedom, equality, and solidarity remains at the heart of politics. How can large numbers of people, separated by diverse interests stemming from their class, race, and gender identities, join together to shape their collective future in a manner that limits or curtails forms of social and political domination? In other words, how can mediated political authority be democratically legitimated? And what role does the modern mediascape play?

Jürgen Habermas's influential response has been to establish forms of noncoercive social solidarity through an appeal to an ideal standard of rational argument. His theory of democratic communication is grounded on the ideal that people come together as equals—with the shared interest of reaching mutual agreement—to engage in face-to-face dialogue using mutually understandable validity claims. Communicative action is thus distinguished from strategic action (the sphere of promotional activity) by its reliance on noncoercive, intersubjective deliberation. "Everyday communication," says Habermas, "makes possible a kind of understanding that is based on claims to validity and thus furnishes the only real alternative to exerting influence on one another in more or less coercive ways" (Habermas 1990: 19).

Habermas has characterized the commercialization of the press and the influx of advertising and publicity interests into the public sphere as a "refeudalization" of the public sphere. As the laws of commodity exchange pervaded the public sphere, commercial interests transformed the critical potential of a debating public. The public sphere became "the court *before*" which one's public prestige could be "displayed—

rather than *in* which public critical debate is carried on" (Habermas 1989: 201). Critically argued consensus is replaced by competition between "privileged private interests" and consumption (195, 161).

As I have stated, Habermas's reliance on face-to-face communication as an ideal standard of judgment is highly problematic for large-scale modern societies. Nonetheless, one must acknowledge the extent to which Habermas's pessimistic assessment of a public sphere colonized by promotional discourse rings true. Politics *does* to an increasingly large extent involve the circulation of promotional symbols designed to win public support for particular policies, causes, and interests; and it often does so using strategies formed out of the requirements imposed by commercial media. This does not mean, however, that we must accept Habermas's "refeudalization" thesis.

I resist Habermas's claim that the assessment of democratic communication be anchored in an ideal speech situation; but I do so not because I reject rationality; far from it. First, Habermas, by basing his theory on a model of dialogical face-to-face communication, fails to account for the historically contingent and mediated context in which public life unfolds. The efficacy of political performance—i.e., the extent to which it is democratic—cannot be separated from the existence of the social institutions in which the conditions of performance are determined. By social institution I mean a set of rules, resources, and social relations that invests individuals with power and status (Thompson 1995: 12). These *conditions of performance* are constitutive of media and political practice and cannot be analyzed properly by reference to an ideal type of speech. We require a more historically sensitive approach. If we are to judge the performance of politics, we must first understand the rules, conventions, and predispositions that guide political actors and that make political performances intelligible to others. We must also interrogate the social relations that contribute to the division of resources (cultural, symbolic, and economic) required to engage in political practice. It is by understanding the social conditions of political performance that we can determine how symbolic power is used to impose systems of meaning that legitimate structures of social inequality. This assessment, I argue, involves an exploration of the integrated media spectacle.

Second, an examination of democratic-will formation must be able to account for the sundry hopes and fears of historically situated individuals (Agacinski 2001: 131–132). People are not motivated to engage in politics (i.e., to support a particular set of policies) purely based on abstract reason alone. Democratic communication necessitates a process in which individuals and groups make public their claims for political support, and, therefore, open to scrutiny. Any study of this process must allow for the complex moral, psychological, and material reasons individuals may have for accepting or rejecting competing explanations of social reality (Edelman 1988; Curran 1996). In other words, Habermas fails to account for the ways in which individuals and groups use "arational" (Dahlgren 1995: 101) forms of communication, such as rhetoric, storytelling, and myth to represent themselves and "narrate the social" (Alexander and Jacobs 1998).

Consequently, we must appreciate how competing groups use practices and *"systems of representation"* to advance their interests (Curran 1996: 101). To insist on using an abstract ideal standard of intersubjective reason as the *one* way of measuring the democratic efficacy of political communication and political performance automatically rejects, undemocratically in my view, alternative forms of public communication. A variety of rhetorical and discursive strategies can be used in public discourse. Dramatic narratives that incorporate vernacular language and popular image-making techniques can broaden access to political discussion. Michael Moore's short-lived *TV Nation,* and his follow-up program, *The Awful Truth,* with its entertainingly satirical reporting style, are good examples. These shows were in many ways more critically informed than the network newsmagazine programs Moore was spoofing.[3] And I think we can make this claim and still eschew journalistic practices that reproduce hearsay evidence and reduce reporters to purveyors of unsubstantiated gossip. To have journalistic standards does not mean one must be boring.

The performance of politics and the narratives and cultural texts employed by political actors are part of a struggle to narrate the social. This is the state of actually existing political communication. Murray Edelman describes the situation well.

> The spectacle constituted by news reporting continuously constructs and reconstructs social problems, crises, enemies, and leaders and so creates a succession of threats and reassurances. These constructed problems and personalities furnish the content of political journalism and the data for historical and analytic political studies. They also play a central role in winning support and opposition for political causes and policies. (Edelman 1988: 1)

The news spectacle is, in partial form, about the dramatization of collective life, not its direct experience. It is a dramatic representation of social relations. News narratives, according to Edelman "objectify," in dramatic form, the hopes and fears of people (96). The news spectacle dramatizes a political world beyond the everyday experiences of people while simultaneously offering explanations, admonitions, and reassurances for social problems ranging from unemployment and crime to healthcare and abortion.

Recognition of this point is the strength of the cultural-anthropology tradition that draws upon the work of Victor Turner. Researchers in this tradition suggest that underlying the social conflict dramatized by the news media is a four-staged ritual sequence: social norms are breached, followed by a crisis, redressive action, and eventually reintegration or schism (Schechner 1985: 310). These researchers are interested in phatic communication—the ways in which cultural performances can strengthen social relationships through storytelling. Moreover, neo-Durkheimian theorists (Carey 1992; Dayan and Katz 1992; Chaney 1993; Alexander and Jacobs 1998) suggest that these dramatic representations have "existential utility" in that they provide individuals and groups with resources to interpret their everyday social reality. In some cases, the media events attached to these dramatic narratives create "liminal" moments in which the norms of society are held up to scrutiny.

Dramatic storytelling—whether it be tales of deceased modern princesses, political sex scandals, or the hagiography of political image making—is constitutive of the process by which cognitive maps are constructed and used by individuals and social groups to assess social life and to make sense of the seeming chaos of the modern world. It is through the news spectacle that social actors are characterized using a binary code of the sacred and profane. In politics, actors are viewed as democratic/antidemocratic, trustworthy/deceitful, or populist/elitist, ally/enemy, etc. The news spectacle represents social reality by telling stories about collective life that make it possible to imagine political communities based on class, race, and gender, and to mobilize these communities in support or opposition to particular public-policy initiatives, political candidates, and the platforms they represent.

Earlier I noted that a fundamental weakness of the cultural-anthropology approach lies in its limited treatment of the concept of power. In addition, while it is true that news discourse dramatizes social conflict, researchers in this tradition overestimate the degree of consensus regarding social norms within society. Their focus on social integration occludes examination of legitimate challenges to those norms. As David Harvey suggests, "emancipation is best defined by a condition in which we can be both rule makers and rule breakers with reasonable impunity" (Harvey 2000: 209). The meaning of news spectacles, from presidential elections to the death of a princess, is always ambiguous because people draw upon different narratives' explanations of events. "It is the ambiguity and the controversy that make developments political in character" (Edelman 1988: 95). The clichéd adage that one group's freedom fighter is another group's terrorist is true. Or, as in the case of the 2000 U.S. presidential election, one group's legitimate presidential winner is another's usurper. That is, until—as happened following the tragic events of September 11, 2001—the nationalist battle cry to rally around the flag gained ascendancy.[4] Researchers need to ask which groups possess the ability to define social and political deviance and its legitimate limits. In other words, *one must understand which individuals, social groups, and institutions have the resources to represent rival groups and their interests as deviant* (i.e., undemocratic, unpatriotic, elitist, etc.). This struggle involves the exercise of symbolic power.

I am not arguing that truth is completely relative to the "play" of dramatic narratives. There is a real material world; and the explanatory adequacy of dramatic narratives, like rational validity claims, can be compared and judged. Some are better than others.[5] But because the meanings of dramatic narratives are ambiguous, the question of whose narratives become dominant is of central political importance. As Darnell Hunt suggests in his study of the media coverage of the O.J. Simpson trial, not all readings of cultural texts are equal. Those readings "gaining the upper hand in the struggle to set the conditions of belief" are often those that are "hypermediated by mainstream news media" (Hunt 1999: 28). The performance of politics is constitutively connected to struggles over the definition of reality—what ought to be taken seriously or taken for granted—e.g., the obvious necessity of tax cuts versus properly funded social programs, or the guilt or innocence of a former football star. Following John Street, we can say that the performance of politics and the dramatic narratives deployed by political and social actors involves "the exercise of power and the attempt to legitimate that power" (Street 1997: 176). The question of crucial importance, then, is which groups have the requisite cultural, economic, and symbolic resources to help define the range of legitimate disagreement over social norms that may exist in society? And which of those groups is best positioned to take political advantage of those legitimating narratives to advance their own particular interests?

Ericson, Baranek, and Chan (1987, 1989) and Mark Fishman (1980) have gone a long way toward answering this question by examining negotiations between news and source bureaucracies. They have, in my view, provided a more sociologically grounded explanation of Stuart Hall et al.'s (1978) "primary definer" thesis. Ericson, Baranek, and Chan, and Fishman argue that those "official" news sources (police, courts, governments, etc.) that share a "bureaucratic affinity" (Fishman) with news organizations, stand a better chance of having their definitions of social and/or procedural deviance legitimated. Ericson, Baranek, and Chan argue that deviance is the prime characteristic of newsworthiness for journalists. Deviance is defined as straying from a norm, but it also refers to straying from "organizational procedures and violations of common-sense knowledge" (Ericson, Baranek, and Chan 1987: 4). Deviance, therefore, becomes the defining characteristic of journalism and its methodological approach. As watchdogs, journalists make sense of their stories by relating them back to an assumed normal state of affairs, or community consensus. Anti–World Trade Organization protesters can be framed as democratic populists who are breaking down the walls of political cynicism, or as anarchistic thugs. Deviance can be defined positively or negatively.

By focusing on deviance, news organizations accomplish two immediate tasks: they develop a method of entertaining audiences by detailing moral, ethical, and procedural transgressions of the established order, and they act as "agencies of social control." Journalists use commonsense language to demarcate the boundaries of acceptable behavior through entertaining dramatic narratives.

> The focus on deviance is also a primary vehicle for entertaining the consumer and evoking emotive aspects of human interest. Visualizing deviance is a matter of the heart as well as the head, sustaining the interest of the audience whatever the thrust of the news story. In the process, journalists become part of the phenomenon they report on, enacting their organizational environment as an agency of stability, reform, and change. (5)

The reliance on authoritative sources who are often associated with bureaucratic institutions means that audiences experience social reality largely "through the eyes of the existing authority structure" (361).

> For citizens who are not elite members of the knowledge structure, politics is a spectator sport. They are left to consume symbolic spectacles, which tell them what to think about if not what to think. . . . Physical reality seems to recede in proportion as man's symbolic activity enhances. (361)

The social construction of reality through news directs our attention to those organizations and/or individuals that have the financial, cultural, and symbolic resources to interact with the media. It is they who have the enhanced opportunity to participate in the construction of the news spectacle.

In addition to this literature, I want to argue that the promotional logic of the spectacle has come to play an important role in determining the chances for dramatic narrative success in the integrated news spectacle. I argue that the reification of dramatic narratives, and in some case, political actors, plays a constitutive role in the "play" of political performance.

### Aestheticization, Politics, and Reification

The issue of social relations of power and mediated politics—what form it takes and whose interests are served—must be investigated through a historical analysis of the *use* of dramatic narratives and the social relations of which they are a part. In other words, one must examine how the mediated production of political representation is structured by social relations while simultaneously investigating how the mediated production of symbolic forms itself is a structuring process that contributes to the maintenance of social relations. One must refer dramatic narratives back to historically situated interests and the media apparatus in which the struggle to legitimate political agendas is played out. Dramatic narratives used in political struggles over such things as social or fiscal policy reform, and the social norms in whose name this practice is conducted, are the tools of "perception and expression" offered by the political field; as such, dramatic narratives, contribute to " the universe of political discourse, and thereby the universe of what is politically thinkable" (Bourdieu 1991: 172). One's ability to play the game of politics, therefore, is linked to one's access to the resources of the political field.

Dramatic narratives fall under the rubric of the integrated system of news production and distribution to the extent that commercial news media remain the primary site through which competing social forces appeal for support within civil society. The logic and structure of the integrated news spectacle is thus a factor in determining which individuals or groups have the resources to fully pursue their agendas, represent their interests, and potentially have them accepted as common sense. It is also responsible, in part, for the style of politics. The organizing mechanism of our image-saturated media culture—and therefore, image politics—is the impersonal network of market exchange. The cultural texts stemming from the promotional packaging of political life have been aestheticized through marketing and advertising in an attempt to bridge the gap between consumers and producers—i.e., the broader public and political professionals. Dramatic narratives—mediated through a particular set of market transactions—have become constitutive of economic competition and the rational organization of journalistic institutions and political professionals; they have become objects of rational and strategic action by commercial and political interests. Political practice has become reified and susceptible to forms of domination to the extent that: (1) political life is conducted according to the logic and rules of the integrated spectacle; and (2) politics favors particular social actors and dramatic narratives—*those more fully integrated within the promotional logic of the system of production, distribution and exchange.*

When I talk of the aestheticization of politics, I am not trying to equate modern politics with fascist spectacles. As I have indicated, we need to investigate the historically contingent ways in which dramatic narratives are aestheticized within the integrated news spectacle. We need to demonstrate "how political presentation interacts with historically contingent patterns of perception, and how imperatives of power and money may colonize the specific ways of what and how we see" (Koepnick 1999: 237).

What I seek to do here is tease out the relation between the habitus of political actors and groups and the political and journalistic fields in which they must operate. In particular, I want to argue that the ability of political actors to utilize the tools of "perception and expression" depends on their access to economic capital, but also cultural and symbolic capital specific to the political field—a social field of interaction that, increasingly is characterized by flexible and integrated systems of image/commodity production, distribution, and exchange. I am less concerned here with individual performances—interesting as they may be—than I am with how actors and groups are suited to political life in the integrated news spectacle. Who possesses the requisite skills and resources required for the "play" of politics? What are those skills and resources? And how do they relate to the practical logic of the integrated news spectacle?

### *Flexibility, Control, and the Politics of Performance*

The communication resources available to political actors have changed over the years. As previously noted, during the mid-20th century there was a shift away from volunteer political labor towards professional consultants specializing in the marketing and public-opinion management. In addition, the role of newspapers as vehicles for political messages, while still vitally important, decreased. In the United States, the big-three television network newscasts became the locus of political campaigns. Image management took center stage as politicians were packaged for national and regional audiences based on frequent public-opinion polling.

Beginning in the 1980s, the mediascape began to undergo further significant changes that affected the type and availability of communication resources. The advent of new information and communication technologies (ICT) such as cable and satellites were integral to this change. These technologies helped spawn new entertainment and news genres, ranging from TV tabloid programs such as *A Current Affair* to the birth of 24-hour news with CNN. The result was a fragmentation of audiences for both media organizations and political actors. Talk-radio and talk-TV formats also flourished following the U.S. government's decision to scrap the content regulations contained in the FCC's Fairness Doctrine. Moreover, a greater emphasis was being placed on profits at major U.S. news organizations in the wake of government liberalization and market-regulation policies. Focus was trained on cheaper, more flexible programming that could reduce the risk of capital accumulation. News-magazine programs that emphasized so-called softer and more entertaining stories featuring dramatic storylines with interesting characters and lifestyles were part of this strategy. These general trends continued with the popularization of the Internet in 1994. The seminal moment came in January 2000, when the AOL Time Warner merger convinced the media elite of the necessity of cross-media corporate convergence.

The ultimate home for these melodramatic tales was found in the 24-hour news channels: CNN, MSNBC, and Fox. These stories were homologous with the flexible production requirements of the all-news giants: (1) the death of Princess Diana and the Monicagate scandal were easily transposable and appealed across gender, class, and racial lines; (2) they allowed for the smooth repurposing of news resources from one program to the next; and (3) these aestheticized events provided fulcrum points that allowed integrated media properties to administer their promotional system on a global scale. As systems of production and consumption become more and more integrated, economies of scope and scale are developed. Audiences are divided into niches and shared among the various strands of the integrated system of production and distribution—broadcast, print, and new media. The melodramatic narratives of these Big News stories provided the hook needed to establish promotional synergies among cross-media properties and programs.

Political actors responded by trying to control the flow of images in the political field. During the 1991 Gulf War, the U.S. government exerted enormous control over the content and flow of information about the Gulf conflict using three basic tactics: (1) restrict media access to the war "theater"; (2) provide "information subsidies" by inundating news organizations with regularly scheduled news conferences that offered carefully scripted explanations of the war effort, including antiseptic screenings of so-called smart bombs striking their targets; and (3) supply news organizations with a dramatic narrative that allowed for an easily transposable and "episodic framing" (Iyengar and Simon 1994: 179) of an emotional confrontation between good and evil, personified in the characters of U.S. President George Bush and Iraqi President Saddam Hussein.[6]

Pippa Norris tells us that in the early 1990s, professional politicians in America tried to reassert control over the fragmented media universe and its 24-hour rolling-news cycle through a so-called permanent campaign that utilizes rolling polls, focus groups, and newly developed forms of voter-politician interaction over the Internet (Norris 2000: 147). The political consulting firm Aristotle International compiled a mammoth databank for the 2000 U.S. presidential election that included the names of 150-million registered voters. The company combines its list of names, addresses, telephone numbers, party affiliation, and voting records with information collected and/or purchased from commercial vendors and other sources to provide political professionals with detailed voter profiles. Aristotle's promotional literature boasts the capability of targeting Republican women voters older than 65, in specific precincts, who have voted in the last three primaries and made campaign contributions (Wayne 2000). This information, in turn, informs the promotional, negative advertising, and direct-mail campaigns of political hopefuls.

The intensification of personalized politics—already well established—was part of the response to audience fragmentation. Bill Clinton's 1992 appearance on Arsenio Hall was a successful attempt to reach out to younger voters who did not pay close attention to politics and for whom popular culture was a zone of comfort. Clinton appeared on MTV for the same reason. He was not alone. That same year the irascible Ross Perot, speaking through his Texas twang, announced his intention to run for president on CNN's popular talk show *Larry King Live*.

The permanent campaign was in essence a combination of two long-standing strategies of power: administrative surveillance and spectacular display. As Peter Wollen (2000) argues, contrary to Foucault (1980: 155), systems of surveillance and spectacle are not necessarily opposed to each other. Wollen says they first merged in the French court of Louis XIV. "The former seeks to gather the maximum information and, for this reason, to improve and elaborate the means and techniques of perception, particularly optical perception. . . . The latter seeks to reach the maximum audience for a performance or an exhibition and, for this reason, to improve and elaborate the means of optical display" (Wollen 2000: 102). Political actors operating in the political field make use of these integrated strategies. In fact, this combination of power captures, in part, the meaning behind Debord's integrated spectacle in which the diffuse spectacle of commodity production, distribution, and exchange is merged with bureaucratized forms of rational administration and control. There is no single centralized power, as Foucault suggests. Instead, we see disparate institutions, social groups and individuals (some with more opportunity and ability than others) trying to harness the power of the integrated news spectacle to their own ends. At the level of the habitus, individuals and groups have, to some extent, internalized (or not) the prerequisites of participation in economic and political life by taking on both the "mentality of bureaucracy" and the imperative of self-promotion. "Like the king of France, the president of the United States seeks, through his Office of Communications, to produce and control a constant flow of favorable images. Similarly, he receives a constant flow of sensitive intelligence" (103). The main difference between Louis the XIV and the president, says Wollen, is that he must deal with public opinion. The practical logic of politicians on the cusp of the new millennium is, once again, "doubly determined."

### Tapping into the Integrated News Spectacle

Certainly, economic wealth has played, and continues to play, a fundamental role in determining the power of social actors in relation to one another. The same can be said of one's relation to social institutions. Membership in state (political office, bureaucracies), legal (law societies) and cultural institutions (the arts, journalism) confers access to economic, cultural, and symbolic capital not available to those social actors outside those institutions. There is evidence, however, to suggest that the integrated news spectacle offers historically unique opportunities for political actors to pursue their own interests by tapping into the new cultural and symbolic resources offered in the political and journalistic fields.

Michael Delli Carpini and Bruce Williams (2001) argue that a series of related factors are changing the social relations of power within the new media environment. First, the introduction of new technologies, including cable, satellite, and the Internet, has increased the volume and speed of information processed by the media. These technological developments combined with economic changes such as the downsizing of news organizations and increased pressure for profits have blurred the traditional boundaries between news and entertainment genres. Delli Carpini and Williams argue that this blurring of boundaries has contributed to an erosion of authority for elite practitioners of politics—i.e., journalists, politicians, policy experts, and academics. Moreover, they argue that this erosion of authority has decreased the power of elite groups to act as gatekeepers. Second, they suggest that the new 24-hour news cycle creates unique opportunities for social actors. These changes have created space for "new or marginalized groups, along with new or formerly nonpolitical media" to play "a central role in setting and framing the public agenda" (167).

Delli Carpini and Williams illustrate their argument by reference to the Lewinsky-Clinton scandal. They point to expanded coverage and commentary about the scandal by late-night comedians, tabloid news programs such as *A Current Affair,* cable and right-wing radio talk shows, and over the Internet by gossip-maven Matt Drudge as evidence of the blurring boundaries of authoritative commentary. This authority, they suggest, was formerly centered in elite publications such as the *New York Times,* the *Washington Post,* as well as the big-three television networks. Moreover, they argue "the new media environment, with its multiple points of access and more continuous news cycle, has increased the opportunities for less mainstream individuals and groups to influence public discourse" (175).

I want to pursue this line of thought. Unfortunately, Delli Carpini and Williams greatly exaggerate the counter-hegemonic potential of this shift in the media environment. Most glaringly, they describe the successful "insurgency movement" of a coalition of well-funded conservative publications, foundations, and religious groups to keep alive various scandalous stories concerning President Clinton's personal and professional life (176). To describe this coalition as marginal is quite a stretch. The ability of this conservative network to merge the Gennifer Flowers, Paula Jones, and Monica Lewinsky stories with the investigation by White House Special Prosecutor Kenneth Starr, involved the exercise of cultural capital, but it also speaks loudly to their position as well-heeled actors within the political field. After all, as Carpini and Williams make clear, they had access to print and video production and distribution resources not available to many. Having said this, there is truth to the claim that fresh opportunities exist for political actors to exploit dramatic narratives while simultaneously turning the power, intensity, and speed of the 24-hour news cycle to their advantage.

Republican Senator John McCain's campaign for his party's 2000 presidential nomination provides us with a valuable example of how one politician adapted himself to the changing nature of the journalistic and political fields. It is generally acknowledged that McCain's campaign became *the* story of the U.S. primary season. In fact, many political observers credited the McCain campaign with boosting voter turnout in the Republican primaries (Cohen 2000b). In a year when George W. Bush was touted as the shoe-in candidate of the party establishment, McCain became the media darling and possible giant slayer of the Republican primary contest. He fostered an image of himself as the populist antipolitician, admittedly not a particularly novel idea. The Arizona senator appeared on the covers of *Time, Newsweek,* and *The Economist.* At one point, *Newsweek* hailed McCain as the "rock star of politics." Alan Lichtman, an oft-quoted presidential historian, dubbed the campaign a "populist rebellion," saying at the time of the campaign that "McCain has tapped into a vein of discontent about politics as it is practised" (Cohen 2000c).

What lay behind McCain's success? Three factors came into play: (1) McCain's brand identity; (2) McCain's flexible media strategy meshed with the needs of media organizations; and (3) McCain's strategic use of the quirks of the American primary system. First, McCain successfully branded himself as the outsider candidate, despite his many years of service as senator and before that as house representative. He declared his opposition to "special interests" and argued in favor of campaign-finance reform, even though he continued to lobby for funds. The key to his branding strategy, and the reason he was able to overcome these contradictions, was the stress placed on his personal character. His story as a prisoner of war in Vietnam who survived five and a half years of captivity and torture became the backbone of the "McCain narrative." The story of his survival, after the U.S. Navy jet he piloted was shot from the sky, is recounted in his best-selling autobiography, *Faith of My Fathers*. It was his status as an American patriot who endured unspeakable horror that infused credibility into his brand message of authenticity and trust. The narrative, reproduced repeatedly by the mainstream media, enabled McCain to appeal to a cross section of voters who did not necessarily share his conservative ideology. McCain told anyone who would listen that he was a "Reagan Republican," suggesting that he was capable of repeating Ronald Reagan's record of attracting the support of Democrats and Independents (Saunders 2000). One long-time Democratic voter told the *Globe and Mail*, "I don't even agree with everything he stands for, but McCain has a moral compass, a real sense of maturity" (Koring 2000).

McCain also skillfully played the dual "politics of authenticity" and "redemption" through his willingness to apologize in public for past personal and political mistakes. The subjects of how he was responsible for the failure of his first marriage and how he voted against making Martin Luther King's birthday a national holiday in the United States were two apparent favorites. There is no reason to suggest McCain's regret was not genuine, but it must be said that these admissions had the added benefit of bolstering his support among women and the country's sizable black minority. McCain projected the image of a man who was steadfast in his honesty, but who was also flexible enough to admit when he had been wrong (Henneberger 2000). As Bill Clinton proved before him, the politics of redemption can reap powerful rewards.[7] The McCain narrative resonated for many Americans, especially at a time when trust in the two major political parties was weak. One market-research firm reported that both the Democratic and Republican party brands "tied for last place on a 'relationship monitor'" with 60 other consumer brands. Consumers contacted indicated stronger commitments to Burger King, Oreo cookies, and Clorox bleach than to either political party (Winters Lauro 2000).

Secondly, the McCain narrative was a boon to the excitement and information-starved news media. "The primary," said Bill Press, former cohost of CNN's *Crossfire*, "was this year's Monica Lewinsky, where every night we did some variation of the same topic." The McCain narrative was such an important part of the news coverage for the all-talk cable programs that when the Arizona senator was eventually forced from the race, following a loss in the New York primary, Press and other media figures could not contain their disappointment. "Postpartum depression is what I'm feeling right now," Press told the *Washington Post*. "I hope we're not going to talk about Al Gore and George Bush for the next six months. We may have to go back and talk about serious issues" (Kurtz 2000e).

McCain received so much favorable media coverage that representatives from the Bush camp began to complain. What marked his relationship with the media as different was that he provided a potent dramatic narrative that was tailor made for personality-driven TV news. McCain also adapted himself to the new 24-hour news cycle. He eliminated the short 10- to 15-minute media availability sessions that have become the norm in politics. Instead, McCain made himself available to reporters throughout the day and night aboard his campaign bus, christened the "Straight Talk Express." *Washington Post* reporter Howard Kurtz referred to McCain's campaign performance as "the political equivalent of a 24-hour Webcam" (Kurtz 2000f). The strategy was not without its risks, chief among them the increased chance of making a political gaffe. But for a political underdog who lacked the deep financial pockets of his opponent (Bush's mammoth campaign kitty stood at a record $70 million during the primaries), the risk was more than justified. McCain's willingness to endlessly brave the media horde allowed the self-styled outsider to reinforce his central brand message of authenticity and trust. At the same time, the strategy ingratiated McCain with the quote-hungry media, while enabling his campaign team to appear more nimble in the increasingly high-speed "spin-wars" among political candidates. Bush eventually adopted the style in his winning electoral battle with Vice President Al Gore.

The brand-new reality of election campaigns is that political reporters are routinely bombarded by e-mail, sometimes hourly, from party handlers trying to influence the latest news update or to create a sense of momentum and buzz about their candidate's electoral chances. "Everyone's being spun all the time in real time," *Newsweek* correspondent Howard Fineman told the *Washington Post*. "Because everyone's on cell phones, you can be out with one candidate and someone from the opposing campaign will call and he can spin you almost while you're listening to the other guy speak" (Kurtz 2000g). The ability to douse political brush fires before they grow into large infernos depends, in part, on being able to respond quickly and decisively to allegations made by one's political opponents. Often, this spin battle degenerates to the level of trading insults between political camps. For example, McCain repeatedly implied that Bush was in some way anti-Catholic. The innuendo stemmed from a speech Bush gave at Bob Jones University. The institution's founders have been pilloried for writing anti-Catholic screeds. In return, Bush labeled McCain anti–New York, during that state's primary race.

The McCain team also enjoyed immense success integrating the Internet into their campaign. Organizers used multiple Internet sites in the targeted states of New Hampshire, South Carolina, Arizona, New York, and California to solicit support. The Web sites allowed potential supporters to register by congressional district. This provided strategists with targeted databases for further e-mail and telephone contact (Ledbetter 1999). Close to 100,000 people used McCain's main Web site to volunteer for the campaign. Of that group, 37,000 signed up after his first primary victory in New Hampshire. On the night of the New Hampshire win, credit-card donations came pouring in through the Web site (www.mccain2000.com) at a rate of $20,000 per hour (Van Natta Jr. 2000). McCain suddenly had the Midas touch. His cultural and symbolic capital had converted into economic capital.

The final factor in McCain's relatively successful challenge of Bush—the dominant GOP candidate—was that he capitalized on the unique quirks of the U.S. primary and caucus systems. Under the sometimes-byzantine U.S. electoral system, voting rules can vary from state to state. McCain's wins in the New Hampshire and Michigan primaries were helped along, in no small part, by the fact that they were open primaries. That meant Democrats were allowed to vote in the Republican primary, and vice versa. It also permitted those individuals without a fixed party affiliation to vote. This contingency allowed McCain to attract crossover votes from Democrats and independents—the so-called Reagan Republicans. In the end, however, the Bush juggernaut won the day. The brand strength of the Bush's name (the son of a former president), his enormous financial resources (due in no small part to the support of his family's contacts in the oil industry), and his deep-seated support among registered Republicans and the religious right made the difference. Perhaps most important, 70 percent of Republican delegates to the party's national convention were selected in states that did not allow crossover voting.

McCain was able to tap into the unique resources of the integrated news spectacle, but it was not enough, in the end, to overcome the enormous advantages of his principal opponent. Nonetheless, the McCain signifier remained a potent political force after his withdrawal from the presidential race. Despite the very real enmity that existed between the two men as a result of campaign mudslinging, the Bush camp insisted their candidate be seen in a friendly setting with McCain. In a tightly scripted media event May 9, 2000, the two former foes met and held a joint press conference in Pittsburgh where they shook hands for the cameras (Milbank 2000).

Not to be outdone, Vice President Al Gore tapped into the McCain narrative in an attempt to replicate McCain's deft use of the politics of authenticity and redemption. "I have learned from my mistakes," he told the *New York Times*. "Like John McCain, I bring the passion that comes from personal experience to the battle for campaign finance reform" (New York Times 2000).[8]

McCain was no pauper. He raised US$21 million in 1999 through a combination of fund-raising, money transferred from his Arizona senatorial campaign and federal matching funds (CNN 1999). His fund-raising efforts disqualify him, therefore, from being considered a marginal political actor in the sense meant by Delli Carpini and Williams. Nonetheless, John McCain represents a good example of how someone with a *relative* disadvantage in financial resources (remember Bush raised close to $70 million in 1999) can become a legitimate political contender by turning stores of cultural and symbolic capital to their advantage. His success was linked to, but not necessarily determined by, economic capital. The McCain team had creatively integrated the melodrama of popular culture with on-the-ground political strategies and fund-raising.

In 1999, celebrity developer Donald Trump flirted with the possibility of running for president; so did Hollywood-lady-killer-turned-political-activist Warren Beatty. Beatty toyed with the idea after being nominated by his friend Arianna Huffington, a celebrity journalist in her own right in Los Angeles. Beatty was the star and director of *Bulworth,* the 1998 movie about a politician who decides to reinvent himself by telling the truth. The actor, who once played the male lead in *Bonnie and Clyde,* used his celebrity to call for the Democrats to renew their commitment to liberal values in a September 1999 speech. The talk, part satire and part political activism, was delivered at a fund-raising dinner of the Southern California Americans for Democratic Action, an action group on the left of the Democratic party. Beatty and Trump were able to dally in the world of politics because of the promotional draw of their celebrity. However, unlike action-movie star Arnold Schwarzenegger who in 2003 successfully joined a recall ballot to replace California Governor Gray Davis, neither man actually took a real step toward high office.

A pop-culture icon who did make the successful leap to electoral politics is Jesse "the Body" Ventura. The former professional wrestler was elected governor of Minnesota in 1998. A past winner of the World Wrestling Federation Tag Team Championship, Ventura was a bad-boy wrestler with a penchant for wearing pink feather boas. "Governor Body," as Ventura has described himself, epitomized the promotional logic at the heart of the integrated news spectacle. A former Navy SEAL in Vietnam, Ventura has also worked as a bouncer, provided security for the Rolling Stones, hosted a shock-jock call-in radio program, provided commentary for Wrestlemania II through VIII, and costarred alongside Schwarzenegger in the movie *Predator.* During the campaign, Ventura was able to draw upon these different personas to embellish his populist credentials and deflect criticism. Ventura continued to embellish his credentials while governor by moonlighting as a commentator for the now-defunct Extreme Football League (XFL). Apparently running a state is not a full-time job.

Ventura is a commodity-sign in the sense meant by Andrew Wernick (1991: 15–16). He was produced by the entertainment industry as an object of spectacular display. At the same time, "the Body" acts as an advertisement for himself. The populist governor even had his own action-figure doll (originally produced in the 1980s during his time as a wrestler), a version of which appeared in one of his campaign television advertisements. In the TV ad, the miniature Ventura does battle with evil "Special Interests Man" and "Lobbyist Man" (Cass 1999: 68). Ventura, literally and figuratively, "embodies" the promotional logic of the integrated spectacle.

The wrestler's political capital is related to his credentials as an aestheticized figure from popular culture. Ventura defeated his Democratic and Republican opponents, neither of whom took him seriously, even though together they raised $4.3-million dollars for their campaigns. In contrast, Ventura rejected contributions of more than $50 and spent $250,000. Exit polls indicated that many of the people who cast ballots for Ventura would not have otherwise voted. In fact, voter turnout in Minnesota that year was twice the national average. Ventura did particularly well with young men under 30. His penchant for quoting dead rock-music legends such as the Door's Jim Morrison and Jerry Garcia of the Grateful Dead apparently resonated with young males (Fisher 1998; Glynn 2000: 237), as did his famous line from *Predator:* "I ain't got time to bleed." The quip eventually became the title of the governor's autobiography.

What was behind Ventura's success? Kevin Glynn argues that Ventura's iconoclastic populism resonated precisely because it mocked the "power-bloc" of official elite culture.

> I want to claim that Ventura's political substance lies partly though significantly in his style—a style that is as tabloidized as any: sensationally populist, ironically playful, laughingly skeptical, wildly outrageous, sometimes self-mocking and sometimes self-satisfied, inclusive and participatory, blusterous and averse to euphemism, scandalous, offensive, and in your face. (Glynn 2000: 241)

Ventura's quasilibertarian election platform was without a written tax plan. He talked in broad terms about returning the state's budget surplus back to the people.[9] Ventura's brand of populism defended gay rights, he was pro-choice on abortion, he pondered whether to legalize prostitution, he talked of the need to legalize marijuana and speculated about the possibility of catching JFK's real killers (Cass 1999: 67). Needless to say, Ventura is a fan of Hollywood director Oliver Stone. "He possessed," writes Dennis Cass, "a Reagan-like ability to make his critics sound like nitpicking elitists" (67). Ventura accomplished this effect through his deft use of popular culture and vernacular rhetoric. "The Body's" campaign theme music was "the title track from the blaxploitation classic *Shaft,*" a choice that Glynn suggests "reflects the power and resource imbalance between himself and his opponents" (Glynn 2000: 235). When reporters questioned whether his four-year term as mayor of the Minneapolis suburb of Brooklyn Park gave him the qualifications to be governor, Ventura quipped: "What's the difference between a city and the state—it's just the amount of money. Instead of millions, you're dealing with billions" (67). In one television advertisement, Ventura posed as Rodin's "The Thinker," this after he had jokingly renamed himself "The Mind" (Fisher 1998).

Ventura's credentials as a bonafide media star conferred upon him a great deal of cultural and symbolic capital. He used these resources to mobilize public support among a populist faction of the public. As Bourdieu says, "the power of a discourse depends less on its intrinsic properties than on the mobilizing power it exercises—that is, at least to some extent, on the degree to which it is *recognized* by a numerous and powerful group that can recognize itself in it and whose interests it expresses" (Bourdieu 1991: 188).[10] Ventura even had an amateur Web designer create a site that helped mobilize volunteers and thousands of voters for a series of last-minute rallies (Neal 1999).

Once again, Vice President Al Gore, ever the savvy opportunist, was ready to tap into the Ventura narrative. In March 2000, the usually wooden Gore appeared with Ventura in Minneapolis for a photo-op in which both politicians wore black shirts, blue jeans and cowboy boots. The performance was a mixture of brand extension and brand differentiation. The vice president, an admitted policy wonk, noted the governor's boots were tan ostrich, while his were black leather. True to form, Ventura told reporters the ostrich hid the dirt. Gore responded: "That makes them cooler." Ostensibly, the meeting was scheduled to talk about their mutual interest in campaign-finance reform (Seelye 2000). It is more fruitful, perhaps, to view it as an attempt to tap into a particularly potent populist narrative. Jesse Ventura, in his dual role as popular entertainer and politician, represents a complex distillation of cultural, economic, and symbolic power. Governor Body was a promotional fulcrum point, for himself and for others. He would later offer his sage political advice to Arnold Schwarzenegger, whose status as an object of spectacular display drew enormous media attention to California's recall campaign.

### Autonomy, Professionalism, and the Performance of Politics

In the political field certain narratives are favored over others. Because the political field is partially structured by the promotional logic of the integrated spectacle, there is a bias towards those narratives that are homologous with that promotional system and the specific needs of integrated news-media organizations. News media favor simplified storytelling. This is not a novel state of affairs, to say the least; but with the onset of 24-hour cable news, this requirement has taken on revivified importance. Narratives that can be turned into long-running "never-ending" stories, such as Monicagate, become central to strategies of capital accumulation for news organizations. These stories make possible the efficient operation of promotionally integrated news organizations. As promotional fulcrum points they also become sites of struggle among competing social actors. The result is that some narratives are more equal than others; that is, some fit the requirements of news media, while other more complicated stories do not. There is enormous incentive to provide news media with the kinds of dramatic performances and stories they crave. The pressure to do so forms a basic condition of entry into the commercially mediated sphere of political discourse.

That is not to say that narrative types do not predate commercial media. These stories also meet the standards established by the professional culture of journalism. The populist narratives used by Senator John McCain and Governor Jesse Ventura can be read as dual versions of the Hero myth—the man born into humble circumstances who goes forth on a quest, and wins a victory to return home triumphant (Lule 2001: 82). Stories of rugged individualists who act, sometimes defiantly, in the name of the common man and woman appear under various guises in popular fiction, movies, and television. The John McCain and Jesse Ventura narratives are simply given different inflections; one is the stolid warrior-patriot, the other the brash, if cartoonlike, working-class hero. These narratives are easily identified and understood by audiences across gender and racial cleavages. And, like the Diana and Monicagate narratives, they can be easily reproduced by reporters for whom these stories are practically second nature. Additionally, in the case of Ventura, his brand of libertarianism (pro-choice on abortion, supportive of gay rights, pro–tax cuts), resonates powerfully within a consumer culture that promises total freedom of choice. This fact surely comes to the chagrin of social conservatives, for whom Ventura arguably embodies the "cultural contradictions of capitalism" bemoaned by Daniel Bell (1976).

Bourdieu argues that the "journalistic field, which is more and more dominated by the market model, imposes its pressures more and more on other fields" (Bourdieu 1998: 56). The need to attract audiences and the daily grind of competition impose a discipline on journalism and other fields related to journalism, such as politics. I have argued this point myself, throughout the book, by situating promotional media events within a broader economic, social, and historical context. I have suggested that the *link* between popular culture, journalism, and politics—what makes these fields of social interaction homologous—is the promotional logic of the integrated spectacle. It is the logic of the integrated spectacle that makes both John McCain and Jesse "the Body" Ventura transposable pop icons that can easily slide among the fields of culture, journalism and politics. Along with Bourdieu we can say that "certain kinds of habitus find the conditions of their realization, indeed of their blossoming, in the logic of the apparatus; and, conversely, that the logic of the apparatus 'exploits' for its own profit tendencies that are inscribed in the different kinds of habitus" (Bourdieu 1991: 200). The Monicagate, McCain and Ventura texts were produced as promotional cultural texts; at the same time, they were reified and made subject to rational organization and control.

I have accepted Bourdieu's contention that political performances are doubly determined. Political professionals must meet the standards and expectations established by the rules of the political game. These rules, I have suggested, are heavily influenced by the logic of the integrated spectacle. On the other hand, politicians must appeal to the public and mobilize a sizable political constituency. It is the willing recognition offered by a sizable public constituency that confers symbolic power upon political actors. These actors, and the social movements to which they are sometimes attached, lose autonomy to the extent that there is a disconnect between the interests of political professionals and the interests of those being represented. In other words, autonomy is lost when political representatives pursue the separate interests imposed on them by the structure and logic of the political field as opposed to satisfying the interests of those whom they represent.

It is clear that Jesse Ventura's political performance was able to tap into the tools of "perception and expression" available in the fields of culture, journalism and politics. The Ventura performance resonated with a well-spring of populist sympathies in Minnesota. Notwithstanding these points, Glynn's celebration of the "counterhege-monic" potential of the Ventura style of politics goes too far. To say, as Glynn does, that Ventura's articulation and rearticulation of popular images and ideological rep-resentations gave rise to a newly emergent social movement (241) grossly "exaggerates the radical character" of tabloid forms of representation (Thompson 2000: 244). As John Thompson argues in his analysis of political scandals, post-structural theory (of the kind practiced by Glynn) goes overboard with claims of popular culture's ability to engage in political subversion.

First, it fails to adequately acknowledge that while Ventura thumbed his nose at the so-called elite power bloc in the name of "the people," he did so as a result of his privileged position within a commercially organized and funded media system. "Gov-ernor Body" owed his political capital to his high level of integration within consumer culture, not to the resources of an established political party. Second, as Thompson argues, the "broad opposition between 'the people' and the 'power-bloc' is a breath-takingly simple way of viewing the nature and organization of power in contemporary society." It excludes an understanding of the multiple forms of power and complex ways it can be exercised (Thompson 2000: 243).

Todd Gitlin, in his groundbreaking book *The Whole World Is Watching,* describes in great detail how the New Left antiwar movement of the 1960s eventually was un-done by its overreliance on a mass media that was fully integrated with the logic of consumer culture. Movement representatives that best met the imposed needs of the news media were able to climb the leadership ladder. These were people savvy in the ways of media articulation, theatrics, and sound bites. Yippies Abbie Hoffman and Jerry Rubin are perhaps the two best examples of movement representatives who be-came media stars. The reliance on celebrity representatives, argues Gitlin, created new vulnerabilities. Representatives could rise to national prominence without being held accountable to a movement base. "The celebrity leaders were squeezed into a situation of contradictory logics as they tried to serve the media and their constituencies at once. At any given moment, one or the other had to be sacrificed" (Gitlin 1980: 162). Gitlin concludes that the New Left was undermined because its leadership started "thinking like promoters, specialists in headlines. . . . The pace of events, the rush of mass-mediated, distanced, and distorted experience, helped disorient the movement, deprive it of a sense of political context" (235). The movement's core values of egali-tarianism and consensus came into conflict with the cults-of-personality constructed by the celebrity system.

We are confronted with a double bind. The political and journalistic fields are extensively integrated with the promotional logic of the spectacle. Under these circumstances, is it possible for social actors to enter the political field to play the game of politics and remain autonomous of the integrated promotional system? My answer is a heavily qualified yes. If social actors wish to reach a broader constituency within civil society, they must enter the political field. This means they become subject to the logic of the integrated news spectacle. However, there are opportunities for progressive politics within the integrated news spectacle. Social actors are able to *use* the resources at their disposal to pursue their own particular interests, but they do so under circumstances not of their own choosing.

# CHAPTER SIX

# The Integrated Spectacle of War

*I have invited my fellow documentary nominees on the stage with us. They're here in
solidarity with me because we like nonfiction. We like nonfiction, yet we live in fictitious
times. We live in a time where we have fictitious election results that elect a fictitious
president. We live in a time where we have a man sending us to war for fictitious reasons.
Whether it's the fiction of duct tape, or the fiction of orange alerts. We are against this
war, Mr. Bush. Shame on you, Mr. Bush, shame on you. And any time you got the Pope
and the Dixie Chicks against you, your time is up. Thank you very much.*
MICHAEL MOORE, UPON ACCEPTING THE ACADEMY AWARD FOR BEST
DOCUMENTARY FEATURE, MARCH 23, 2003

### Shock and Awe

On March 21, 2003, millions of television viewers around the world watched the
night sky light up over Baghdad as U.S. and British forces rained close to 1500 bombs
and cruise missiles down on the ancient Iraqi capital. One could be forgiven for
thinking the focus of news coverage would be on the plight of civilians frantically taking what shelter they could find from the bombardment. Such was not the case. The
aerial attack was the beginning of a much-anticipated military spectacle dubbed
"Shock and Awe." Reporters, both in Baghdad and those safely tucked in their network studios, were bursting with excitement. "The sky is lit up, Tom!" shouted veteran war correspondent Peter Arnett to NBC News anchor Tom Brokaw. "Just like
out of an action movie, but this is real, this is real, this is shock and awe, Tom!"
Brokaw took his cue. "The overture is over," he replied. "This is the main piece"
(Rosenthal 2003a). Jingoistic U.S. cable leader Fox News would not to be outdone.

"It's fascinating and amazing," enthused conservative host Brit Hume, "to see this with the lights on in Baghdad" (Barnhart 2003). CBS took a few minutes before the network broke from its NCAA basketball coverage, but once it had made the switch, channel surfers looking for a sense of the potential human cost of the attack would be similarly frustrated. CBS News anchor Dan Rather did feel the need to comment on what he thought was the "somewhat historic" nature of waging war "when we have 24-hours-a-day" media coverage worldwide. In contrast, a less spectacular attack on one of Saddam Hussein's palaces two days earlier—the object of Brokaw's overture remark—received less glowing reviews. "If You Have to Ask, It's Not 'Shock and Awe,'" read a graphic on Fox News. "It could be called 'Shock and Pause,'" said NBC reporter Jim Miklaszewski (Rosenthal 2003b). Although Dan Rather, known for his over-the-top one-liners, could not contain his own enthusiasm, comparing the air raid with "the rocket's red glare, and bombs bursting in air" (Houston 2003a). Rather's corny patriotism notwithstanding, the lack of "awe" generated from the earlier, and much smaller, air raid had left broadcasters with a palpable sense of disappointment. They had been primed for a full-blown spectacle, a performance that, in their view, had not been delivered. So when it finally *came,* as they had promised viewers it would, they could not contain themselves.

The now-infamous branding slogan first gained public notoriety in January when CBS News aired a report by correspondent David Martin. The story contained information leaked by unidentified Pentagon sources who confirmed that "Shock and Awe" was indeed the label given to the attack plans being prepared for the anticipated invasion of Iraq. Alongside a "Showdown with Saddam" logo that was set against an American flag and a combination gunsight/radar-screen graphic, Martin told viewers that "Shock and Awe" is predicated on a spectacular, and overwhelming, display of military might aimed at destroying an opponent's will to fight. It centers on the psychological intimidation of the enemy and downplays the need for traditional military ground forces. The concept is associated with Harlan Ullman, coauthor of the book titled *Shock and Awe: Achieving Rapid Dominance.* Ullman acknowledges his debt to famed military strategists Sun Tzu and Carl von Clausewitz, both of whom wrote about the importance of extinguishing an adversary's will to fight. What makes Ullman's use of the concept unique is its attachment to an integrated information environment that combines high-speed technological surveillance, communication, and spectacular display.

> Battlefield awareness requires three information technologies: collection, fusion, and dissemination of real-time actionable information to a shooter. Rapid Dominance requires an unprecedented level of real-time information collection. . . . It would be hard to overstate the importance of information dissemination within Rapid Dominance. Administering Shock and Awe requires a spectrum of attacks that the adversary is unable to fathom. (Ullman and Wade 1996)

If successful, Ullman told Martin, there would be no ground war involving large-scale tank battles, as was the case in the 1991 Gulf War, and fewer lives would be lost (Martin 2003). The aestheticized discourse of "Shock and Awe" promises the "surgical" use of "smart bombs" and other weaponry in order to create a strong psychological effect while minimizing the material destruction of military and civilian infrastructure. War without blood. That is to say, viewers at home would not be exposed to blood, especially American blood. The online version of the story contained a personal note from anchor Dan Rather, who reassured the public that the report contained no information that the Defense Department thought could help the Iraqi military.

There were two intended audiences for the discourse: foreign military adversaries and their civilian populations, and domestic citizens. "Shock and Awe" is designed to strike fear in the enemy, while at the same time reassure those on the home front concerned about the carnage of war. The phrase was quickly added to the popular lexicon. A flood of trademark applications for the term began to appear for products and services ranging from teddy bears and ski boots to men's and women's underwear. Sony backed off plans to market a "Shock and Awe" video game following accusations of war profiteering (BBC News Online 2003a; Harper's 2003).

"Shock and Awe" is simultaneously a battle strategy and an ideological discourse connected to what military strategists call the "Revolution in Military Affairs" (RMA), or as Kevin Robins and Frank Webster prefer, "Information Warfare" (1999). Robins and Webster contrast Information Warfare with Industrial Warfare to highlight the heightened importance information and communication technologies play in the rational administration and control of warfare. They admit that the use of information has always been an integral part of warfare. Nonetheless, Robins and Webster argue that important differences exist. First, in the modern industrial period, roughly from the First World War through to the Vietnam War, warfare involved the mobilization of large elements of the general population with a commitment to total warfare. Since the end of the Vietnam War, citizens have become more apprehensive about sanctioning large-scale human casualties. As a result, it has become more difficult to mobilize an entire society for war—both in terms of shifting industrial production from domestic to military products and in the curtailment of the consumption of everyday goods and luxury items. Meanwhile, a shift has occurred, particularly following the collapse of the Soviet Union, toward what Manuel Castells calls "Instant Wars." These are relatively short-lived conflicts that are waged without conscription by professional forces, and that rely upon technological improvements in weaponry and information management to limit public knowledge of the material and human consequences of battle (Robins and Webster 1999: 154–157; Castells 2000a: 486). The 1991 Gulf War, it is argued, provided the most fully developed example. Power was in effect operationalized, not simply by brute military force and large-scale industrial production, but through administrative surveillance—the monitoring of enemy forces and domestic political opposition—and spectacular display.

Well-trained, well-equipped, full-time, professional armed forces do not require the involvement of the population at large in the war effort, except for viewing and cheering from their living rooms a particularly exciting show, punctuated with deep patriotic feelings. (Castells 2000a: 486)

In a sense, the "Gulf War did not happen" for most viewers of the war spectacle—to borrow Baudrillard's well-known line—that is, when compared to women who gained their first work experience in factories during the Second World War, and who, while waiting for their husbands, sons, and brothers to return from abroad, went without many everyday comforts. The mediated version of the war was experienced at a distance through self-referential discourses, such as Shock and Awe.

The use of perception management by nation-states is not, of course, particularly novel. And we must be cautious not to overstate the extent of the historical shift represented by the so-called RMA. After all, as John Downey and Graham Murdock remind us, the use of information contained in maps was integral to the swift movement of Napoleon's forces in the early-19th century, while "the stubborn persistence of core features, and failures of Industrial Warfare" remain (Downey and Murdock 2003: 75). Technology fails, humans make errors, and people still die in large numbers, particularly those unfortunate enough to be the target of the world's only superpower. The Associated Press estimated that 3,240 civilians perished from the war's beginning March 20 to the end of large-scale military conflict on April 20 (Bedway 2003). A running tally by the Web site iraqbodycount.net, which used a different methodology, more than doubles that estimate. Notwithstanding these warnings, I want to argue that spectacular narrative forms such as "Shock and Awe" are constitutive of the political field. These narratives are fully integrated into military, government, and corporate public-relations campaigns along with the daily production regimes of mainstream news media, particularly 24-hour cable news channels.

The experience of warfare is, for a majority of Western citizens, limited to spectacle. Western liberal democracies require the support of public opinion to wage war. The bulk of the population is mobilized, not as soldiers and producers of war armaments, but as "spectators of war," who are sold on the rightness of battle in the name of sacred universal values. Citizens are told the so-called War Against Terrorism is undertaken in the name of security, democracy, freedom, and human rights, not to secure vital oil interests. The Manichean struggle between good and evil was engaged, not only on the battlefield (or in "battlespace," as proponents of RMA prefer), but also through the spectacle of dramatic narrative forms. America—a "target of hate because of its freedoms"—takes on "evildoers" in a just global struggle that will require eternal vigilance and flexibility of response. "Perception management," conducted by war-time governments, says Frank Webster, "must therefore attempt to combine ways of ensuring a continuous stream of media coverage that is positive and yet ostensibly freely gathered by independent news agencies" (Webster 2003: 64). Governments need to appear to practice what they preach. Perception management of this type is achieved most efficiently by tapping into the resources made available to political actors by the integrated news spectacle. My argument is that the administration of George W. Bush enjoyed an enormous amount of political success packaging and selling the America-led invasion of Iraq under the rubric of the "War on Terror" narrative by making deft use of those resources.

### Branding War

September 11 was a spectacular example of "mass-mediated terrorism," planned and executed to attract media interest in order to further a political agenda (Nacos 2002). It was also the promotional fulcrum point for a host of major policy initiatives from the Bush administration, including arguments justifying the U.S. invasion of Iraq. From the beginning, the events of September 11 and the declared war on terror were invoked as justification for the Bush doctrine of "preemptive military strikes." As Douglas Kellner makes clear, the Manichean logic used by Bush, and he correctly adds, radical Islamists, rhetorically empowers those who wield it with a flexibility of purpose. "This amorphous terrorist Enemy. . . allows the crusader for Good to attack any country or group that is supporting terrorism, thus promoting a foundation for a new doctrine of preemptive strikes and perennial war" (Kellner 2003a). Part of the appeal of the discourse of terror, among those who would deploy it, is that it trumps international law that explicitly prohibits nation-states from engaging in unprovoked invasions. As one Fox News.com headline put it: "Why Now? A Better Question Is Why Wait?" (Adelman 2002). To be against the invasion of Iraq, following this logic, is to side with evil. It implies that one is callously willing to put the lives of one's fellow citizens at risk. It, in turn, conveniently brands opponents as unpatriotic.

The Bush administration tapped into America's newfound vulnerability to terror to push through a series of draconian security measures that stripped citizens of civil liberties and awarded powers of surveillance to the state previously thought intolerable. The USA Patriot Act, backed by the bureaucratic muscle of a new secretariat ominously named the Office of Homeland Security, gave the state power to eavesdrop on private phone and e-mail communications and detain citizens without warrants, all in the name of their own security. Color-coded terror alerts issued by the Homeland office soon became institutionalized, each warning receiving a ritual media response. Reports accusing police of misusing their authority began to accumulate, including abuse of prisoners and the creation of police databases containing names of people arrested during antiwar protests (McCool 2003; Shenon 2003). Bush would eventually cite the "national emergency" created by September 11 to justify his decision to limit scheduled pay increases for federal workers (King 2003).

The Bush administration was not alone in its desire to tap into the spectacle. Following September 11, Washington lobbyists wasted no time in connecting their pet issue to the tragedy. "No self-respecting lobbyist," said Democratic Representative Edward J. Markey, has failed to "repackage his position as a patriotic response to the tragedy." In one of the more ridiculous examples, the *New York Times* reported that the American Traffic Safety Service Association, whose members make traffic signs, petitioned the federal government for increased funding to install more signage. The reason offered was that they would prevent potential traffic jams after terror attacks (Rosenbaum 2001). Selling fear made good business sense. The *Guardian* newspaper quoted *PR Week* as offering this bit of advice: "The trick in 2002, say public affairs and budget experts, will be to redefine your pet issue or product as a matter of homeland security. . . . If you can convince Congress that your company's widget will strengthen America's borders, or that funding your client's pet project will make America less dependent on foreign resources, you just might be able to get what you're looking for" (Rampton and Stauber 2003).

Public-relations analysts Sheldon Rampton and John Stauber argue that while the Bush administration failed to convince the UN Security Council and other NATO allies such as Germany, France, and Canada to endorse its unilateral attack on Iraq, it enjoyed incredible success at home. "And a key component has been fear: fear of terrorism and fear of attack" (Rampton and Stauber 2003). Kellner has dubbed the strategy "Terror War" (Kellner 2003b).

Fear, according to Michael Hardt and Antonio Negri, is the glue that holds together the society of the spectacle.

> The society of the spectacle rules by wielding an age-old weapon. Hobbes recognized long ago that for effective domination 'the Passion to be reckoned upon, is Fear.' For Hobbes, fear is what binds and ensures social order, and still today fear is the primary mechanism of control that fills the society of the spectacle. (Hardt and Negri 2000: 323)

But the spectacle of war, and its corollary fear, does not simply intimidate and pacify citizens. At the heart of the spectacle is a promise to reunite what has been sundered, to return what is feared to have been lost; and this promise is resolved at the level of myth. Samuel Weber argues that "the spectacle" of terror and war, "at least as staged by the mainstream broadcast media, seeks simultaneously to assuage and exacerbate anxieties of all sorts by providing images on which anxieties can be projected, ostensibly comprehended, and above all *removed*" (Weber 2002: 457). That is why, he argues, it is imperative that the object of one's fear must be named and located. "In the images of catastrophe that dominate broadcast media 'news,' the disunity is projected into the image itself, while the desired unity is reserved for the spectator off-scene (and for the media itself as global network)" (455).

Again, there is no centralized "man behind the screen" whose job it is to manipulate the spectacle, although the spectacle's unity of appearance may give the impression that one exists. The integrated news spectacle is both concentrated and diffuse. It operates through the efforts of disparate social actors, some (governments and corporations) to be sure with more power than others, but each pursuing its own interests. What unifies them is their adaptation and use of the spectacle's logic. As for spectators, one might say, following Debord, that what unites them is the same thing that maintains their separateness from one another—the image of the spectacle.

CBS News reported September 4, 2002, that Defense Secretary Donald Rumsfeld told aides that he wanted them to draw up plans to attack Iraq a mere five hours after doomed American Airlines Flight 77 crashed into the Pentagon. The report by correspondent David Martin cited notes taken by aides who were with Rumsfeld on September 11. Despite intercepted phone calls, airline passenger manifests, and other information linking the Al Qaeda organization to the terror attacks, Rumsfeld reportedly insisted that attempts be made to connect Saddam Hussein to the suicide hijacking. "Go massive," he is said to have written, "Sweep it all up. Things related or not" (CBS News 2002). Rumsfeld's determination is all the more striking given that reports quoting CIA sources indicate two top-level Al Qaeda leaders had told U.S. interrogators, months prior to the invasion of Iraq, that their organization had no links with Saddam Hussein (Bruce 2003). A leaked British Intelligence Staff report had also cast doubt on any connection, suggesting that Al Qaeda's "aims are in ideological conflict with present-day Iraq," itself a secular dictatorship (Rangwala and Whitaker 2003). Moreover, hawks within the Bush administration had been pushing for an American military presence in the Persian Gulf region prior to the September 11 attacks in order to secure American strategic interests, including oil supplies. The policy was contained in a well-publicized 2000 report prepared for the Project for a New American Century—a neoconservative think tank whose members include Vice President Dick Cheney, Defense Secretary Donald Rumsfeld, and Deputy Secretary of Defense Paul Wolfowitz.[1] The terror attacks in New York and Washington simply provided the administration with a useful promotional hook for a long-standing desire, on the part of senior administration officials, for a military presence in the region via "regime change" in Iraq.[2]

As Kellner indicates, the dominant media frame following September 11 characterized the attack as an act of war that required a swift military response. The merits of alternative, nonviolent policy responses were minimized. Discussion of how historical context, including the U.S. military presence in Saudi Arabia, and past American funding of Islamic fundamentalist groups, might have played a role in sowing the seeds of Al Qaeda was discouraged and readily condemned as "blaming the victim." Fox News led the charge among cable networks. On September 13, only two days after the tragedy, the host of the network's leading prime-time program, *The O'Reilly Factor*, admonished the former Clinton administration for security lapses and pinned blame for the actual attack on Saddam Hussein. His Republican guests Jeane Kirkpatrick and Newt Gingrich agreed (Kellner 2003b: 59). Credible evidence for either charge was not presented.

The die was cast in January 29, 2002, when President Bush used the State of the Union address to include Iraq, along with Iran and Stalinist North Korea, as a member of the "Axis of Evil." All three "rogue states," argued Bush, possessed "weapons of mass destruction" (WMD) and presented a threat to American security. Osama bin Laden and the Al Qaeda movement were not mentioned. The protean quality of "rogue" states allowed for the construction of an abstract form of secularized evil for which there are no historical "root causes." Unlike more civilized nation-states, rogues do not pursue rational interests. As Weber argues, these states and their leaders are defined as pathological, "whose roguishness consists in their refusal to follow the norms of international behaviour as laid down by the United States government" (Weber 2002: 456). By now international law had been relegated to an arbitrary "opt-in" status by the U.S. administration. A year later in his January 28, 2003, State of the Union speech, Bush made clear his administration's intentions regarding "regime change" in Iraq: "A brutal dictator, with a history of reckless aggression . . . with ties to terrorism . . . with great potential wealth . . . will not be permitted to dominate a vital region and threaten the United States."

### Weapons of Mass Distraction

The 2003 State of the Union address contained a now infamous 16-word sentence that raised the specter of a nuclear mushroom cloud: "The British government has learned that Saddam Hussein recently sought significant quantities of uranium from Africa." The now thoroughly discredited story—based on forged documents, and dismissed as unsubstantiated by CIA intelligence—returned to haunt the president in the months following the occupation of Iraq. The administration eventually was forced to concede it should never have been in the speech. It had also been revealed that the British report cited by Bush contained plagiarized portions of a graduate-student paper lifted from the Internet. What is clear, however, is that this claim, along with a series of dicey allegations tied to the terror narrative of September 11, was used as justification for swift action to topple the Hussein regime.

Following the State of the Union address, Bush and his British ally, Prime Minister Tony Blair, cranked up the rhetoric of fear in order to win public approval for an invasion. "If you leave Saddam Hussein with his chemical, biological and potentially nuclear weapons," said Blair on February 21, "the link between that and international terrorism is so obvious that it hardly needs to be stated." Speaking from Rome, Blair went further and assured reporters that a link between Saddam Hussein and Al Qaeda was not part of the distant past, but was becoming stronger. "It's probably true historically going back some years, the links between Al Qaeda and Iraq probably weren't very significant. But it is also true that increasingly over the past period of time there is greater evidence of that" (Darlington 2003). Blair, whose policy faced ferocious opposition within his own Labour Party, went on famously to suggest that these WMD could be deployed in 45 minutes. The discredited claim was repeated twice by President Bush, in a White House Rose Garden appearance and in a September 2002 radio address (Milbank 2003). "Is it really smart to wait until after Saddam goes nuclear to entice other states to join in?" questioned Kenneth Adelman, a Fox News commentator, former assistant to U.S. Secretary of Defense Donald Rumsfeld and U.S. ambassador to the United Nations under President Ronald Reagan. "Is that the ideal time for American troops to go in? It would seem a lot smarter and safer to act before the world's vilest ruler gets a hold of the world's vilest weapon" (Adelman 2003).

In the time leading up to the March invasion, the U.S. and British governments staged a series of performances designed to win over international and domestic public opinion. One highlight came February 5, when U.S. Secretary of State Colin Powell made the case for war to members of the U.N. Security Council. Powell waved a vial of yellow powder in the air during his address, frightening some in attendance who worried it might actually contain traces of anthrax. Powell claimed the vial symbolized the deadly toxins the Hussein regime had in its possession. The 80-minute presentation, which included blurry satellite photos of ammunition storage bunkers alleged to contained chemical weapons, received glowing reviews from most of the mainstream U.S. media. "Powell masterfully choreographed an accessible, reasoned and relentless assault on Iraq and its role in befriending terrorists and producing and hiding weapons of mass destruction," wrote attorney Andrew Cohen for CBSNews.com (Cohen 2003). Powell used his performance, broadcast live by CNN, to outline the U.S. case that Iraq presented a clear and present danger to the world community. Cohen readily compared Powell's address to diplomatic theater, but most stunning perhaps is his admission that the presentation contained no proof: "If he did not prove that Iraq has active weapons of mass destruction, he certainly proved that Iraq is *acting* [my emphasis] like it has weapons of mass destruction. . . . No smoking gun? So what." High standards indeed for the justification of war leading to the deaths of thousands of people. A less-charitable review came from veteran Canadian foreign-affairs columnist Eric Margolis, who called Powell's proof "smoke and mirrors" (Margolis 2003). What received less media attention was a "dirty tricks" campaign launched by the United States against U.N. Security Council delegations. Britain's *Observer* cited a leaked memo written by a National Security Agency official that indicated the delegations of Angola, Cameroon, Chile, Mexico, Guinea, and Pakistan had their phone and e-mail bugged and intercepted. It was all part of an unsuccessful attempt to win the necessary votes in the Security Council to sanction the invasion (Bright, Vulliamy, and Beaumont 2003).

Efforts made to connect Saddam Hussein to September 11 and portray him as an immediate threat to world peace were hypocritical and riddled with potential conflicts of interest. Ignored by the White House in its march to war was the troublesome fact that Hussein's acquisition and use of WMD in its war with Iran had been supported by the U.S. George Schultz, the former secretary of state under Ronald Reagan, added his voice to the prowar chorus in an op-ed piece for the *Washington Post.* Schultz, chairman of the prowar Committee for the Liberation of Iraq, argued there was an urgent need to not only remove Saddam Hussein, but to start "a multilateral effort to rebuild Iraq after he is gone" (Herbert 2003a). Schultz is a past president and current board member of the Bechtel Group, a San Francisco–based construction giant with strong ties to the Republican Party. The Bush administration awarded Bechtel, whose vice president, Jack Sheehan, also sits as a member of the government-appointed Defense Policy Board, a construction contract worth up to US$680 million (Herbert 2003b). Halliburton, the Texas oil company where Vice President Dick Cheney was CEO during the late 1990s, won contracts worth more than US$1.7 billion. The Bechtel and Halliburton deals were part of an increasing trend by the U.S. government to contract out overseas support operations (Dobbs 2003). Moreover, an executive order signed by President Bush on May 22 appeared to grant U.S. oil companies operating in Iraq blanket immunity to civil and criminal liability (Girion 2003). The charge was denied by the White House.

Bush's dubious 16 words linking Iraq to Al Qaeda became the focus of many skeptical stories in the American media beginning in July, but it was clear the statement was only a part of a much larger campaign. A lengthy account of the events published August 10 in the *Washington Post* concluded "the danger of a nuclear-armed Saddam Hussein" used as "an argument for war" started with weak evidence that "grew weaker still in the three months before the war" (Gellman and Pincus 2003). Britain's *Independent* compiled a list of what it called "20 Lies about the War," which it published July 13 (Rangwala and Whitaker 2003). In addition to the claim that Iraq maintained links with Al Qaeda, the paper listed 19 other discredited assertions including: that Iraq had tried to obtain aluminum tubes suitable for nuclear weapons, that previous weapons inspections had failed, and that British and U.S. claims were supported by U.N. weapons inspectors, a contention contradicted on numerous occasions (Irving and Whitaker 2003).

On January 27, 2003, the day before Bush's presidential address on the State of the Union, the head of the International Atomic Energy Agency (IAEA) told the United Nations Security Council that, after a two-month search, investigators had discovered that no nuclear activities were conducted at Iraq's former nuclear sites. When Mohammed El Baradei delivered his final report to the Security Council on March 18, he reaffirmed the earlier findings and concluded that no further evidence had been found that Iraq had revived its nuclear-weapons program (Pincus 2003). But it wasn't until July 8, roughly two months after the toppling of the Saddam Hussein regime, that the Bush administration retreated from the African uranium-purchase statement and admitted it should never have been included in the address.

The WMD that Blair and Bush had claimed could be deployed in 45 minutes had not been found. "It is sort of puzzling," said the U.N.'s former chief weapons inspector Hans Blix, "that you can have 100 percent certainty about weapons of mass destruction, and zero certainty about where they are" (Van Rijn 2003). Perhaps most telling, wrote columnist Lawrence Martin, is that Hussein never used WMD when faced with certain defeat. "This makes a mockery of the stated American reason for the aggression—that with his 'deadly' arsenal, he was an immediate threat" (Martin 2003). The White House would later lay blame for the nettlesome 16-word sentence on the shoulders of CIA director George Tenet, who conceded it was his responsibility. Allegations that the "Dodgy Dossier," as it was known in the British press, had been torqued by communication staff had thrown the BBC into a protracted row with the Blair government. The government leveled counter-charges at the BBC, saying the public broadcaster had itself inflated claims that the dossier had been "sexed up." The BBC's principal source on the story eventually killed himself after facing a heated public grilling by a parliamentary committee. A House of Commons committee eventually cleared the government of charges that it deliberately tampered with evidence, while insisting its handling of the information caused Blair to unknowingly misinform Parliament. Across the Atlantic, similar allegations were made by former diplomatic and intelligence officials, who pointed out the Africa yellowcake story was bogus (Buncombe and Woolf 2003; Wilson 2003). Bush's first impulse was to employ unintended irony: "I know there's a lot of revisionist history now going on, but one thing is certain," Bush said. "He [Hussein] is no longer a threat to the Free World, and the people of Iraq are free" (Allen 2003).

By July 2003, reasons for the invasion were in flux. "The coalition did not act in Iraq because we had discovered dramatic new evidence of Iraq's pursuit of weapons of mass murder," Rumsfeld testified before the U.S. Senate Armed Services Committee. "We acted because we saw the evidence in a dramatic new light, through the prism of our experience on 9/11" (Boyd 2003). It was a curious reversal for Rumsfeld who pronounced in January that: "There's no doubt in my mind but that they [the Iraqi government] currently have chemical and biological weapons" (Boyd 2003). Only three days before the invasion began Vice President Dick Cheney appeared on NBC's *Meet the Press* saying: "We know he's been absolutely devoted to trying to acquire nuclear weapons, and we believe he has, in fact, reconstituted nuclear weapons" (Pincus 2003). Bush would later tell reporters the United States decided to invade Iraq after he had offered Hussein "a chance to allow [weapons] inspectors in, and he wouldn't let them in." The false statement—inspectors had been in the country, but Bush had opposed letting them continue working—was passed over by most media with little comment (Priest and Milbank 2003).

The media brouhaha over whether or not the British and U.S. governments inflated the immediate risk to the world posed by Saddam Hussein erupted in the months following the occupation of Iraq—after the desired foreign-policy objective had been secured. There had been reports casting doubt on the evidence prior to the invasion (Dreyfuss 2002), but they were marginal to the dominant prowar news frame. The WMD saga is an example of what Curtis White (2003) calls the "New Censorship." Stories that challenge official commonsense understandings of the world are available in an information-saturated media environment. It wasn't the first time a government had used misleading information to win political and public support for a war. In 1964, a false report of an unprovoked attack on an American destroyer was used by President Lyndon Johnson to win congressional support to prosecute the war in Vietnam. In 1991, false testimony was given by a Kuwaiti diplomat's daughter that Iraqi soldiers were taking babies out of incubators and leaving them to die. Both these lies were exposed after the fact and should have stood as reminders of how easy it is to manipulate media frames during times of military tension. Yet, in the post–September 11 political context, the use of terror as a promotional fulcrum point was stunningly successful. A social and cultural space had been negotiated in which challenging White House claims meant one risked being labeled unpatriotic. In a *New York Times*/CBS News poll, conducted over the weeks leading up to the invasion, 45 percent of respondents said Hussein was directly involved in the attacks. A second poll, conducted before the second anniversary of the September 11 attacks, found the number had increased. The *Washington Post* poll reported that nearly 7 in 10 respondents thought Hussein was involved in the attacks—a troublesome figure considering there is no evidence to support the opinion. A Knight Ridder poll reported that 44 percent of respondents believed that some of the September 11 hijackers were Iraqi citizens. No Iraqis were involved. (Feldmann 2003; Milbank and Deane 2003; Nagourney and Elder 2003). A more detailed survey conducted by researchers at the University of Maryland reported that audience misperceptions about Iraq-al Qaeda links varied significantly depending on their source of news. Americans "who receive most of their news from Fox News are more likely than average to have misperceptions. Those who receive most of their news from NPR or PBS are less likely to have misperceptions" (Kull 2003: 12). Information used to build support for war would be exposed as misleading, but only after the window of opportunity to intervene in policy implementation had passed. "While few shed tears for the exit of the murderous Saddam Hussein," wrote Joe Strupp in June 2003, "the press needs to remind the public that the war was sold to them not on the basis of 'regime change' but on the personal threat to Americans posed by Saddam's so-far-missing weapons" (Strupp 2003). Virtually all major U.S. newspapers backed Bush's decision to attack Iraq in their editorial pages.

## *Promoting Patriotism*

From the beginning, the invasion of Iraq was a cable-TV affair. Significantly, 70 percent of Americans polled reported they had relied on cable as their main source of news about the conflict. Ratings were great. Nielson data indicate that the number of average daily viewers had jumped 300 percent for CNN and MSNBC. Fox enjoyed a 288-percent spike (Sharkey 2003). The Pentagon was prepared. It understood the importance of television and contracted a designer who had worked for Disney, MGM, and *Good Morning America* to build a $250,000 studio for the daily media briefings. The first Gulf War made CNN a global leader in 24-hour news. In this conflict the all-news pioneer would not be alone. In addition to Fox and MSNBC, 24-hour competition for scoops came from Qatar-based Al Jazeera, which used the international reputation it first gained reporting on the Afghanistan conflict to pursue plans for an English-language Web site.

The war commodity is problematic; many sponsors, such as Proctor & Gamble, were worried that their brands could be damaged if associated with body bags (Cassy and Milmo 2003; Chunovic 2003). The U.S. networks had to forgo $77 million in advertising revenue in order to air commercial-free news during the first week of the conflict. The cable-news networks sacrificed roughly 71 percent of their weekly ad revenue. But after the initial "awe" had worn off, commercials returned (Beard 2003). Despite obvious financial hurdles, the spectacle of war is in the long-term interests of all-news networks seeking to extend their brand, and expand their audience. China's state-run China Central Television (CCTV) was openly trying to court some of the marketing magic enjoyed by CNN in 1991. CCTV-1, the network's main news channel, ran nonstop coverage on the first day of the war that carried video of advancing U.S. forces. Senior editors talked about the need to adopt Western professional standards of "objectivity" as a way of attracting and holding audiences in what was becoming an increasingly competitive global commercial-television market (Chang and Hutzler 2003). Military pundits would also do well. The expanded number of 24-hour cable outlets meant there was more need than ever for commentary. Whereas in 1999, retired generals provided opinion without pay, for the most part; by 2003 those same experts were striking lucrative, and exclusive, contracts with networks (Tugend 2003). The crucible of war coverage would also lend much-desired gravitas to ambitious reporters, such as CBS News correspondent Lara Logan—a former model—hoping to boost their careers.

The U.S. news media were in Iraq to cover the invasion, but they were also engaged in a vicious branding war, each network trying to project an image of itself as more patriotic than the competition. CNN and MSNBC were feeling the ratings pinch after watching the aggressively patriotic Fox News grab the top spot. Graphics with fluttering flags were ubiquitous, as were the words "we" and "us" when identifying U.S. military personnel. "The conveying of actual news often seems subsidiary to their mission to out-flag-wave one another and to make their own personnel, rather than the war's antagonists, the leading players in the drama," wrote Frank Rich in the *New York Times* (Rich 2003). Both MSNBC and Fox News branded their news coverage with the U.S. government's logo for the conflict: "Operation Iraqi Freedom." Fox allowed soldiers to go on camera and send personal messages to loved ones at home. MSNBC created a video-montage bumper in which still photos of military personnel were overlayed with the motto "May God bless America. Our hearts go with you" (Sharkey 2003). CNN boasted loudly after its medical correspondent, Sanjay Gupta, performed emergency brain surgery on a mortally injured young Iraqi boy. Gupta, an accomplished neurosurgeon, was traveling as an "embedded" reporter with a U.S.-military medical unit known as the "Devil Docs." What received less attention was news the boy , who didn't survive surgery, was among three people killed by U.S. Marines when they opened fire on a taxi passing through a checkpoint (MacDonald 2003). One of the more sensational moments in the branding war involved rivals MSNBC and Fox News. Both networks broadcast news items and promotional spots that took patriotic digs at each other. The promotions came after Fox's charismatic Geraldo Rivera ran afoul of the U.S. military by revealing troop locations when he drew a map in the sand while on camera. Veteran Peter Arnett, who had been filing reports for NBC, MSNBC, and National Geographic Explorer, was fired after granting an interview with Iraqi state TV. He had told the interviewer that President Bush was facing a "growing challenge" to the "conduct of the war" at home. At the time, this was factually correct, but by granting an interview that could be used by the Iraqi regime for propaganda purposes, he had opened himself up to attack. After running a story about Rivera's run in with the U.S. military, MSNBC broadcast a spot assuring its audience that it would never "compromise military security or jeopardize a single American life." Upset, Fox responded with its own spot that showed a portion of Arnett's Iraqi TV interview. "He spoke out against America's armed forces," said an announcer, "he said America's war against terrorism had failed; he even vilified America's leadership. And he worked for MSNBC" (Rutenberg 2003a).

On the morning of March 26, CNN led newscasts with a report that U.S. forces had killed 200 Iraqis in a large land battle. That same day, at least 15 Iraqi civilians died after an apparent U.S. bombing of a Baghdad marketplace. The marketplace bombing was reported, but attention quickly faded among the U.S. networks. Coverage shifted to President Bush's visit to the MacDill Air Force Base near Tampa, Florida. The trip was billed as a morale booster for troops one week into the war. "If that rendition of the *Star-Spangled Banner* doesn't stir you, I don't know what will," said CNN's morning anchor Paula Zahn, after Bush was greeted by the singing of the anthem. Zahn would later win her own prime-time show on the strength of her performance during the conflict. Later that day, all the major news channels broadcast live a news briefing from central command's new studio in Qatar. "OK, so, a lot of negative questions there," said Fox's anchor. "But let's focus on the positive" (Burkeman et al. 2003).

Antiwar voices that challenged "Brand America" were hard to find before or during the conflict. Those people who did speak out faced a range of penalties, including threats, job loss, and arrest (Kenna 2003). With the exception of CNN's "Voices of Dissent," a segment created in the weeks leading up to the war, and later renamed "Arab Voices" after hostilities started, antiwar voices were largely absent. "Get the following production pieces in the studio NOW: . . . Patriotic music that makes you cry, salute, get cold chills! Go for the emotion," read a "War Manual" produced by McVay Media, a Cleveland-based broadcast media consultant. McVay advised clients to downplay protests against the war because they drive away viewers (Farhi 2003). One mass "die-in" staged by protesters in New York, was mocked by Fox News. A few blocks away, a message on the news ticker outside Fox's New York headquarters read: "War protester auditions here today . . . thanks for coming" (Cowen 2003). On another occasion, a Fox anchor referred to war protesters as "the great unwashed" (Rutenberg 2003b). The pro-war flack emanating from media organizations was extensive. Radio stations owned by Clear Channel Communications, the owner of close to 1,200 stations across the United States, organized rallies that endorsed the U.S. government's position against Iraq (Jones 2003). Country-music stations owned by the corporate giant, along with radio chain Cumulus Media, stopped playing songs by the popular Dixie Chicks after the group's lead singer, Natalie Maines, criticized President Bush while performing in London.

The usual support came from right-wing talk-radio hosts such as Rush Limbaugh; but there was one TV talk show that regularly included antiwar guests along with supporters of the Bush position. Veteran Phil Donahue had his show cancelled by MSNBC in February 2003, as the build up to war intensified. The official reason offered by MSNBC was that the program trailed Fox's *The O'Reilly Factor* by a wide margin. But while the program was badly behind in ratings for its time slot, it was still MSNBC's top-rated program, ahead of *Hardball with Chris Matthews*. A different reason was offered by Rick Ellis, a columnist with *All Your TV* Web site. Ellis claims he received a leaked internal report from NBC that argued Donahue would be a "difficult public face for NBC in a time of war" (Ellis 2003). MSNBC soon hired conservative radio talk-show host Michael Savage. His views on the war effort were unambiguous. In one program, Savage suggested war protesters were "committing sedition, or treason." On radio, Savage happily swept away hundreds of years of history when he offered his own subtle solution to the Middle East conflict: "We are the good ones and they, the Arabs, are the evil ones. They must be snuffed out from the planet and not in a court of law." Savage apparently went too far and was fired in July of that year after making homophobic remarks on air.

Commentators were now talking about a so-called Fox Effect, whereby CNN and MSNBC were trying to recapture lost market share by singing from the same patriotic song book as Fox (Rutenberg 2003b; Willis 2003). The near monopolization of the meaning of patriotism by Republican and prowar advocates was difficult to break through for anti-war protesters. In San Francisco, a hub of antiwar activity, counter-branding campaigns were launched to "reclaim" the flag using "Peace is Patriotic" bumper stickers (Salladay 2003). While media corporations were openly sponsoring pro-war rallies, one *San Francisco Chronicle* reporter was fired after it was learned he had participated in an anti-war rally on his own time. MSNBC correspondent Ashleigh Banfield, who had been feted by the network during its coverage of the conflict in Afghanistan, was reprimanded by her employer after telling students at Kansas State University that media coverage had not shown the full horrors of battle.

### In Bed with Militainment, 24/7

News organizations' desire to brand themselves as patriotic meshed nicely with the Pentagon's and the White House's desire to choreograph the invasion. "After September 11 the country wants more optimism and benefit of the doubt," said MSNBC President Erik Sorenson. "It's about being positive as opposed to being negative" (Rutenberg 2003b). CBS News President Andrew Heyward said he wanted audiences to know that he was "rooting for the U.S. to win the war" (Bednarski and Higgins 2003). Branding synergy between broadcasting media and the military was at the core of the media/military relationship. Careful attention was given by the Pentagon to make sure that their public-relation needs were integrated with the hour-by-hour organizational requirements of broadcasters. The goal was to produce dramatic and sympathetic stories about the troops. Their solution was to attach, or "embed," more than 600 reporters with specific military units. These reporters traveled 24 hours a day under the protection of the same soldiers they were supposed to write stories about. The decision met with condemnation and praise. Liberal critics worried that reporters would lose their prized "objectivity" while living, eating, and sleeping under the protection of their military keepers. Proponents such as Heyward argued professional distance was maintained. "We had total freedom to cover virtually everything we wanted to cover," claimed Chip Reid, an embedded reporter with NBC (Bauder 2003). Supporters also praised the ability of embedded reporters to bear direct witness to events, and recalled how journalists had been kept far from the battlefield in previous conflicts. "It broadened the lens on the battlefield," said Terence Smith, media correspondent for PBS (Kelley 2003). Others were more defensive. "Let them try not showering for a week, sleeping out in the desert, living through sandstorms, being under fire—I don't see these people out there," said embedded CBS correspondent John Roberts, speaking of critics of the program. "All they do is criticize" (Kurtz 2003a).

Reporters who chose to go it alone, the so-called unilaterals, were seen as a problem. Some unilaterals were harassed and detained by soldiers as they tried to move around the country (Houston 2003b; York 2003). During the advance into Baghdad, the main hotel housing journalists was shelled by U.S. tanks, killing two cameramen.

"It is in fact a brilliant, persuasive conspiracy to control the images and the messages coming out of the battlefield and they've succeeded colossally," un-embedded Canadian TV reporter Paul Workman concluded, when speaking of efforts to restrict the movement of journalists (Ward 2003). Stories by embedded reporters were also subject to censorship if they revealed information deemed sensitive by military overseers. Many commentators added that "embeds" could only see what military handlers allowed them to see.

American and British military media minders did try to restrict story frames to the governments' daily "message track." The lack of valuable information coming out of the daily briefings at the central-command media center in Doha, Qatar, was particularly frustrating. *New York Magazine* writer Michael Wolff captured a sentiment held by many journalists who were annoyed by the successful efforts to organize and control coverage.

> It takes about 48 hours to understand that information is probably more freely available at any other place in the world than it is here. At the end of the 48 hours you realize that you know significantly less than when you arrived, and that you're losing more sense of the larger picture by the hour. Eventually you'll know nothing. (Wolff 2003)

Reporters had complained during the conflict in Afghanistan about restrictions placed on their movement. Moreover, government communication teams were overwhelmed by the challenge of managing a 24-hour global news cycle. American and British media specialists responded during the Afghan conflict by creating Coalition Information Centers (CICs). With offices in Washington, London, and Islamabad, the centers coordinated the release of information and rebutted opposition allegations across time zones. The CICs were modeled on the so-called war rooms used in domestic political campaigns (DeYoung 2001; Stanley 2001b; Brown 2003). The approach has since been institutionalized. The daily briefing in Doya were timed for 2:00 p.m. so as to coordinate with morning-news programs in the United States.

After the Hussein regime collapsed, U.S. General Tommy Franks gave the embedding program a thumbs up. "Embedding will happen again," he said, "and I remain a fan" (Moses 2003). The British government had struggled to persuade a skeptical public to support its decision to participate in the invasion. But during the conflict, Defence Secretary Geoff Hoon gave credit to embedding for a swing in public opinion in favor of the war. "The imagery they broadcast is at least partially responsible for the public's change in mood," he said (Cozens 2003). Hoon had identified the core issue. Fear that reporters would lose their "objectivity" missed the point. What really mattered were the lasting images of the fight against terror. Despite tensions between British and American PR staff over this strategy, the U.S. approach carried the day, according to John Kampfner, who helped produce a BBC documentary that was highly critical of military propaganda during the conflict.

The American strategy was to concentrate on the visuals and to get a broad message out. Details—where helpful—followed behind. The key was to ensure the right television footage. The embedded reporters could do some of that. On other missions, the military used their own cameras, editing the film themselves and presenting it to broadcasters as ready-to-go packages. The Pentagon had been influenced by Hollywood producers of reality TV and action movies, notably Black Hawk Down. (Kampfner 2003)

One could remain true to the "regime of objectivity" and still provide the Pentagon spin machine what it wanted—dramatic stories, sometimes mythic tales, about the heroic efforts of men and women in uniform. In fact, while the embedding program was backed by coercive force, its success ultimately depended on reporters doing their jobs as they saw fit. It was important that stories produced by Western media have an air of verisimilitude. Iraq's hapless information minister, Mohammed Saee al-Sahhaf, was nicknamed "Comical Ali" by wags in the Western media for his obvious disinformation. But while he provided suitable fodder for late-night comics, his presence had an ideological dimension. If Disneyland exists, as Baudrillard suggests, to make the rest of the United States appear real, then "Comical Ali's" outbursts—"We defeated them yesterday. God willing, I will provide you with more information"—marked the sophisticated American and British propaganda as truth.

There is no reason to believe that military personnel twisted the arm of embedded *New York Times* bio-terrorism reporter Judith Miller to write the numerous stories she filed, both before and during the invasion, on the search for Iraq's WMD program. Her stories were cited by the White House to justify swift military action. And the imprimatur of the *New York Times* brand gave them enormous credibility. The unnamed source used in the stories turned out to be Ahmed Chalabi, leader of the Iraqi National Congress (Kurtz 2003b). Chalabi was the Pentagon's favored replacement as a possible new Iraqi leader and, therefore, had a substantial interest in the war's outcome. Reports that Chalabi was the principal source for the stories raised obvious questions as to whether the *New York Times* was manipulated to make it appear *as if* the White House was citing an independent intelligence source, instead of one of its own Iraqi proxies.

The Pentagon did not force the embedding program on an unwilling news media. Their relationship was symbiotic. Moreover, "military and entertainment types have been meeting and greeting over the last ten years or so" at conferences geared towards merging entertainment and military-training simulation technologies (Burston 2003: 166). Hollywood executives, including top people from Warner Brothers television, CBS, and Fox were meeting with White House officials about participating in counter-terrorism initiatives as early as one month after the September 11 attacks. "We have not done a good job communicating to people about who we are," said Bryce Zabel, chairman of the Academy of Television Arts and Sciences. "It's possible the entertainment industry could help the government formulate its message to the rest of the world" (Rutenberg 2001f). Indeed, the idea to embed reporters came out of a program produced for ABC by action-movie king Jerry Bruckheimer *(Black Hawk Down),* and coproducer Bertram van Munster (reality-TV show *Cops*), with the cooperation of the Pentagon. The premise behind *Profiles from the Front Line* was to get "up close and personal" with soldiers fighting in Afghanistan in order to tell dramatic human-interest stories from their perspective (Seelye 2002; Holson 2003; Kakutani 2003; Kampfner 2003). It was a basic story formula first made popular in the 1970s by ABC Sports maven Roone Aldridge. The Pentagon liked the show so much that the embedding program was born.

Some stories were produced that did not show soldiers in a particularly fond light, but the overwhelming flow of live-broadcast pictures tended to produce decontexutalized tales of heroism, or simply gripping live video. Armed with portable satellite video phones, reporters were able to keep pace with advancing military forces while filing dramatic footage of troops on the move, or fearless paratroopers leaping out of aircraft into the pitch-black night. These live shots were often given the added patina of authenticity by their fuzzy green quality. Perhaps the most famous embedded reporter was NBC correspondent David Bloom, who transmitted live pictures while strapped atop his specially outfitted vehicle, nicknamed the "Bloom Mobile." A content analysis of embedded coverage found that most reports were anecdotal, combat focused, mostly live and unedited. That is to say, most reports involved a live standup (49.1 percent; audio-only 12.1 percent), with the reporter describing military action (27.8 percent), combat results (13 percent), or pre-combat activity, such as troop movements (31.5 percent). Stories about troop morale, the work soldiers did and details about weaponry accounted for another 16 percent. "In general," read the report by the Project for Excellence in Journalism, "the embedded reports tended toward immediacy over reflection" (Project for Excellence in Journalism 2003). "The dead and dying were always kept at PG-13 distances" (Bart 2003). Even the Pentagon and White House officials admitted, in their more grumpy moments, that media coverage tended to view the conflict "through a soda straw."

### The Myth of the Saving of Private Lynch

Perhaps the most memorable story of the war was the rescue of Private First Class Jessica Lynch from an Iraqi hospital. In this story, the potential for the spectacular integration of military propaganda, the commercial interests of converged-media conglomerates, mythic storytelling, and the organizational requirements of their 24-hour broadcasters were fully realized. A documentary produced for the BBC's *Correspondent* program went as far as to call the story "one of the most stunning pieces of news management ever conceived."

Lynch was traveling with the Army's 507th Maintenance Company March 23, when the convoy was ambushed after taking a wrong turn. The 19-year-old soldier was taken prisoner after she sustained serious injuries to her legs and spine. Five others were captured and held separately from Lynch. Eleven soldiers were killed. That much of the story remains undisputed. Almost two weeks into the conflict, there was mounting pressure on the White House and Pentagon. Some media coverage had gone negative. Reports from mainstream American news outlets were not challenging the validity of the invasion. That would have damaged "Brand America." Instead, retired generals and other elite sources were starting to question whether the United States and Britain had underestimated the strength and determination of Iraqi soldiers who, at that moment, were putting up much stiffer resistance than anticipated. Many journalists had been swept up by the promise of "Shock and Awe" and expectations were high that there would be a swift and painless victory march into Baghdad. That would change. Negative images of frightened U.S. POWs released by Iraq as propaganda had become front-page news. Word that Iraqi civilians, including women and children, had been shot after the vehicle they were in failed to stop at a U.S. checkpoint, was also making headlines. Some reports dared to raise the possibility that the military operation might slip into a Vietnam-like quagmire.

It was in this media context that reporters embedded with Centcom, in Doha, were raised from their beds April 1. Some reporters thought the military might have captured Saddam Hussein. The story was better. They were briefed on the dramatic tale of Lynch's rescue. Edited video of the operation was distributed by the military to eager broadcasters, who quickly beamed the images around the world. The video showed Lynch, draped in a U.S. flag, being carried on a stretcher into a helicopter that would fly her to a U.S. military hospital in Germany. Soon family photos of the photogenic private would be released. The image of a pretty blond American teenager, with humble roots from Palestine, West Virginia, grabbed media attention. "She Was Fighting to the Death," shouted an April 3 headline in the *Washington Post*. That story went on to quote unnamed Pentagon sources who said Lynch, despite having sustained multiple gunshot wounds at the hands of Iraqi soldiers, had "fought fiercely," discharging her weapon until she ran out of ammunition. "She did not want to be taken alive," said one official. "Talk about spunk!" said U.S. Senator Pat Roberts, who was also quoted in the *Post* story. "She just persevered. It takes that and a tremendous faith that your country is going to come and get you" (Schmidt and Loeb 2003). Other broadcast and print outlets quickly followed the *Post*'s lead and wrote similar stories that would mark Private Lynch as a national hero—an icon of American grit, determination, and patriotism (Chinni 2003). Seemingly overnight, Private Lynch had entered the pantheon of American heroes. And, just as suddenly, media coverage changed. "Boy, one little POW rescue can sure change the tone of the press coverage," wrote *Post* media critic, Howard Kurtz. "By the time Ari Fleischer [White House press secretary] faced reporters yesterday, many of the questions were about who would be running Iraq once Saddam is permanently sidelined. Goodbye, quagmire" (Kurtz 2003c).

The "good news" was soon complicated. Within days reports began to appear that contradicted the storyline as portrayed in the *Post*. Named sources at the hospital in Germany denied that Lynch had been shot and stabbed. The extent and cause of her injuries were being questioned. "Interestingly though," writes Dante Chinni, in a detailed chronology of media coverage of the story, "given the choice between the two stories, many news organizations chose the more theatric set of circumstances, even though the other version of events had better sourcing" (Chinni 2003). It appears the story of a pretty blond soldier displaying courage and patriotism under fire was simply too good to pass up, particularly for broadcasters predisposed to wrapping coverage in the flag. It was later confirmed that, while Lynch suffered serious leg and spinal injuries due to a motor-vehicle accident, she was never shot or stabbed. Neither did she participate in a gun battle, because her gun jammed. Further information indicates that Iraqi troops that had been guarding the hospital had left before the rescue. This means that the special forces team did not meet any significant resistance during the rescue mission, as first reported—a fact that seriously dampens the dramatic tension required for successful melodrama. On June 17, a chastened *Washington Post* published a lengthy reassessment of the Lynch saga on its front page, in which it corrected many of the errors contained in its heavily quoted story of April 3 (Priest, Booth, and Schmidt 2003).

The patriotic mythology of "Saving Private Lynch" was a made-for-Hollywood script. Unlike Specialist Shoshana Johnson, a fellow POW whose frightened image was also widely broadcast, Lynch was, as one columnist put it, the "archetypal blonde-in-peril" (Zerbisias 2003). Shoshana had humble origins, but she was a black single mother. The Lynch mythology was so compelling that a bidding war erupted among news media thirsting for the first interview with the "plucky" private—what is known in the industry as "the get." It is the most-prized interview among celebrity journalists. Katie Couric, NBC's popular host of the *Today Show* reportedly sent Lynch "a bundle of patriotic books, including Rudolph W. Giuliani's memoir, *Leadership*. Diane Sawyer, of ABC News, sent a locket with a photograph of Private Lynch's family home." At CBS News the interview pitch was on a much larger scale. A letter written by CBS News senior vice president Betsy West offered to bundle a two-hour TV movie along with other possible media projects with CBS Entertainment, MTV, and book publisher Simon & Schuster—all of which are owned by parent company Viacom. "From the distinguished reporting of CBS News to the youthful reach of MTV, we believe this is a unique combination of projects that will do justice to Jessica's inspiring story" (Rutenberg 2003c). The proponents of media convergence at Viacom recognized a platinum promotional opportunity when they saw one. Unfortunately, after the conglomerate's plans were revealed in a page-one story in the *New York Times,* CBS News was accused of "checkbook journalism." The news organization fought back by accusing the *Times* of selectively quoting from its offer, and it insisted that the editorial independence of CBS News was never in question. A month later, CBS chairman Leslie Moonves would finally concede that linking the interview pitch to an integrated multimedia entertainment package may have gone too far. In a moment of astounding honesty, Moonves blamed the new competitive environment created by large media conglomerates. "As these companies become more and more vertically integrated, you know, sometimes you do go over the line," Moonves said (BBC News Online 2003b).

Lynch returned home to a choreographed hero's welcome July 22, that was broadcast live. She was greeted by thousands of flag-waving well-wishers who lined the streets of the tiny Appalachian town for a glimpse of their home-grown celebrity. Some displayed entrepreneurial spirit. Souvenir hunters could purchase a "Welcome Home Jessica" t-shirt or a CD including a song about her ordeal made by an employee of a local market. It was titled: "She Was Just Nineteen, Became America's Queen" (Dao 2003; Whoriskey 2003). For $24.95, online shoppers could visit jessica video.com and purchase "Faith and a Community"; promotional copy for the video/ DVD promised to "tell the untold story of not just one individual but a whole community that pulled together during a time of war. . . . This dynamic video tells the story of Jessica's rescue and those who believed for [*sic*] a miracle."

Media were forbidden from taking pictures of Lynch struggling to get off a Black Hawk helicopter, nor were they permitted to film her at the family home. Reporters were directed to the parade route and a media tent constructed for the occasion. Sitting in front of the stars and stripes, Lynch nervously read from a prepared statement in which she thanked all those people who helped "save" her, including special forces soldiers and a handful of Iraqi civilians, one of whom was Mohammed Odeh Rehaief. The 32-year-old lawyer is said to have tipped the military as to Lynch's whereabouts. He and his wife were swiftly granted political asylum in the United States. Rehaief began "working on a book for Harper Collins and with NBC" for an unauthorized TV movie about the rescue (Priest, Booth, and Schmidt 2003). Lynch declined overtures made by NBC to cooperate with the film, but later signed a deal with publisher Alfred A. Knopf that would see her share a reported $1-million advance with former *New York Times* writer Rick Bragg.

All the reports about Lynch's homecoming produced by major U.S. news broadcasters failed to mention the controversy over her story. However, during her statement, Lynch did make a cryptic comment connected to the media controversy. "I've read thousands of stories that said when I was captured I said, 'I'm an American soldier, too.' Those stories were right. Those were my words. I am an American soldier, too." With these comments, Lynch's carefully crafted statement provided a testimonial as to the veracity of her story, without making specific claims that could be proven factually incorrect. It testified to the truth of her story at the level of myth. Significantly, controversy over whether the Pentagon manipulated the news media in order to construct a convenient war-time hero was not considered to be a problem by locals gathered to view the parade. "Every war needs a hero," 77-year-old James Roberts told the *Washington Post*. "Rickenbacker . . . Kennedy . . . she's the hero in this war. The facts don't particularly matter" (Whoriskey 2003). The view was shared by others. "No matter what happened, she deserves every good thing she can get," said a local restauranteur. "We just love her" (Dao 2003). These neighbors were concerned with phatic communication, not factually accurate reporting. The power of the "Saving Private Lynch" drama is connected to how it is used by people to reinterpret everyday social reality and strengthen social relationships. The myth of "Saving Private Lynch" had "existential utility," that was historically situated, and structured in domination.

To Lynch's credit, she eventually cast doubt on her status as a mythic hero during an interview on the ABC News program *Primetime*. The Pentagon "used me as a way to symbolize all this stuff," Lynch told host Diane Sawyer. "I mean, yeah, it's wrong . . . I don't know what they had . . . or why they filmed it" (ABC News 2003). The interview was broadcast November 11, Veterans' Day, to coincide with the launch of her co-authored book—*I am a Soldier, Too: The Jessica Lynch Story*.

### Falling Statues and Flexible Memory

The symbolic ending to the Iraq invasion, and the regime of Saddam Hussein, came April 9. That day U.S. soldiers strapped a chain around the neck of a statue of the deposed Iraqi dictator in central Baghdad, and hauled it to the ground. The event was, of course, broadcast live by the 24-hour news channels. The image of the falling statue was repeated endlessly throughout the day. The message was simple and crystal clear: Iraq and its long-suffering people had been liberated, by the benevolent actions of the United States and its allies. The tightly framed pictures showed a crowd of men rejoicing while they smashed the remnants of the colossal bronze figure. They were well-composed photographs that helped convey a sense of action and dramatic tension. The statue invariably appears in contrast to the soldiers, or the crowd of people gathered to witness, what viewers were told was, a truly historic moment. The dramatic video was cited by defenders of the invasion as vivid proof that the United States had done the right thing. Immediate comparisons were made to the fall of the Berlin Wall as a symbol of popular enthusiasm for the end of a long dictatorship. "The Iraqi people are well on their way to freedom," said U.S. Defense Secretary Donald Rumsfeld (McKenna 2003).

But, as with the story of Jessica Lynch, appearances were deceiving. Within days of the U.S. military triumph, a counter-narrative began circulating among e-mail users. The messages contained hypertext links to a series of photographs depicting the tumbling statue. One photograph in particular depicted a very different scene from the one repeated endlessly by cable-news networks. The photo, available on the Web site globalresearch.ca, showed a wide-angled shot of the scene. Taken from above, it revealed a largely empty plaza, where the bronze statue sat, in the middle of an automotive roundabout. The plaza was surrounded by at least four American tanks, which had apparently sealed off the area. In contrast to the tightly framed picture, this shot did not support the dominant narrative of a city rejoicing in its newfound freedom. Without close-up action shots, it also lacked dramatic tension. The wide-angle picture exposed the inevitable editorial selection that is made when framing a photograph. What is included and excluded from the frame affects the range of possible meanings to be gleaned. There is no reason to believe that photojournalists and videographers were in league with the military. They were simply practicing their craft in an effort to produce "good" photos—i.e., dramatic action shots of individuals caught up in the emotion of the moment. Just as tightly framed photos of stadium bleachers can create a false impression of crowd size at a football game, the pictures of a toppled statue created an ideologically partial view of events. A crowd of about 150 people was amplified through framing and sheer repetition of images. In a gesture of patriotism, one Marine had draped the statue in a U.S. flag. It was later replaced with an Iraqi flag. According to a BBC report, the Stars and Stripes was replaced after people in the crowd complained. One person reportedly told a U.S. soldier that he was exercising his right to free speech to say he wanted U.S. forces out of Iraq as soon as possible (Omaar and Wood 2003).

The falling statue was inserted into the production flow of a global 24-hour news cycle. As such, it became part of what Manuel Castells calls the "culture of real virtuality." A protean flow of images and sound was created as these pictures became a part of the flexible production regime of cable news. In this way, 24-hour news organizations help construct a "timeless" media environment. Time and space are compressed. Far-flung audiences simultaneously watch the fall of the statue, but only after the images have been processed. The fall of the statue is broadcast "live," but it is instantly reinserted into the news flow as edited tape. The edited images and live commentary of anchors and military experts mix, then blur, as they mesh with the rolling-news format, which simultaneously acts as a "temporal collage" without linear sequence. There is no beginning or end. "History is first organized according to the availability of visual material, then submitted to computerised possibility of selecting seconds of frames to be pieced together, or split apart, according to specific discourses" (Castells 2000a: 492). In this high-speed media context, historical memory or consciousness is fragile, at best. The justification for war also becomes flexible. Official emphasis shifted from the threat of WMD to the joy of a battered nation shaking off the yoke of a vicious regime. Through the continuous flow of rolling news, the falling statue can be situated within a range of discourses. One could choose to situate the event within the context of Iraq's colonial past, in which case emphasis could be placed on similarities between the British occupation following the defeat of the

Ottoman empire in the First World War. Instead, the event is associated, most prominently, with the crumbling of the Berlin Wall, itself a symbolically charged media event that also unfolded within the flow of 24-hour news. As such, it is much more likely to be recognized by audiences familiar with the tropes and conventions of cable news. In this way an ideologically partial reading is constructed that privileges a discourse of freedom and liberation, over colonial oppression and expanding empire.

One hundred days after President Bush stood aboard an aircraft carrier to declare an end to major combat, a large number of Iraqis were making their displeasure known. By that time, 56 U.S. soldiers had died as a result of hostile fire from guerrilla forces. The total number of U.S. troops killed in postwar Iraq would grow and eventually surpass the number killed in major combat. Under U.S. and British occupation there had been widespread looting, and protests, some turning violent, by citizens angry about the lack of clean drinking water, electricity, and fuel. Disgruntled Shia Muslims, long oppressed under the brutal rule of Saddam Hussein, were so upset that they announced a decision to form their own army to oppose U.S. occupation forces. (Halpern 2003; Harper 2003). The material consequences of "Shock and Awe" had become increasingly painful for U.S. forces.

# CONCLUSION

# Spectacular Integration and Autonomy

*The inability to find an "optimism of the intellect" with which to work through alternatives has now become one of the most serious barriers to progressive politics.*
DAVID HARVEY

I have argued throughout the book that the integrated news spectacle can be properly understood only if we adopt a historical perspective that focuses on the *practical use* of cultural texts and other forms of cultural capital available to journalists, news organizations, political professionals, and audiences. I began by rejecting the widely held tabloidization thesis. I suggested its adherence to a linear model of communication and the assumption that spectacular media events represent moments of displaced or distorted communication fails to understand the complex ways news stories are constructed and circulated by modern news media. I then argued that approaching news as a dramatic form of ritual takes us partway towards understanding these complexities and how news media feed off and back into popular culture. In doing so, I have made qualified use of scholarly work in the cultural-anthropology tradition, influenced by Victor Turner. The news spectacle is a dramatic representation of social relations beyond everyday experience that offers people explanations, criticisms, and reassurances for the problems of society. In this way, cultural texts, such as popular news stories about deceased princesses, can be used by members of society to strengthen social relationships through storytelling, envision communities based on class, race, and gender, and mobilize those groups for collective action.

The problem with research into ritualized dramatic narratives is that it lacks a historical dimension. I have argued that the cultural texts produced by news media cannot be fully appreciated if they are separated from material reality as reified ideal forms of the sacred. They must be referred back to specific historical contexts in which they are produced, distributed, exchanged, consumed and/or contested by disparate groups of social actors. Yes, popular forms of news are involved in the reproduction of social norms—the sacred and profane of social life. But, I have argued, these cultural texts must be referred back to a broader social totality. I have used the Monicagate, Diana, and McCain texts as entry points into a discussion of this broader social totality. The name I have given to this broader set of cultural, social, economic, and political relations is the integrated news spectacle. The term has been used throughout to refer to the "constellations" of social forces, new technologies, and institutional logics that have converged in unique and contingent ways to produce a highly complex integration of the cultural, economic, social, professional, and political realms. I argue that the representation of social life by the news media is only a partial manifestation of the broader social mediation of experience.

The study of journalism and news media in general cannot be separated from the study of modernity, consumer culture, the logic of capital accumulation, globalization, and technological development. I have shown that media events do not represent the spectacle in its entirety; instead, spectacular media events are component parts of a much larger integrated promotional system of commodity production, circulation, and exchange. It is for this reason that the integrated news spectacle defies easy categorization and definition. I have tried, instead, through an analysis of the practical strategies adopted by individuals, news organizations, and political professionals, to tease out the underlying logic of practice within the integrated news spectacle. I have referred to this as the promotional logic of spectacle—a logic characterized by the transposable circulation and promotion of cultural commodities. All social actors, I have suggested, whether they be private individuals, news workers, or political professionals, find themselves in a social context in which the logic of promotion is constitutive of strategies of capital accumulation (where capital, in the broad sense used by Bourdieu, is understood as cultural, symbolic, and economic). In this agonistic model of social relations, individuals, social groups, commercial, and noncommercial organizations utilize the tools and resources available to them in the social fields of popular culture, journalism, politics, and the economy to further their own particular interests.

I have further suggested that the logic of promotion is structured in domination. As commodities, the cultural texts produced within the integrated news spectacle are aestheticized through marketing and other forms of promotion in order to bridge the gap between anonymous producers and consumers. The arbitrary meanings associated with cultural commodities are then used by social actors in their quest for self-realization and political or economic gain. There is no direct correspondence between the associations ascribed to commodities in the production process and the meanings appropriated by those who consume them. Consumers are not simply dupes of the production process. Meanings must resonate with the real needs and desires of social actors. Nonetheless, the key point I have developed is that social identities, mediated through market transactions, become essential to economic competition, rational organization, and political practice. In doing so, they become objects of rational and strategic action by commercial interests and institutions. It is in this sense that personal autonomy is under the constant threat of domination. To the extent that social actors must use the resources of the integrated news spectacle, they run the risk of conducting their lives according to *its* rules, not their own.

Cautionary tales about marital infidelity, or the conflict between good and evil, are used, modified, and inserted into integrated strategies of capital accumulation, producing large-scale media events, such as Monicagate and the Gary Condit/Chandra Levy scandal. These stories then act as promotional fulcrum points for disparate interests. Individual, commercial, and political actors scramble to tap into these promotional fulcrum points, further expanding the scope and scale of the spectacle. This shared logic of promotional integration exists in stories mourning the death of Princess Diana and in those describing the U.S.-led invasion of Iraq. In this context, distinctions between high and low culture are no longer relevant.

Meanwhile, journalists working in integrated news organizations that seek to maximize the benefits of promotional integration find themselves fragmented and ramified. Increasingly, journalists are viewed as providers of content for converged multimedia organizations whose strategies of capital accumulation are predicated on the efficiencies found in economies of scale and scope. The professional culture of journalism retains its semi-independent status. Many news workers remain skeptical of the brave new world of convergence. They fear layoffs as a result of the rationalization of journalistic resources and they distrust cross-promotional practices that serve the particular interests of their employer, as opposed to the broader public interest. But this resistance is already being met with attempts to reintegrate or "re-brand" reporters and editors in order that they believe the goals of integrated newsrooms remain compatible with journalism's legitimating ideal of social responsibility and public service.

We are left finally with the problem of locating spaces and fissures within the integrated news spectacle for autonomous practice. I will conclude this study by exploring, in a preliminary fashion, the question of autonomy. To say that the integrated news spectacle is structured in dominance does not mean that there is no space left for autonomous agency. Both the neo-Durkheimian and Marxist scholarly traditions I have drawn upon in this study seek to explain the historical and social structures that stand over human agency. The hope offered by scholarly research is that an understanding of these structures will allow social actors to overcome them. Anthony Giddens (1971) reminds us that freedom, for both Durkheim and Marx, is equated with autonomy. One is autonomous if one is "not impelled by either external or internal forces beyond rational control" (227). In Durkheim's functional system of analysis, rational autonomy is regained when individuals understand their place within the social whole—when they understand and accept the unity of purpose behind the division of labor and their role in it (230). This is the function of dramatic news rituals, such as the mourning of Diana. Less optimistically, we see here a striking resemblance to the branding strategies encouraged by the gurus of corporate convergence and the public-relations campaigns launched by the Pentagon. For Marx, the goal is not simply to understand one's role in the division of labor, and by extension the broader social totality. Instead, it is to take control of the practices of individual and social reproduction in order that social actors may use them, instead of being used by them. It is to the latter goal that I now turn my attention.

The integrated news spectacle is not hermetically sealed. The same technologies that make possible the protean blur of the spectacle of war are used by social actors who resist "the logic of timelessness" (Castells 2000a: 497). The circulation of the wide-angle view of the toppled statue of Saddam Hussein is a good example, as are leaked reports concerning the veracity of U.S. and British government claims that the Hussein regime presented an imminent nuclear threat. It is increasingly difficult in a high-speed, global media environment to suppress storytelling. The struggle is over whose stories become dominant.

Nick Dyer-Witheford (1999) argues persuasively that there is a contradiction at the core of networked global capitalism. The diffusion of information technologies furthers the reach of both capitalism and social movements opposed to capitalism's advancement. Money rules as global capitalism becomes increasingly integrated with quicker and more flexible production, transaction, and delivery systems. Today's high-volume flexible production systems offer both economies of scale and scope. The central link of these new high-speed networks of capital flows is the ability to process information and communicate among elements of the integrated network. However, before this flexible production system can operate efficiently, it requires that communication technology be dispersed throughout society, and along with it, the knowledge of how to use it.

> This means that on occasion corporate control can be interrupted and spaces opened within which a multiplicity of social movements, all in different ways contesting the dominance of the market, can be connected and made visible to each other. New information technologies therefore appear not just as instruments for the circulation of commodities, but simultaneously as channels for the circulation of struggles. (121–122)

The transnational networks of social movements that held anti-WTO demonstrations in Seattle in 1999 and other so-called antiglobalization protests that followed in Quebec City, Prague, Goteburg, Washington, and Genoa, worked precisely because widely dispersed information technologies allowed disparate activists to coordinate their activities.

It was in Seattle that the first Independent Media Center (IMC) was established. IMC Web sites have since sprung up around the world. The site's open access allows interested people to post their own news reports and commentary on economic, social, and environmental issues. The Vancouver IMC provided extensive coverage of local opposition to a proposal to privatize water-treatment facilities. The story was virtually ignored by the local mainstream media outlets until a decision was made by authorities to forego the plan. The Vancouver IMC also won approval to Webcast arguments made in a British Columbia court challenging a NAFTA panel ruling that awarded financial compensation to a U.S. firm. Metalclad had been blocked from opening a waste-disposal site in Mexico by local authorities.[1] Other alternative Web sites have emerged, including the Guerrilla News Network (GNN), which uses the grammar of music videos to produce critical videos about the aftermath of September 11 and other issues. The use of e-mail lists has also fostered unique protest forms, such as "flash mobs," whereby large groups of people are mobilized by sending single e-mail messages.

The hope is that these newly opened autonomous spaces fostered by networks of social movements provide a home for alternative forms of identity formation critical of spectacular consumer culture. According to Ian Angus (2000), it is within the spaces created by new social movements that anticonsumer identities are able to articulate their critical sense of a "lack of fit" with dominant culture. In short, Angus argues that new social movements have contributed to the diffusion of a counterhegemonic common sense, what he calls new "primal scenes of communication."

> The emergence of social movement politics originates from a process of *undiscounting* what is left by dominant explanations. The process of the disruption of common sense by social movements is now well underway and our current society is traversed by the rhetoric of consumer society, critical rhetoric emerging from movements, and counter-rhetoric in opposition to movements. (140)

The task set before demonstrators in Seattle and Quebec City was to explain the downside of the new informational global economy. The demonstrators, in essence, sought to highlight the new social cleavages produced and *discounted* by the dominant economic order. Manuel Castells (2000b) identifies three basic social cleavages produced by the so-called network society: (1) a rift between the usefully information-rich and less useful information-poor; (2) highly educated "reprogrammable" professional labor versus unskilled "generic" labor; and (3) the cruel "separation between the market logic of global networks of capital flows and the human experience of workers' lives" (377). The last cleavage is perhaps best exemplified by the Indonesian sweatshops producing Nike running shoes. Social movements work to reintroduce the experience of this "lack of fit" back into mainstream political discourse.

As with the 24-hour cable networks, the transnational networks of social movements are forced to find ways of communicating their messages that transcend different cultural and linguistic boundaries. And to accomplish this goal, many groups utilize dramatic storytelling techniques that propose stark choices between right and wrong (Keck and Sikkink 1998: 226). One memorable example came when local activists in Seattle dressed as sea turtles. They donned the costumes to dramatize their belief that the World Trade Organization's 142 members were doing little to protect the environment. Sometimes, the renaming of an issue can have great dramatic effect. This was the case when a network of woman's groups and human-rights organizations replaced the term "female circumcision" with "female genital mutilation" in their campaign. The association with the less-threatening male procedure was eliminated (225). Nonetheless, the possibility remains that dramatic protests will lose contact with the grassroots. As media frames become highly aestheticized through dramatic storytelling, local social actors run the risk of losing control of their own stories (227).

In an effort to mobilize support in civil society, competing social actors must utilize the resources available to them, be they economic, cultural, or symbolic. This will entail the symbolic representation of particular interests. Social life will, in part, continue to be mediated and experienced at a distance. The spectacle of dramatic storytelling in news discourse is not in itself to be lamented. The mediated representation of political and social life is a necessary part of large-scale societies. It can be creative, inspiring, and yes, confrontational. What is not inevitable is that the unique tales of people—the stories we *use* to communicate our histories, our individual and group identities—be subject to the dictates of a promotional logic that serves the interests of particular social actors while cloaked in the myth of universal good.

# Notes

*Chapter 1*

1. As far back as the ancient writings of Tertullian's *De Spectaculis,* there has been ample evidence to contradict the suggestion that the elite tastes are inherently more moral than those of the masses. Elites also enjoyed the bloody displays of the gladiatorial games (Brantlinger 1983: 78).
2. For a thorough social theory of political scandal, see John B. Thompson's *Political Scandal: Power and Visibility in the Media Age.*
3. The March 2000 funeral of Olympic curling champion Sandra Schmirler, who died of cancer, was broadcast live across Canada by CBC Newsworld, the network's 24-hour cable channel. The touchstone theme of the programming suggested that Schmirler was both representative of the average Canadian woman and mother, and yet, as an Olympian, was uniquely gifted. Implied throughout the broadcast was the notion that curling is somehow representative of Canadian culture. Reporter Colleen Jones—a competitive curler in her own right and a friend of Schmirler—gave a live report later in the afternoon during an audience phone-in program entitled *Remembering Sandra Schmirler,* in which she said that "there are no superstars in this sport. This is a blue-collar sport played in small-town rinks across this country." Anne Petrie, the host of the broadcast extended the point by making reference to how simple and authentic she thought the ceremony was, just like curling in Canada—and one might add Canadians in general.
4. The British Royal family sustained much criticism in the popular press about their seemingly unfeeling response to the news of Lady Diana's death. Many of the stories on this subject suggested the reticence on the part of the Queen was due to rifts created by Lady Diana's airing of Royal dirty laundry in public.
5. The *Globe and Mail* newspaper updated the narrative of the self-reliant entrepreneur for the tight-labor market of the late 1990s by giving it a post-Generation X spin: "Generation Xers are stereotyped. But that's not the real story. The fact is, young adults are demanding more from a job than a pay cheque these days. And if Mr. Corp. won't give it to them, they'll do it themselves" (Chiose 1997). The title of the piece: "You're Going to Make It After All!" along

with a photo of someone throwing their hat in the air, is a successful play on the opening theme song from the popular 1970s sitcom *The Mary Tyler Moore Show*. Here we have an example of a well-worn narrative form that has been reproduced in popular entertainment and that is once again reproduced as a feature piece for the paper's weekend edition. Possible structural determinants of the tight labor market are downplayed while an emphasis is placed on the responsibility of the individual to act, to pull oneself up by one's own bootstraps, to borrow another well-worn phrase.

6. In his opposition to hand recounts of Florida ballots, George W. Bush maintained that technology was more reliable than people. Remember, this is the man whose opposition to a federally operated health-care plan is predicated on his trust in the American people to decide how best to invest in their own future. Moreover, in his capacity as the governor of Texas, Bush signed a bill into law that makes hand recounts possible in that state. Historically contingent doesn't begin to capture the willful hypocrisy at play.

## *Chapter 2*

1. Former Canadian Alliance leader Stockwell Day learned this lesson the hard way during the first two days of the 2000 federal election. Day's message that Canada's high taxes were contributing to a so-called brain drain of talented young people to the United States was obscured by two gaffes in which the grammar of his photo ops contradicted the party's message. First, Day visited a high-tech firm whose president recently left the U.S. for Canada. Undeterred, Day held another news conference the next day in an attempt to use the spectacular backdrop of Niagara Falls to give visual emphasis to his argument. His message drowned as a result of a bad sense of direction over which way the water flowed. Day was trying to use the visual to draw a parallel between the flow of Niagara Falls and Canadians who go south to the United States for work. Unfortunately, Day's handlers were unaware that the falls flow toward Canada, not away from it. The two gaffes became the focus of most stories about Day during that 48-hour news cycle. The point here is that political success or failure often hinges on the successful deployment of media logic or grammar and not the factual strength of particular arguments. Added to this situation is the relatively new 24-hour news cycle created by all-news cable channels and the Internet, and its tendency to amplify gaffes and other dominant narratives.

2. A thorough examination of the cultural variability of media systems is found in a collection of comparative essays edited by James Curran and Myung-Jin Park (2000), *De-Westernizing Media Studies,* Routledge.

3. The people of Taber did not receive the media as openly as the people of Columbine did. Many blamed media coverage for the so-called copycat shooting in their rural community. One student was killed and another seriously wounded in the incident. A 14-year-old male student was arrested and later pleaded guilty (Mitchell 1999, Harrington 2000). In contrast, Littleton is a well-off suburban community of Denver where many of the people being interviewed shared similar demographics with reporters. In Jonesboro, Arkansas, a rural community, angry locals threw rocks at reporters covering a school shooting in that community, a year earlier (Siegel 1999).

4. All citations of *The Society of the Spectacle* refer to thesis number, not page number.

5. Debord's personal biography indicates that he and other members of the Situationist movement, of which he was a key member, engaged in a prodigious amount of sexual activity. On more than one occasion these acts were incorporated into the creation of "situations" aimed at fulfilling the Situationist creed. See Len Bracken's (1997) account of Situationist life.

6. The magazine *Brill's Content,* which debuted August 1998 amidst wall-to-wall coverage of the Clinton-Lewinsky scandal, devoted itself entirely to this purpose. One study (Bishop 2001) found that news stories about media performance were "clustered" around stories such as the O.J. Simpson trial and the death of Princess Diana (28). Ronald Bishop suggests that the increasing use of certain pundits, such as the *Washington Post's* Howard Kurtz, is "tied to the fact they wrote well-received books about the media's effects on politics, books that later became part of the coverage of these issues. Thus, we find Disney-like synergy in an arena that calls for in-depth, sober analysis" (36).

7. The princess's image has appeared on coffee mugs, t-shirts, plates, even tubs of margarine. A three-hour Diana walking tour of London that explored tenuous connections to the Princess, including an apartment in which she took elocution lessons, cost £4.50 (about C$11, US$7) (Leeman 1998).

8. Sometimes the fulcrum point of the moment can be stretched far beyond the time of its initial construction. An Associated Press story, December 11, 2000, reported that Madonna had tried to hold her much-publicized wedding at the Spencer family estate where Princess Diana is buried. Madonna and the Spencers could not come to a mutual agreement; but if they had it would have marked yet another promotional coup for the self-proclaimed "material girl" (Associated Press 2000a).

9. NBC's *Tonight Show* host Jay Leno would later confide in a taped interview with an NBC reporter that his profession has never been so flush with material as it was during the peak of the Monicagate scandal.

10. For the record, Lewinsky wore "nude lip liner and "glaze" lip color. *The Province* newspaper, a Vancouver tabloid, reports that "Club Monaco stores in New York, Chicago, Seattle, San Francisco, and Beverly Hills racked up hundreds of backlog orders for the lipstick and lipliner, which sell for $13 (US) and $10 (US)" (Province 1999).

11. There was some resistance to the promotional circulation of the Lewinsky commodity-sign. Not all of the Jenny Craig franchisees were happy with the choice of Monica Lewinsky as a dietary role model. Some of the U.S. franchisees made their displeasure known, but remained tied to a nationwide advertising deal to which they were obliged to contribute (Southerst 2000).

12. Writing in the *New York Times,* Jeffery A. Krames, editor in chief of the trade-books division of McGraw-Hill, suggests the timing of the book's publication date, June 2003, was predicated on the possibility that Clinton will make a presidential bid in 2004. "That possibility was undoubtedly factored into her advance," said Krames (Krames 2000). Clinton's *Living History* was an immediate bestseller with close to 200,000 copies sold the first day the book was available (Martin 2003). Like Lewinsky before her, Clinton granted an interview to Barbara Walters to promote the book.

13. Lizzie Grubman, daughter of an influential entertainment lawyer, became the subject of intense media scrutiny during the summer of 2001. Grubman was arraigned on charges of assault, reckless endangerment, and leaving the scene of an accident after her father's car backed into a crowd of people outside a popular nightclub in the Hamptons—the playground of the wealthy.

14. Users of the Internet auction house eBay took advantage of Elián's celebrity by listing various items the sellers claimed were linked to the boy, including: the inner tube he clung to as a raft when shipwrecked, a used coloring book and, perhaps most absurdly, a jar of air that was purported to contain the smells of tear gas and cigar smoke from Elián's Miami neighborhood (Thomas 2000).

15. Pirandello's 1921 play, *Six Characters in Search of an Author: A Comedy in the Making,* is, as the title suggests, about the struggle of six character "types" to convince a group of actors rehearsing a play to *use* them—and in so doing, put them to work in a work of art. The play begins with the characters (including, "the father," "the mother," "the step-daughter," and "the boy") confronting the actors with their demand as they begin rehearsal.

1. The three-way news-agency cartel remained in place until the First World War. Following the war, it was broken with the expansion of two American news agencies: Associated Press (AP) and United Press Association (UPA). Havas was reorganized and became Agence France-Presse (AFP). Wolff disappeared following the end of the Second World War and the defeat of Nazism.

2. Rantanen underlines the importance of time and place by providing the example of Russian news wires that provided stories in random order and without headline. All that was used to differentiate the stories was "transmission place (not country) and date (i.e., Turin 10 December 1866)" (Rantanen 1997: 613).

3. Michael Massing drives this point home when he writes: "CBS is by far the most emotional of the three networks. When there is joy, CBS celebrates. When there is sadness, CBS consoles. When man overcomes adversity, CBS is there to marvel. And when emotions are mixed, CBS tries to sort them out. Thus, when the national Christmas tree was lit on the same day on which 256 [American servicemen died in an air crash near Gander Newfoundland], Dan Rather signed off with this epiphany: 'Tragedy knows no season; but today's tragedy is especially painful. It comes at a time of traditional joy and celebration, celebration of rebirth of faith, celebration of the miracle of the flame that refused to be snuffed out: the trappings of joy all around the President. But now, added to the traditional trappings, the unexpected symbols of grief, unfurled and half staffed, on flagpoles and on faces, in a season of faith, remembering that those who died in the service of their country today were coming home from a mission of peace in the Sinai'" (Massing 1986, cited in Bennett 1988: 6). News here is framed as dramatic ritual; and its chief currency, emotion, is commodified and made subject to rational organization and control in order to produce stories that are attractive to a broader audience.

4. As James Curran (1998) points out, the trend towards audience fragmentation is less severe in Britain, where four channels attract 90 percent of total viewing time. Two of those channels, BBC 1 and ITV, account for two-thirds of all TV viewing.

5. CBS increased its news and current-affairs programming from 770 hours in 1979 to 2,400 hours in 1990 (Owen and Wildman 1992: 176).

6. The Prime-Time Access Rule (PTAR) was eliminated in the mid-1990s. This further lessening of government regulation provided enormous incentives for networks to vertically integrate with the producers of entertainment content—that is, Hollywood studios. In 1996, Disney bought ABC (Budd, Craig, and Steinman 1999: 47).

7. Other controversial conservative talk-show hosts who followed Limbaugh's lead include crazed Watergate burglar G. Gordon Liddy, and Oliver North, better known for his involvement in the Iran-Contra arms-for-cash scandal. Both men received presidential pardons before embarking on successful broadcast careers.

8. In fact, the talk shows' love/hate relationship with Bill Clinton continued after he left office. Clinton's controversial pardon of fugitive financier Marc Rich and allegations that Rich's former wife, Denise, funnelled hundreds of thousands of dollars into the coffers of the Democratic party and Clinton's presidential library project made for a messy departure. NBC Nightly News began leading their newscasts with the "Clinton Watch." The "event" overshadowed the policy announcements of newly elected U.S. President George W. Bush in the first month of his term in office.

9. Herman and McChesney cite data taken from Tunstall and Palmer (1991: 94) that indicate between 1980 and 1987 advertising in Europe more than doubled. The growth in ad spending continued into the 1990s, spurred on by the creation of a Single European Market (Herman and McChesney 1997: 39).

10. The CNN coup embarrassed rival CBS. On the night the bombing began a technical problem left CBS anchor Dan Rather interviewing a correspondent on the telephone who could only talk about "rumors" the bombing had begun. The humiliation forced CBS to pull out all the stops in the "media-war" to be the first to report from Kuwait that allied troops had "liberated" the tiny Arab emirate. Correspondent Bob McKeown won the race for CBS by breaking from the official press pool. McKeown used a "flyaway" transmitter to broadcast the news live. His reports were carried by news organizations around the world (MacGregor 1997: 11; McKeown 2001).

11. Cable News Egypt (CNE) was approved by the Egyptian government in 1990. CNE, later re-named Cable Network Egypt, is operated in a cooperative arrangement with CNN. It rebroad-casts Cable News Network International (CNNI) within Egypt (Amin and Napoli 2000). In 1996, Al Jazeera became the first 24-hour satellite news network in the Arab world. Referred to by staff as the "CNN of the Arab world," the Qatar-based all-news channel has been the target of criticism from some Arab governments for its relatively free-wheeling discussions of sex, government corruption, and Islamic fundamentalism. It was also criticized by the U.S. govern-ment for its coverage of the American-led invasion of Iraq in 2003. The station is operated under a quasi-BBC model that provides it with a US$30-million annual subsidy from Qatar's emir. It also receives advertising and subscription revenue and reaches an audience of 35 mil-lion (el-Nawawy 2001; Miladi 2003). There is also a 24-hour broadcast channel that caters to a worldwide Iranian audience. NITV, a Farsi-language news, lifestyle, and cultural program-ming station, started broadcasting in June 2000 from Los Angeles. It also employs recombi-nant program formats, including a morning show in the style of ABC's *Good Morning Amer-ica*. NITV repeats its 12-hour program cycle during daytime hours in Tehran. It too is trying to skim the cream off of a relatively small worldwide affluent Iranian audience. Some of the station's sponsors include Porsche and Sharp Electronics (Raphael 2000).

12. The successful export of Mexican and Brazilian telenovelas provides another example of the transposable nature of melodrama. As Chris Barker argues, many of these programs, such as the Brazilian *Beto Rockefeller*, combine the specificity of local ambiance with a more interna-tional production style that utilizes familiar character types, high-production values, and mel-odramatic plot lines (Barker 1997: 95).

13. Networks have also begun to offer services in local languages and dialects, although the pro-gram formats remain similar to those seen on the parent networks (Barker 1997: 40–42; Thussu 1999: 127).

14. U.S. conservative commentator Bill Kristol is a good example of the new breed of omnipresent media pundits on the cable talk-show circuit. The former chief of staff for former U.S. Vice President Dan Quayle began his pundit career on ABC's *This Week* and is now courted by all the network talk shows. "He's become part of Washington's circulatory system," says Howard Kurtz, "this half-pol, half-pundit, full-throated advocate with the nice-guy image"(Kurtz 2000d).

15. Two newspaper columnists, Dan Guthrie with the *Daily Courier* in Grant Pass, Oregon, and Tom Gutting with the *Texas City Sun,* were fired for writing mild criticisms of President Bush's behavior immediately following the attacks. Well-known conservative pundit Anne Coulter also had her column in the *National Review* axed after writing that any Arab countries that supported the terrorists should be invaded and "converted to Christianity." FedEx and other companies withdrew their advertising from the ABC talk-show *Politically Incorrect* after host Bill Maher quipped that only those people who attack others beyond the range of retalia-tion could properly be labeled cowardly, not people who were willing to die for a political or religious cause.

In Canada, Sunera Thobani, a critic of U.S. foreign policy, became the subject of police scrutiny. An unidentified complainant alleged that the assistant professor of Women's Studies at the University of British Columbia had contravened Canada's hate-crime laws when she described U.S. foreign policy as being "soaked in blood." Her comments attracted considerable attention in the United States after they were featured prominently on the infamous *Drudge Report* Web site. The complaint was later dismissed as unfounded.

16. The results of the study remain disputed. Members of the consortium, including the *New York Times* and the *Washington Post*, wrote stories that indicated George Bush would have won the race by a slender margin even if the United States Supreme Court had not ordered a recount of disputed Florida ballots be discontinued. However, the study also indicated that Al Gore would have won if there had been a full recount of all Florida ballots. See Greg Palast's (2002) report, first published in Britain, for a complete account of how Florida Republicans were involved in excluding a sizable number of eligible, but poor, Floridians from voting. As pointed out by Robert McChesney (2003) and others, these excluded voters were more than enough to give Gore the presidency.

17. *Newstand* was not alone. ABC's *20/20* and NBC's *Dateline* also were starting to lose viewers. According to Tom Rosensteil, director of the Project for Excellence in Journalism, "People are too busy with other appointments to show up for these generic newsmagazine shows. . . . "It's also a very difficult thing to do. The last time someone put on a successful appointment show, they had to put a bunch of castaways on an island" (Farhi 2000).

## Chapter 4

1. Rupert Murdoch boasts that he launched the Fox News Channel as a counterbalance to the perceived liberal bias of CNN. The 24-hour news channel has been widely criticized for the hypocrisy of its conservative slant (Hickey 1998; Rutenberg 2000c). The Fox News slogan "We report. You decide" is an obvious claim to fairness and balance. A similar strategy was employed at the *Calgary Herald* newspaper. A strike in 1999 by editorial staff at the paper was sparked, in part, by management's decision to implement a new system of "FAB reporting," which stood for "fair, accurate and balanced." FAB reporting was adopted by management, of the then Hollinger-controlled broadsheet, after it was determined the paper's editorial position had been too left wing. "It [the paper's news coverage] was not reflective of the city," said former *Herald* publisher Ken King. "If Calgary was an entrepreneurial, enthusiastic, upbeat city with a robust economy, the newspaper was not reflecting that" (Craig 1999). At both Fox News and the *Herald*, the standard of objectivity was redefined to allow for the presentation of more right-of-center opinion; yet, it was branded as fair and balanced.

2. Miami news organizations are incredibly integrated. NBC's station WTVJ also has a partnership with the *Miami Herald* newspaper to share news content. And the prepackaged newscast that appears on WBZL using WTVJ anchors and reporting can be seen on the Paxton affiliate WPXM. In addition, the Tribune's *Sun-Sentinel* has a partnership with the CBS O & O, which also owns the Miami Viacom/Paramount station that broadcasts a newscast during the same 10 p.m. slot in which WBZL's prepackaged rehash of WTVJ news appears (Fitzgerald 2000).

3. Gilder, a former speechwriter for U.S. President Ronald Reagan, has become rich by using his religious hyperbole to promote technology stocks on his own Web site <www.gildertech.com>. After successfully branding himself as an Internet/market guru, Gilder rode the high-tech stock bubble and charged subscribers $295 a year for the privilege of reading his unique mixture of free-market mythology and stock picks (Rothstein 2000).

4. Research in the United States indicates that socioeconomic disparities continue to affect Internet usage. In 1998, only 37 percent of production and agriculture workers owned a home computer. Conversely, 62 percent of white-collar professionals had computers in their homes

(Wilhelm 2000: 56). Race and ethnicity also play a role. In fall of 2000, the U.S. Department of Commerce found that White (50.3 percent) households enjoyed Internet access levels nearly double those of Black (29.3 percent) and Hispanic (23.7 percent) households. Internet use rates were also higher in homes with higher incomes. Seventy percent of people living in homes with incomes greater than US$75,000 reported using the Internet. That figure dropped to roughly 19 percent for individuals who lived in households with annual incomes of less than US$15,000 (U.S. Department of Commerce 2000).

5. Officials at AOL now say the 25-percent cancellation provision has been scrapped.

6. The measurement of Internet audiences is not an exact science. Competing measurement firms employ different methodologies, resulting in different numbers. Media Metrix, for example, includes users two and older in its samples. PC Data limits its samples to people age 13 and older (Eunjung Cha 2001).

7. The Media Metrix data cited here can be reviewed at: <mediametrix.com>.

8. The Excite.ca site was closed after parent company Excite@Home filed for bankruptcy in October 2001. Excite.com was later purchased by iWon.com, an Internet rival among second-tier Internet portals, which uses contests to attract Web users.

9. Perhaps the most extreme case of a news organization using personality traits to brand their news file comes from the computer-generated character of Annanova—the world's first virtual newscaster. Created by Britain's Press Association, Annanova.com repurposes news bulletins, which are read by Annanova, the Web site's fully animated green-and-blue-haired newscaster. Her profile is that of a single 28-year-old "girl about town." She loves the pop-band Oasis and the TV show *The Simpsons,* and is programmed to read the news in "a pleasant and quietly intelligent manner" (BBC News Online 2000). Annanova newscasts can be viewed at <www. annanova.com>.

10. Media General took a particularly aggressive approach to the melding of different newsroom cultures when it created a central news desk for the *Tampa Tribune, Tampa Bay Online* (TBO.com) and its NBC affiliate, WFLA-TV. The company staged a series of so-called pre-nuptial meetings to iron out any lingering difficulties among the three newsrooms. Gil Thelen, the *Tribune*'s senior editor and vice president, makes it clear that he wanted to infuse the newly formed joint newsroom with the values of the business community. "An ongoing concern is how to integrate the entrepreneur into a traditional culture," said Thelen. "This will be a challenge for the company to adjust to. We want to place a high value on experimental risk-taking, rather than on the tried and true journalism story" (Colon 2000). The clash of newsroom cultures also posed a problem in the convergence partnership between the *Dallas Morning News* and that city's ABC affiliate, WFAA (Moses 2000).

11. Canadian census data is available online at <www.statscan.ca>. U.S. census data is available online at <factfinder.census.gov>.

12. Media Metrix has reported that local news sites have had trouble attracting visitors. The audience-monitoring service says not one local TV station in the United States attracted more than 200,000 unique visitors per month. And none of the TV Web sites have reported making a profit (Anzur 2001).

13. Both the *Globe and Mail* and the *National Post* created useful online packages during the 2000 Canadian federal election that contained links to Web sites run by political parties, as well as basic information about individual ridings. The *Washington Post* also created hyperlinks to Web sites of opponents of the World Trade Organization as part of its coverage of the opposition to the expansion of neoliberal trade policies.

14. A survey by Don Middleberg and Steven Ross (1998) found that original content published by newspapers with Web sites increased during the 1990s. "By late 1997 almost 20 percent of newspapers with web sites said original content was at least 50 percent" of the site's content. That figure was up considerably from 1996 when only seven percent of newspapers with online

sites reported that original content accounted for 50 percent of their online news file (cited in Pavlik and Ross 2000). Still, despite the optimistic tone of the Middleberg and Ross report, wire copy remains prominant on many online news sites.

15. Some media apologists point to the fact that the existence of the dress was later proven. While true, this does not absolve news organizations from publishing unsubstantiated claims and hearsay.

16. VNS was thrown into disrepute in 2000 after all five U.S. networks used the faulty numbers provided by the service to prematurely award the presidential election to Gore, only to give it to Bush two hours later. Finally, the networks ended the evening admitting they didn't know who had won.

17. Another noteworthy partnership involves CBS's New York station WCBS-TV. The station, along with close to a dozen media partners, has created the CBS 2 Information Network. The deal involves the sharing of resources and reporters from *U.S. News and World Report.* Other partners are CBS News, VH1 News, Court TV, CBS Healthwatch, CBS Marketwatch, CNN, Hollywood.com, the *New York Daily News,* and The Learning Channel (TLC).

18. At the time, *Saturday Night Live* was enjoying renewed vigor on the strength of cast member Will Ferrell's impersonation of George W. Bush. Drehle related a story about how one night Bush's staff members were watching the program in a hotel room. Bush, well known for his early bed times, reportedly burst into the room during one of Ferrell's impersonations, demanding that the program be turned off. According to Drehle, Bush's staff scattered.

19. The FCC's comment period on the proposed changes to cross-ownership rules came during the U.S.-led bombing raids on Afghanistan. Schechter points out that 10 years earlier during the Gulf War, the broadcast industry had been lobbying the FCC to change financial syndication rules. The industry eventually won the changes, and much more, in the 1996 Telecommunications Act. Schechter speculates that brass in the broadcasting networks were loath to criticize government policy during the Gulf conflict because of their own "economic agenda." As part of the chill on news coverage, Schechter cites a 1991 speech by FCC commissioner James Quello in which Schechter says Quello questioned "the patriotism of TV journalists for demanding hard information about the war."

20. The short life of *Brill's Content* provides a concise history of the ups and downs of adopting the logic of promotional integration. The magazine's 1998 premiere issue successfully used Steven Brill's cover story of the media coverage of the Clinton-Lewinsky scandal to create a media buzz. Brill had tapped into the big promotional fulcrum point of the moment. However, the magazine was unable to convert that early success into a consistent readership. Early in April 2001, Brill Media announced plans to merge *Brill's Content* to form a co-branded hybrid called *Inside Content.* The plan was scrapped a month later. Brill cited the depressed advertising market as the reason. As part of the announcement, the magazine would no longer be published 10 times a year. It was relaunched as a quarterly, before its eventual demise in October 2001. The flat dot-com economy, and a depressed advertising market that only got worse following the terrorist attacks of September 11, 2001, also affected the prospects of Contentville and Inside.com, which was reduced to the status of a Web portal.

## Chapter 5

1. The Verus Group, a Vancouver-based public-relations firm, bragged in its mid-1990s promotional literature that its accomplishments include: "9 chemical spills explained . . . 6 industrial deaths explained . . . 450 negative stories prevented . . . and 23 environmental protests managed."

2. See Leiss, Kline, and Jhally's (1990) chapter entitled "Fantasia for the Citizen" for a concise summary of the political marketing literature.

3. In one episode of *The Awful Truth,* Crackers, the Corporate Crime-Fighting Chicken, visits Disneyland. Crackers advises Mickey Mouse about Disney's alleged unfair labor practices. This "gonzo" style of reporting has a celebrated tradition. It owes its origins to the humorously nonobjective and critical work of Hunter S. Thompson. His book *Fear and Loathing: Campaign Trail '72,* closed out a list of 100 best examples of American journalism in the 20th century. The list was compiled in 1999 by experts assembled by the New York University Department of Journalism & Mass Communication.

4. The dominance of the patriotic good-versus-evil framing of the events related to September 11, 2001, was brought home two months later. On November 12, during coverage of the crash of an American Airlines airbus into the New York suburb of Queens, many broadcasters removed the ubiquitous red, white and blue logos from their broadcasts. "We did not think that there was any kind of America-against-the-rest-of-the-world issue with this story," said Erik Sorenson, MSNBC president. Fox News kept its stars-and-stripes logo because, according to a spokesperson, the country was "still at war" (Stanley and Rutenberg 2001).

5. It is possible to determine the clear winner of the U.S. presidential election, if standards of measurement can be agreed upon.

6. In 2001, the same media strategy was applied by the U.S. administration during the early stages of the so-called War on Terrorism. It is worth noting that it was precisely at the moment when the U.S. administration's control over coverage began to slip, that members of the Bush cabinet adopted more overtly authoritarian tactics. The Bush administration pressured the emir of Qatar, Sheikh Hamad Khalifa al-Thani, to exert influence on the Al Jazeera cable-TV network. The United States government wanted the Qatar-based network to tone down coverage the administration claimed was fanning the flames of Arab extremism in the Middle East. Likewise, the American and British administrations leaned on major media outlets in their respective countries to not broadcast video supplied by Al Qaeda to Al Jazeera. The pretext used was that the video may contain secret messages for members of the Al Qaeda terrorist network.

   In an unprecedented move, the five major U.S. television-news organizations agreed to follow the wishes of the administration. They agreed to not broadcast Al Qaeda video live, as had been done October 7, 2001, the day American forces launched bombing raids in Afghanistan.

   Worried that the American-led coalition was losing the propaganda war in the Arab world, the U.S. administration hired a well-known Washington public-relations firm to shape its message in the Middle East and Central Asia. The Rendon Group was retained to alter the impression shared among many Arabs that the war in Afghanistan was a war against Islam (Strobel and Landay 2001).

7. Bill and Hillary Clinton's 1992 appearance on CBS's *60 Minutes* arguably salvaged the future president's campaign. At the time, Clinton's candidacy was reeling from allegations made by Gennifer Flowers that she had been his mistress. It was during the televised interview that Clinton made his now famous admission of guilt: "I have acknowledged wrongdoing," he told interviewer Steve Kroft. "I have acknowledged causing pain in my marriage." As John Thompson argues, Clinton knew that a public denial of the affair could fuel a torrent of stories and eventually sink his run for the presidency (Thompson 2000: 149–151). Ironically, Clinton's lack of candor regarding his relationship with Monica Lewinsky fueled reports of the so-called Monicagate scandal. Congressman Gary Condit was ruthlessly attacked by the "punditocracy" following his televised interview with ABC's Connie Chung. Many critics felt Condit was evasive about the nature of his relationship with missing intern Chandra Levy. Condit had hoped to use his appearance on *Primetime Thursday* to launch his political comeback. Instead, the interview was a public-relations disaster.

8. Al Gore's attempt to tap into the McCain narrative becomes obvious when one is able to see his repetitious references to the Arizona senator's style of politics. Gore made the following comments in a *New York Times* interview aboard Air Force II: "Like John McCain, I took from my personal experience a deeper commitment to the battle for campaign finance reform, and I think this is the year it's going to happen." Again, on campaign finance reform: "I have acknowledged my mistakes in the past, and I am applying the lessons of those mistakes to a call for change now, so that this campaign and all future campaigns will be conducted differently." Once more, on personal growth: "Making mistakes and acknowledging them. When you acknowledge a mistake, that is an opportunity for learning and growth. And that is what I experienced." (*New York Times* 2000).

9. Ventura eventually "made good" on his promise by having rebate checks mailed to Minnesota residents.

10. Bourdieu goes on to say that a social group's recognition of its own interests is "in more or less transfigured and unrecognizable form." I do not share Bourdieu's belief that the use of symbolic power implies a form of "misrecognition" on the part of individuals. I agree, instead, with John Thompson who argues that "these beliefs may be erroneous or rooted in a limited understanding of the social bases of power, but these should be regarded as contingent possibilities rather than necessary presuppositions" (Thompson 1995: 269n.8).

## *Chapter 6*

1. The report is available online at <www.newamericancentury.org>.

2. David Armstrong (2002) argues that Dick Cheney had been developing plans for U.S. domination of the Persian Gulf region as far back as 1992 when he authored the Defense Planning Guidance, a draft paper in which the Bush administration's unilateral foreign policy was first fleshed out.

## *Conclusion*

1. Beginning in 1987, the Institute for Global Communication (IGC) and its partner the Association for Progressive Communications (APC) helped establish numerous activist sites on the Web (Downing et al. 2001: 212).

# Bibliography

ABC News (2003) "Fear and Relief: Jessica Lynch Was about to Be Rescued; She Thought She Was about to Be Killed," ABCNews.com, November 11, <abcnews.go.com/sections/Primetime/US/Jessica_Lynch_031111-1.html>.

Adelman, Kenneth (2002) "Why Now? A Better Question Is Why Wait?" Foxnews.com, <www.foxnews.com/story/0,2933,65146,00.html>.

Adorno, Theodore (1976) [1957] "Sociology and Empirical Research," in Paul Connerton, ed., *Critical Sociology,* Harmondsworth, UK: Penguin Books, pp. 237–257.

Agacinski, Sylviane (2001) "Stages of Democracy," in Marcel Hénaff and Tracy B. Strong, eds., *Public Space and Democracy,* Minneapolis: University of Minnesota Press, pp. 129–143.

Ahrens, Frank (2000) "What Will They Talk About Now?" *Washington Post,* November 14, C2.

Ahrens, Frank (2002) "These Giants Hope to Dump Angels and More," *Washington Post,* October 24, E1.

Ahrens, Frank (2003a) "Court Blocks Media Rules," *Washington Post,* September 4, A1.

Ahrens, Frank (2003b) "Panel Fires Shot across FCC's Bow," *Washington Post,* September 5, E5.

Ahrens, Frank (2003c) "Compromise Puts TV Ownership Cap at 39%," *Washington Post,* November 25, A19.

Ahrens, Frank and Alec Klein (2003) "Parent Firm May Drop AOL from Its Name," *Washington Post,* August, E1.

Alexander, Jeffrey (1988) "Culture and Political Crisis: 'Watergate' and Durkheimian Sociology," in Jeffrey Alexander, ed., *Durkheimian Sociology: Cultural Studies,* Cambridge: Cambridge University Press, pp. 187–224.

Alexander, Jeffrey, and Ronald Jacobs (1998) "Mass Communication, Ritual and Civil Society," in Tamar Liebes and James Curran, eds. *Media, Ritual and Identity,* London and New York: Routledge, pp. 23–41.

Alger, Dean (1998) *Megamedia: How Giant Corporations Dominate Mass Media, Distort Competition, and Endanger Democracy,* Lanham, Maryland: Rowman & Littlefield.

Allen, Mike (2003) "President Assails Iraq War Skeptics," *Washington Post,* June 18, A13.

Altheide, David, and Robert Snow (1991) *Media Worlds in the Post-Journalism Era,* New York: Aldine de Gruyter.

Amin, Hussein, and James Napoli (2000) "Media and Power in Egypt," in James Curran and Myung-Jin Park, eds., *De-Westernizing Media Studies,* London and New York: Routledge, pp. 178–188.

Andersen, Robin (1995) *Consumer Culture and TV Programming,* Boulder, CO: Westview Press.

Angus, Ian (2000) *Primal Scenes of Communication: Communication, Consumerism, and Social Movements,* Albany: State University of New York Press.

Angwin, Julia, and Matthew Rose (2001) "Creating a New Media Concept: AOL, Time Warner Hash Out Exactly What It Means; the Keanu Reeves 'Mistake,'" *Wall Street Journal,* March 9, B1.

Anzur, Terry (2001) "TV News Websites: The Myth of Convergence," *Online Journalism Review,* January 10, <ojr.usc.edu/content/print.cfm?print=521>.

Armstrong, David (2002) "Dick Cheney's Song of America: Drafting a Plan for Global Dominance," *Harper's,* October, pp. 76–83.

ASNE (2000) *Extending the Brand: A Newspaper Editor's Guide to Partnerships and Diversification in a Converging Media World,* Reston, VA: American Society of Newspaper Editors, Publication Fulfilment.

Associated Press (1991) "War-Related Products Face 'Profiteering Tag,'" *Marketing News,* March 18, p. 1.

Associated Press (2000a) "Madonna Wanted to Marry Near Diana's Grave," *Salon,* December 11, <www.salon.com/people/wire/2000/12/11/madonna/print.html>.

Associated Press (2000b) "Tribune Wants Paper Reporting for TV," Excite.com, September 20.

Associated Press (2000c) "Internet Attracting Younger News Audience," CNETNews.com, June 11, <news.cnet.com/news/0-1005-200-2057853.html>.

Associated Press (2001) "Salon.com Seeks Subscriptions," *New York Times,* March 20, <www.ny times.com>.

Auletta, Ken (1998) "Synergy City," *American Journalism Review,* 20 (4), pp. 18–35.

Babe, Robert (1996) "Convergence and the New Technologies," in Michael Dorland, ed., *The Cultural Industries in Canada: Problems, Policies and Prospects,* Toronto: James Lorimer and Company, Publishers, pp. 283–307.

Bagdikian, Ben (2000) *The Media Monopoly,* 6th ed., Boston: Beacon Press.

Barber, Benjamin (1984) *Strong Democracy,* Berkeley: University of California Press.

Barker, Chris (1997) *Global Television: An Introduction,* Oxford and Malden, MA: Blackwell.

Barnhart, Aaron (2003) "On TV, Bombing Induces Awe," *Kansas City Star,* March 22, <www.kansas city.com/mld/kansascity/>.

Barringer, Felicity (2000) "Big News on Little Screens," *New York Times,* April 10, C1.

Barringer, Felicity (2001) "Growing Audience Is Turning to Established News Media Online," *New York Times,* August 27, C1.

Bart, Peter (2003) "Iraq Passes Its Screen Test," Variety.com, April 13, <www.variety.com/index.asp?layout=print_story&articleid=VR1117884504&categoryid=1019>.

Bauder, David (2001) "Geraldo Rivera Goes from CNBC to Fox," *Associated Press,* November 1, <news.excite.com/news/ap/011101/19/ent-fox-rivera>.

Bauder, David (2003) "Embedded War Reporters: Experiment Passes Muster," *Globe and Mail,* April 23, B12.

Baudrillard, Jean (1981) *For a Critique of the Political Economy of the Sign,* St. Louis: Telos Press.

Baudrillard, Jean (1995) *The Gulf War Did Not Take Place,* Paul Patton, trans., Bloomington and Indianapolis: Indiana University Press.

Baum, Caroline (2000) "Election and O.J. Mini-Series Vie for Viewers," *Bloomberg News,* November 15.

BBC News Online (2000) "Cyberbabe to Read the News," *BBC News Online,* January 17, <news.bbc.co.uk/1/hi/entertainment/606855.stm>.

BBC News Online (2003a) "Sony in 'Shock and Awe' Blunder," *BBC News Online,* April 16, <news.bbc.co.uk/1/hi/business/2951859.stm >.

BBC News Online (2003b) "CBS Backs Down on Lynch Movie," *BBC News Online,* July 21, <news.bbc.co.uk/2/hi/entertainment/3083235.stm>.

Beard, Alison (2003) "US TV Counts the Cost of War," *Financial Times,* April 7, P. 18.

Bednarski, P.J., and John M. Higgins (2003) "Heyward: Objectivity a Function of Fairness," Broadcastingandcable.com, March 24, <www.broadcasting-cable.com/CA286552.htm>.

Bedway, Barbara (2003) "Why AP Counted Civilian Deaths in Iraq," *Editor and Publisher,* July 24, <www.editorandpublisher.com/editorandpublisher/headlines/articles_display.jsp?vnu_content_id=1920081>.

Bell, Daniel (1976) *The Cultural Contradictions of Capitalism,* New York: Basic Books.

Benjamin, Walter (1968) "The Work of Art in the Age of Mechanical Reproduction," in Hannah Arendt, ed., *Illuminations,* New York: Schocken Books.

Bennett, W. Lance (1988) *News: The Politics of Illusion,* 2nd ed. New York: Longman.

Bennett, W. Lance (1998) "The UnCivic Culture: Communication, Identity, and the Rise of Life-style Politics," *P.S.: Political Science and Politics,* December 31, pp. 741–761.

Bennett, W. Lance, and Murray Edelman (1985) "Toward a New Political Narrative," *Journal of Communication* 35, 156–171.

Bennett, W. Lance, and Jarol B. Manheim (2001) "The Big Spin: Strategic Communication and the Transformation of Pluralist Democracy," in W. Lance Bennett and Robert M. Entman, eds., *Mediated Politics: Communication in the Future of Democracy,* Cambridge and New York: Cambridge University Press, pp. 279–298.

Berke, Richard (2001) "Aftermath: It's Not a Time for Party, But for How Long?" *New York Times,* September 23, D3.

Berkowitz, Dan (2000) "Doing Double Duty: Paradigm Repair and the Princess Diana What-a-Story," *Journalism: Theory, Practice and Criticism,* 1 (2), pp. 125–143.

Beveridge, Dirk (1998) "Diana's Image a Hot Commodity," *Associated Press,* August 13.

Bhabha, Homi (1998) "Designer Creations," in Mandy Merck, ed., *After Diana: Irreverent Elegies,* London and New York: Verso.

Bird, Elizabeth (1990) "Storytelling on the Far Side: Journalism and the Weekly Tabloid," *Critical Studies in Mass Communication,* 7, pp. 377–389.

Bishop, Ronald (1999) "From Behind the Walls: Boundary Work by News Organizations in Their Coverage of Princess Diana's Death," *Journal of Communication Inquiry,* 23 (1), pp. 91–113.

Bishop, Ronald (2001) "News Media, Heal Thyselves: Sourcing Patterns in News Stories about News Media Performance," *Journal of Communication Inquiry,* 25 (1), pp. 22–37.

Black, Conrad (2000) "Don't Write Off Newspapers Yet," *Wall Street Journal,* March 6, A30.

Blackwell, Richard (2003) "Toronto Star and TV Station Join Forces," *Globe and Mail,* September 5, B2.

Bloomberg News (1998) "Clinton Speech Draws Largest TV News Audience Since Gulf War," *Bloomberg News,* August 19.

Bloomberg News (2000) "Salon.com Is Cutting Work Force by 20 Percent," *New York Times,* December 21, <www.nytimes.com>.

Bock, Paula (2000) "The Nike Guru: Weave Your Brand into the Fabric of Life," in ASNE (2000) *Extending the Brand: A Newspaper Editor's Guide to Partnerships and Diversification in a Converging Media World,* Reston, VA: American Society of Newspaper Editors, Publication Fulfilment, pp. 15–21.

Boehlert, Eric (2001) "One Big Happy Channel?" *Salon,* June 28, <www.salon.com/tech/feature/2001/06/28/telecom_dereg>.

Boorstin, Daniel (1992) *The Image: A Guide to Pseudo-Events in America,* New York: Vintage.

Bourdieu, Pierre (1990) *The Logic of Practice,* Stanford: Stanford University Press.

Bourdieu, Pierre (1991) *Language and Symbolic Power,* John B. Thompson, ed., Gino Raymond and Matthew Adamson, trans., Cambridge, MA: Polity Press.

Bourdieu, Pierre (1998) *On Television,* Priscilla Parkhurst Ferguson, trans., New York: The New Press.

Bourdon, Jérôme (2000) "Live Television Is Still Alive: On Television as an Unfulfilled Promise," *Media, Culture and Society,* 22 (5), pp. 531–556.

Boyd, Christine (2003) "U.S. Alters Reason for War on Iraq," *Globe and Mail,* July 10, A10.

Bracken, Len (1997) *Guy Debord—Revolutionary,* Venice, CA: Feral House.

Branch, Shelly (2000) "Product Plugs—'M'm M'm Good?" *Wall Street Journal,* November 14, B1.

Brantlinger, Patrick (1983) *Bread and Circuses: Theories of Mass Culture as Social Decay,* Ithaca, NY: Cornell University Press.

Brill, Steven (1998) "Pressgate," *Brill's Content,* July/August, pp. 123–151.

Bright, Martin, Ed Vulliamy, and Peter Beaumont (2003) "US Dirty Tricks to Win Votes on Iraq War," *The Observer,* March 2, News Section, p. 1.

Brown, Chip (1999) "Fear.com," *American Journalism Review,* June, 21 (5), pp. 50–71.

Brown, Robin (2003) "Spinning the War: Political Communications, Information Operations and Public Diplomacy in the War on Terrorism," in Daya Kishan Thussu and Des Freedman, eds., *War and the Media: Reporting Conflict 24/7,* London: Sage, pp. 87–100.

Bruce, Ian (2003) "Al Qaeda Chiefs Told US They Had No Links with Saddam: Bin Laden Ruled out Iraq Sanctuary Offer," *(Glasgow) Herald,* June 10, p. 2.

Brunelli, Richard (2003) "Cross-Media Partnerships Grow," *Editor and Publisher,* June 3, <www.editorandpublisher.com/editor-andpublisher/headlines/-article_display.jsp?vnu_content_id=1900523>.

Budd, Mike, Steve Craig, and Clay Steinman (1999) *Consuming Environments: Television and Commercial Culture,* New Brunswick, NJ, and London: Rutgers University Press.

Buffalo News (2002) "Newspapers Gaining Acceptance Online," *Buffalo News,* October 25, C8.

Buncombe, Andrew, and Marie Woolf (2003) "Cheney under Pressure to Quit over False War Evidence," *Independent,* July 16, Section 1, p. 1.

Burkeman, Oliver, Ian Black, Matt Wells, Sean Smith, and Brian Whitaker (2003) "Television Agendas Shape Images of War," *Guardian,* March 27, Home Pages, p. 7.

Burston, Jonathan (2003) "War and the Entertainment Industries: New Research Priorities in an Era of Cyber-Patriotism," in Daya Kishan Thussu and Des Freedman, eds., *War and the Media: Reporting Conflict 24/7,* London: Sage, pp. 163–175.

Canada NewsWire (2001) "CRTC Decision Bad for Journalists and Public, Says TNG Canada," August 2.

Canadian Radio-Television and Telecommunications Commission (2001a) Licence Renewals for the Television Stations Controlled by Global (Decision 2001—458), <www.crtc.gc.ca/archive/ENG/Decisions/2001/DB2001-458.htm>.

Canadian Radio-Television and Telecommunications Commission (2001a) Licence Renewals for the Television Stations Controlled by Global by CTV (Decision 2001- 457), <www.crtc.gc.ca/archive/ENG/Decisions/2001/DB2001-457.htm>.

Carey, James (1992) *Communication as Culture: Essays on Media and Society,* London and New York: Routledge.

Carey, James (1998) "Political Ritual on Television: Episodes in the History of Shame, Degradation and Excommunication," in Tamar Liebes and James Curran, eds., *Media, Ritual and Identity,* London and New York: Routledge.

Carr, David (2003) "Slate Sets a Web Magazine First: Making Money," *New York Times,* April 28, C1.

Carter, Bill (2000a) "TV Talk Shows See Hope in the Never-Ending 2000 Election," *New York Times,* November 13, C1.

Carter, Bill (2000b) "The Times in News Deal with ABC," *New York Times,* January 21, C4.

Carter, Bill (2001) "Murdoch Executive Calls Press Coverage of China Too Harsh," *New York Times,* March 26, C8.

Carter, Bill (2003) "Nightly News Feels the Pinch of 24-hour News," *New York Times,* April 14, C1.

Carter, Bill, and Felicity Barringer (2001) "In Patriotic Time, Dissent Is Muted," *New York Times,* September 28, A1.

Carter, Bill, and Allison Fass (2000) "CBS Finally Lures Coveted Young Viewers with Survivor," *New York Times,* June 19, C1.

Cass, Dennis (1999) "An Action Figure for All Seasons," *Harper's,* February, pp. 65–71.

Cassy, John, and Dan Milmo (2003) "Ad Slots Empty as Brands Avoid War," *Guardian,* March 21, City Pages, p. 23.

Castells, Manuel (2000a) *The Rise of the Network Society,* 2nd ed., Oxford and Malden, MA: Blackwell.

Castells, Manuel (2000b) *End of Millennium,* 2nd ed., Oxford and Malden, MA: Blackwell.

CBS News (2002) "Plans for Iraq Attack Began on 9/11," CBSNews.com, September 4, <www.cbsnews.com/stories/2002/09/04/september11/main520830.shtml>.

CBS News (2003) "Iraq Faces Massive Missile U.S. Barrage," CBSNews.com, January 24, <www.cbsnews.com/stories/2003/01/24/eveningnews/main537928.shtml>.

Cernetig, Miro (2001) "Lights, Action, Roll War," *Globe and Mail,* October 2, R1.

Chaney, David (1993) *Fictions of Collective Life: Public Drama in Late Modern Culture,* London: Routledge.

Chang, Leslie, and Charles Hutzler (2003) "CCTV Aims To Be China's CNN," *Globe and Mail,* March 27, B12.

Chan-Olmsted, Sylvia M. (2000) "Marketing Mass Media on the World Wide Web: The Building of Media Brands in an Integrated and Interactive World," in Alan B. Albarran and David H. Goff, eds., *Understanding the Web: Social, Political and Economic Dimensions of the Internet,* Ames: Iowa State University Press, pp. 95–116.

Chinni, Dante (2003) "Jessica Lynch: Media Myth-Making in the Iraq War," journalism.org, <www.journalism.org/resources/research/reports/war/postwar/lynch.asp>, accessed July 26.

Chiose, Simona (1997) "You're Going To Make It After All!" *Globe and Mail,* March 1, D1.

Chipman, Kim (2001) "Disney Keeping Go.com Because of Low Expenses," *Los Angeles Times,* March 15, C4.

Chomsky, Noam (1992) "The Media and the War: What War?" in Hamid Mowlana, George Gerbner, and Herbert I. Schiller, eds., *Triumph of the Image: The Media's War in the Persian Gulf—A Global Perspective,* Boulder, CO: Westview Press.

Chunovic, Louis (2003) "War: Sponsors Take Wait-and-See Stance," *Electronic Media,* September 30, p. 10.

CNN (1999) "Bradley Claims to Catch Gore in Overall Fund-Raising: McCain Quarterly Figures Double," December 29, <www.cnn.com/1999/ALLPOLITICS/stories/12/29/mccain.fundraising>.

Cohen, Akiba A., and Mark R. Levy, Itzhak Roeh, and Michael Gurevitch (1996) *Global Newsrooms, Local Audiences: A Study of the Eurovision News Exchange,* London: John Libbey and Company.

Cohen, Andrew (1999a) "American Tragedy Plays Out Once More," *Globe and Mail,* July 19, A1.

Cohen, Andrew (1999b) "Monica's Story: 'I Cannot Believe' That It's Over," *Globe and Mail,* A11.

Cohen, Andrew (2000a) "Mudslinging Smears U.S. Election," *Globe and Mail,* November 18, A16.

Cohen, Andrew (2000b) "McCain Campaign Brought More Voters into the Booths," *Globe and Mail,* March 15, A12.

Cohen, Andrew (2000c) "The Sudden Superstar," *Globe and Mail,* February 11, A1.

Cohen, Andrew (2003) "Diplomacy As Theater," CBSNews.com, February 5, <www.cbsnews.com/stories/2003/02/05/news/opinion/courtwatch/main539500.shtml>.

Colon, Aly (2000) "The Multimedia Newsroom: Three Organizations Aim for Convergence in

Newly Designed Tampa Headquarters," *Columbia Journalism Review,* May/June, <www.cjr.org /year/00/2/colon.asp>.

Conant, Jennet (1997) "L.A. Confidential," *Vanity Fair,* December, pp. 160–172.

Cowen, Richard (2003) "Die-ins Target War and News Media," *The Record,* <www.common dreams.org/headlines03/0328-10.htm>.

Cozens, Claire (2003) "Hoon Claims PR Victory," media.guardian.co.uk, March 28, <media.guardian. co.uk/marketingandpr/story/0,7494,924642,00.html>.

Craig, Susanne (1999) "The Real Reason Herald Staff Are Hitting the Bricks," *Globe and Mail,* November 16, A14.

Cronauer, Adrian (1994) "The Fairness Doctrine: A Solution in Search of a Problem," *Federal Communications Law Journal,* 47 (1), pp. 51–77.

Curran, James, Angus Douglas, and Gary Whannel (1980) "The Political Economy of the Human Interest Story," in Anthony Smith, ed., *Newspapers and Democracy,* Cambridge, MA: MIT Press.

Curran, James (1996) "Mass Media and Democracy Revisited," in James Curran, and Michael Gurevitch, eds., *Mass Media and Society,* London: Arnold, pp. 81–119.

Curran, James (1998) "Crisis of Public Communication: A Reappraisal," in Tamar Liebes, and James Curran, eds., *Media, Ritual and Identity,* London and New York: Routledge, pp. 175–202.

Curran, James, and Myung-Jin Park (2000) *De-Westernizing Media Studies,* London and New York: Routledge.

Currie, Phil (2000) *News Report to Publishers: We Are Moving Ahead with a New Information Model, Changes in Review, Emphasis on Online,* Report produced for Gannett, <www.gannett.com/go/ newswatch/2000/june/nw0609-1.htm>.

Dahlgren, Peter (1995) *Television and the Public Sphere: Citizenship, Democracy and the Media,* London: Sage.

Dalton, Russell J. (1996) *Citizen Politics: Public Opinion and Political Parties in Advanced Western Democracies,* Chatham, New Jersey: Chatham House Publishers.

Damsell, Keith (2001a) "BCE, Thomson Close Deal, Forming Bell Globemedia," *Globe and Mail,* January 10, B2.

Damsell, Keith (2001b) "CEOs Say Benefits of Media Mergers Far Ahead," *Globe and Mail,* April 4, B4.

Dao, James (2003) "Private Lynch Comes Back Home to a Celebration Fit for a Hero," *New York Times,* July 23, A1.

Darlington, Shasta (2003) "Blair Warns Iraq Ties with Al Qaeda are Growing," *Reuters,* February 21, <www.publicbroadcasting.net/kpbs/news/news.newsmain?action=article&ARTICLE_ID= 457965>.

Darnton, Robert (1975) "Writing News and Telling Stories,' *Daedalus,* Vol. 104 (2), pp. 175–193.

Davis, Aeron (2000) "Public Relations, News Production and Changing Patterns of Source Access in the British National Media," *Media, Culture and Society,* 22 (1), pp. 39–59.

Dayan, Daniel and Elihu Katz (1992) *Media Events: The Live Broadcasting of History,* Cambridge, MA: Harvard University Press.

Debord, Guy (1988) *Comments on the Society of the Spectacle,* Sheffield: Pirate Press.

Debord, Guy (1967) *The Society of the Spectacle,* Paris: Buchet-Castel. Reprinted with translation by Donald Nicholson-Smith. New York: Zone Books, 1995. Page references are references to 1995 edition.

Dedinsky, Mary L. (2000) "An Editor's Primer: Lessons Learned at the Chicago Tribune," in ASNE (2000) *Extending the Brand: Newspaper Editor's Guide to Partnerships and Diversification in a Converging Media World,* Reston, VA: American Society of Newspaper Editors, Publication Fulfilment, pp. 43–46.

Delli Carpini, Michael and Bruce Williams (2001) "Let Us Infotain You: Politics in the New Media Environment," in W. Lance Bennett and Robert M. Entman, eds., *Mediated Politics: Communication in the Future of Democracy,* New York: Cambridge University Press, pp. 160–181.

Dewan, Shaila K. (2001) "Beyond Calamity, Death Goes On," *New York Times,* October 17, D1.

DeYoung, Karen (2001) "U.S., Britain Step Up War for Public Opinion," *Washington Post,* November 1, A1.

Dobbs, Michael (2003) "Halliburton's Deals Greater Than Thought," *Washington Post,* August 28, A1.

Donnelly, Thomas (2000) "Rebuilding American Defenses: Strategies, Forces and Resources," A New American Century, September, <www.newamericancentury.org/RebuildingAmericas Defenses.pdf>.

Dotinga, Randy (2003) "Convergence Gains Critical Mass: Making a Dream a Reality," *Editor and Publisher,* May 12, <www.editorandpublisher.com/editorandpublisher/headlines/article_display. jsp?vnu_content_id=1885814>.

Dowd, Maureen (1998) "With Boomers Fixating on Mortality, Next Step is Inevitable: Death TV," *Globe and Mail,* July 7, A20.

Downey, John, and Graham Murdock (2003) "The Counter-Revolution in Military Affairs: The Globalization of Guerilla Warfare," in Daya Kishan Thussu, and Des Freedman, eds., *War and the Media: reporting conflict 24/7,* London: Sage, pp. 70–86.

Downing, John, with Tamara Villarreal Ford, Genève Gil, and Laura Stein (2001) *Radical Media: Rebellious Communication and Social Movements,* London: Sage.

Dreyfuss, Robert (2002) "The Pentagon Muzzles the CIA," *The American Prospect,* December 16, 13 (22), p. 26.

Durkheim, Emile (1995) *The Elementary Forms of Religious Life,* Karen E. Fields, trans., New York: The Free Press.

Dwyer, Paula (1996) "Can Rupert Conquer Europe?" *Business Week,* March 25, p. 169.

Dyer-Witheford, Nick (1999) *Cyber-Marx: Cycles and Circuits of Struggle in High-Technology Capitalism,* Urbana and Chicago: University of Illinois Press.

Ebner, Dave (2003) "Bell Canada, Microsoft Web Sites Click Together," *Globe and Mail,* June 17, B4.

Edelman, Murray (1988) *Constructing the Political Spectacle,* Chicago: University of Chicago Press.

Editor and Publisher Online (2003) "Newspapers Run 5 of Top Web News Domains," *Editor and Publisher,* May 21, <www.editorandpublisher.com/editorandpublisher/headlines/article_display. jsp?vnu_content_id=1892072>.

Editor and Publisher Online (2003) "MediaNews Group Joins Real Cities Network," *Editor and Publisher,* May 8, <www.editorandpublisher.com/editorandpublisher/headlines/article_display. jsp?vnu_content_id=1883449>.

Effron, Eric (2000) "Promotional Consideration," *Brill's Content,* December/January, pp. 51–52.

Eksteins, Modris (1989) *Rites of Spring: The Great War and the Birth of the Modern Age,* Toronto: Lester & Orpen Dennys.

Elliott, P., and P. Golding (1974) "Mass Communication and Social Change," in E. de Kadt, and K. Williams, eds., *Sociology and Development,* London: Tavistock, pp. 229–254.

Elliott, Philip (1980) "Press Performance as Political Ritual," in Harry Christian, ed., *The Sociology of Journalism and the Press,* Totowa, NJ: Rowman and Littlefield, pp. 141–177.

Elliott, Stuart (1999) "The Internet May Precipitate a Tempest for Traditional Brands and Advertising," *New York Times,* December 20, C43.

Ellis, Rick (2003) "The Surrender of MSNBC," AllYourTV.com, February 25, <www.allyour tv.com/0203season/news/02252003donahue.html>.

el-Nawawy, Mohammed (2001) "A Window on the Arab World," *Baltimore Sun,* July 23, 2A.

Enzensberger, Hans (1974) *The Consciousness Industry*, New York: Seabury Press.

Ericson, Richard V., Patricia M. Baranek, and B.L. Chan (1987) *Visualizing Deviance: A Study of News Organization*, Toronto: University of Toronto Press.

Ericson, Richard V., Patricia M. Baranek, and B.L. Chan (1989) *Negotiating Control: A Study of News Sources*, Toronto: University of Toronto Press.

Eunjung Cha, Ariana (1999) "AOL, Microsoft Set Alliances With Retailers," *Washington Post*, December 17, E3.

Eunjung Cha, Ariana (2001) "Counting Web Traffic: Which Internet Sites Have the Most Visitors? It Depends on Whom You Ask," *Washington Post*, February 4, H1.

Ewen, Stuart (1996) *PR!: A Social History of Spin*, New York: Basic Books.

EXTRA! (1999) "A Tale of Two Entertainment Shows," FAIR/EXTRA! Subscription Service, <www.fair.org/>.

Evans, Mark (2000) "Content Said Not Critical in Web Wars," *Globe and Mail*, March 2000, B3.

Fairchild, Charles (1999) "Deterritorializing Radio: Deregulation and the Continuing Triumph of the Corporatist Perspective in the USA," *Media, Culture and Society*, 21 (4), pp. 549–561.

Falasca-Zamponi, Simonetta (1997) *Fascist Spectacle: The Aesthetics of Power in Mussolini's Italy*, Berkeley: University of California Press.

Fallows, James (1999) "Rush from Judgement: How the Media Lost their Bearings," *The American Prospect*, March–April, No. 43, p. 18.

Fancher, Michael R. (2000) "Seattle: Branding Can Show Path to a Better Newspaper," in ASNE (2000) *Extending the Brand: Newspaper Editor's Guide to Partnerships and Diversification in a Converging Media World*, Reston, VA: American Society of Newspaper Editors, Publication Fulfilment, pp. 6–14.

Farhi, Paul (2000) "Crunch Time," *American Journalism Review*, November, p. 42.

Farhi, Paul (2003) "For Broadcast Media, Patriotism Pays," *Washington Post*, March 28, C1.

Featherstone, Mike (1991) *Consumer Culture and Postmodernism*, London: Sage.

Feldmann, Linda (2003) "The Impact of Bush Linking 9/11 and Iraq," csmonitor.com, March 14, <www.csmonitor.com/2003/0314/p02s01-woiq.html>.

Ferguson, Marjorie (1990) "Electronic Media and the Redefining of Time and Space," in Marjorie Ferguson, ed., *Public Communication: The New Imperatives: Future Directions for Media Research*, London: Sage.

Fisher, Marc (1998) "Minnesota Surprise: Voters Elect 'Governor Body,'" *Washington Post*, November 4, A1.

Fishman, Mark (1980) *Manufacturing the News*, Austin: University of Texas Press.

Fiske, John (1989) *Understanding Popular Culture*, London: Unwin Hyman.

Fitzgerald, Mark (2000) "FCC's Boob-Tube Bobble," *Editor and Publisher*, October 2, p. 20.

Fitzgerald, Mark (2002) "Chicago Trib' Circulation Gets 9/11 Boost," *Editor and Publisher*, October 1, <www.editorandpublisher.com/editorandpublisher/headlines/article_display.jsp?vnu_content_ide=1726110>.

Flint, Joe (1999) "ABC, Fox and CBS Set Up Footage Swap," *Wall Street Journal*, December 21, B8.

Flournoy, Don, and Robert Stewart (1997) *CNN: Making News in the Global Market*, Luton: University of Luton Press.

Foucault, Michel (1980) *Power/Knowledge: Selected Interviews and Other Writings 1972–1977*, Ed. by Colin Gordon, New York: Pantheon.

Fox News (2003) "B-2 Bombers Lead 'Shock and Awe,'" Fox News.com, March 26, <www.foxnews.com/story/0,2933,82262,00.html>.

Franklin, Bob (1994) *Packaging Politics: Political Communications in Britain's Media Democracy*, London: Arnold.

Franklin, Bob (1997) *Newszak and News Media*, London: Arnold.

Fraser, Matthew (1999) *Free-for-All: The Struggle for Dominance on the Digital Frontier,* Toronto: Stoddart.

French, Serena (2001) "Getting the Celebrity to Show Up," *National Post,* August 2, B3.

Gabler, Neal (1998) "Watergate With a Chorus Line," *Globe and Mail,* December 15, A31.

Gaillard, François (1998) "Diana, Postmodern Madonna," in Mandy Merck, ed., *After Diana: Irreverent Elegies,* London and New York: Verso.

Gaither, Chris (2001) "NBC to Shut Most of Its NBCi Web Portal," *New York Times,* April 10, C4.

Gans, Herbert (1979) *Deciding What's News,* New York: Pantheon.

Garnham, Nicholas (2000) *Emancipation, the Media and Modernity: Arguments about the Media and Social Theory,* Oxford and New York: Oxford University Press.

Garreau, Joel, and Linton Weeks (2000) "Visions of a World That's Nothing by Net," *Washington Post,* January 11, C1.

Gellman, Barton, and Walter Pincus (2003) "Depiction of Threat Outgrew Supporting Evidence," *Washington Post,* August 10, A1.

Gentry, James K. (2000) "Tampa: Another Stop on the Road to Convergence," in ASNE (2000) *Extending the Brand: Newspaper Editor's Guide to Partnerships and Diversification in a Converging Media World,* Reston, VA: American Society of Newspaper Editors, Publication Fulfilment, pp. 31–37.

Gerbner, George (1992) "Persian Gulf War, the Movie," in Hamid Mowlana, George Gerbner, and Herbert I. Schiller, eds., *Triumph of the Image: The Media's War in the Persian Gulf—A Global Perspective,* Boulder, Colorado: Westview Press.

Getler, Michael (2000) "The New News Thing," *Washington Post,* December 24, B6.

Ghosh, Peter (1998) "Mediate and Immediate Mourning," in Mandy Merck, ed., *After Diana: Irreverent Elegies,* London and New York: Verso.

Giddens, Anthony (1971) *Capitalism and Modern Social Theory: an Analysis of the Writings of Marx, Durkheim and Max Weber,* Cambridge: Cambridge University Press.

Giddens, Anthony (1990) *The Consequences of Modernity,* Stanford: Stanford University Press.

Gipson, Melinda (2003) "Playing the Online Game to Win!" *Presstime,* July/August, p. 26.

Girion, Lisa (2003) "Immunity for Iraqi Dealings Raises Alarm," *Los Angeles Times,* August 7, A1.

Gitlin, Todd (1980) *The Whole World is Watching: Mass Media in the Making and Unmaking of the New Left,* Berkeley: University of California Press.

Gitlin, Todd (1983) *Inside Prime Time,* New York: Pantheon Books.

Gitlin, Todd (1991) "Bits and Blips: Chunk News, Savvy Talk and the Bifurcation of American Politics," in Peter Dahlgren, and Colin Sparks, eds., *Communication and Citizenship: Journalism and the Public Sphere,* London and New York: Routledge, pp. 119–136.

Gitlin, Todd (2000a) "Dying for Attention," *Globe and Mail,* March 13, A11.

Gitlin, Todd (2000b) "A Look at. . . The AOL Deal; FEARED: It's All About Eyeballs, Baby," *Washington Post,* January 16, B3.

Glynn, Kevin (2000) *Tabloid Culture: Trash Taste, Popular Power, and the Transformation of American Television,* Durham and London: Duke University Press.

Goldoff, Anna C. (1996) "The Public Interest Standard and Deregulation: The Impact of the Fairness Doctrine," *International Journal of Public Administration,* 19(1), pp. 51–74.

Goodman, Peter S. (2001) "Powell Plans Fewer FCC Rules," *Washington Post,* March 30, E3.

Graham, Philip (2000) "Hypercapitalism: A Political Economy of Informational Idealism," *New Media & Society,* Vol. 2 (2), pp. 131–156.

Gramsci, Antonio (1971) *Selections from the Prison Notebooks of Antonio Gramsci,* Quintin Hoare, and Geoffrey Nowell Smith, eds. and trans., New York: International Publishers.

Griffin, Wendy (1999) "An American Paean for Diana, an Unlikely Feminist Hero," in Tony Walter, ed., *The Mourning for Diana,* Oxford and New York: Berg, pp. 241–251.

Gripsrud, Jostein (1992) "The Aesthetics and Politics of Melodrama," in Peter Dalhgren, and Colin Sparks, eds., *Journalism and Popular Culture,* London: Sage.

Gripsrud, Jostein (2000) "Tabloidization, Popular Journalism and Democracy," in Colin Sparks, and John Tolloch, eds., *Tabloid Tales: Global Debates over Media Standards,* Lanham, Maryland: Rowman and Littlefield, pp. 285–300.

Gruneau, Richard (1996) "Introduction: Why TVTV?," in Robert Anderson, Richard Gruneau, and Paul Heyer, eds., *TVTV: The Television Revolution, the Debate,* Vancouver, BC: Canadian Journal of Communication Corporation.

Gruneau, Richard (1983) *Class, Sports, and Social Development,* Amherst: University of Massachusetts Press. Reprinted with foreword by R.W. Connell. Champaign, Il: Human Kinetics, 1999. Page references are references to 1992 edition.

Gurevitch, Michael (1996) "The Globalization of Electronic Journalism," in James Curran and Michael Gurevitch (eds) *Mass Media and Society,* 2nd Edition, London and New York: Arnold.

Habermas, Jürgen (1989) *The Structural Transformation of the Public Sphere: An Inquiry into a Category of Bourgeois Society,* Thomas Burger, trans., Cambridge, MA: MIT Press.

Habermas, Jürgen (1990) *Moral Consciousness and Communicative Action,* Christian Lenhardt, and Shierry Weber Nicholsen, trans., Cambridge, MA: MIT Press.

Habermas, Jürgen (1992) "Further Reflections on the Public Sphere," in Craig Calhoun, ed., *Habermas and the Public Sphere,* Cambridge, MA: MIT Press, pp. 421–479.

Hackett, Robert A., and Yuezhi Zhao (1994). "Challenging the Master Narrative: Peace Protest and Opinion/Editorial Discourse in the US Press During the Gulf War," *Discourse and Society,* 5 (4), pp. 509–541.

Hackett, Robert, and Yeuzhi Zhao (1998) *Sustaining Democracy: Journalism and the Politics of Objectivity,* Toronto: Garamond Press.

Hackett, Robert, and Richard Gruneau (2000) *The Missing News: Filters and Blind Spots in Canada's Press,* Ottawa: Canadian Centre for Policy Alternatives/Garamond Press.

Hall, Stuart, Critcher, C., Jefferson, T., Clarke, J., and Roberts, B. (1978) *Policing the Crisis: Mugging, the State, and Law and Order,* London: Macmillan.

Hallin, Daniel, and Todd Gitlin (1994) "The Gulf War as Popular Culture and Television Drama," in W. Lance Bennett, and David L. Paletz, eds., *Taken by Storm: The Media, Public Opinion, and U.S. Foreign Policy in the Gulf War,* Chicago: University of Chicago Press.

Hallin, Daniel (1996) "Commercialism and Professionalism in the American News Media," *Mass Media and Society,* James Curran, and Michael Gurevitch, eds., London: Arnold.

Halpern, Orly (2003) "A New Iraqi Army Takes Aim at U.S.-Led Coalition," *Globe and Mail,* August 11, A1.

Hamilton, Tyler (2000) "Wireless World Requires Partnerships, Case Says," *Globe and Mail,* March 2, B4.

Hansell, Saul (2000a) "So Far, Big Brother Isn't Big Business," *New York Times,* May 7, C1.

Hansell, Saul (2000b) "TV's Monoliths Learn That the Web Is a Fragmented World," *New York Times,* August 14, C1.

Hansell, Saul (2001) "Disney, in Retreat From Internet, to Abandon Go.com Portal Site," *New York Times,* January 30, C1.

Hanson, Cheri (2001) "BCTV Shuffles its News Team for Re-Launch with Global BC," *Vancouver Sun,* August 16, B1.

Hardt, Michael, and Antonio Negri (2000) *Empire,* Cambridge, MA: Harvard University Press.

Harmon, Amy (2001) "Two Long-Running Internet Magazines Shut Down," *New York Times,* June 11, C7.

Harper, Tim (2003) "U.S. Pleased with Progress in Iraq 100 Days After War," *Toronto Star,* August 9, A14.

Harper's (2003) "Shlock and Awe," *Harper's,* June, 306 (1837), p. 18.

Harrington, Carol (2000) "Taber Shooter Sentenced to Three Years," *Globe and Mail,* November 18, A4.

Harris, Edward (2000) "Remember When . . . Internet Enthusiasts Protest Commercialism at Gatherings," *Wall Street Journal,* October 23, <interactive.wsj.com/archive/retrieve.cgi?id=SB972242613799628425.djm>.

Harvey, David (1989) *The Condition of Postmodernity: An Enquiry into the Origins of Cultural Change,* Oxford: Blackwell.

Harvey, David (2000) *Spaces of Hope,* Berkeley: University of California Press.

Hazlett, Thomas W., and David W. Sosa (1997) "Was the Fairness Doctrine a 'Chilling Effect'?: Evidence from the Postderegulation Radio Market," *Journal of Legal Studies,* 26, pp. 279–301.

Held, David (1980) "The Culture Industry: Critical Theory and Aesthetics," in David Held, *Introduction to Critical Theory: Horkheimer to Habermas,* Berkeley: University of California Press, pp. 77–109.

Hénaff, Marcel, and Tracy B. Strong (2001) "The Conditions of Public Space: Vision, Speech, and Theatricality," in Marcel Hénaff, and Tracy B. Strong, eds., *Public Space and Democracy,* Minneapolis: University of Minnesota Press, pp. 1–31.

Henneberger, Melinda (2000) "The Hobgoblins of Politics: Change and Consistency," *New York Times,* February 20, D1.

Hentoff, Nat (2000) "Can Journalism Survive Synergy?," *Editor and Publisher,* May 1, p. 38.

Herbert, Bob (2003a) "What Is It Good For?," *New York Times,* April 23, A23.

Herbert, Bob (2003b) "Spoils of War," *New York Times,* April 10, A27.

Herman, Edward (2000) "The AOL–Time Warner Merger: Billboarding the Information Superhighway," *ZNET,* January 16, <www.zmag.org/ZSustainers/ZDaily/2000-01/16herman.htm>.

Herman, Edward, and Noam Chomsky (1988) *Manufacturing Consent,* New York: Pantheon.

Herman, Edward, and Robert W. McChesney (1997) *The Global Media: The New Missionaries of Corporate Capitalism,* London: Cassell.

Heyboer, Kelly (2000a) "Cable Clash," *American Journalism Review,* June, p. 20.

Heyboer, Kelly (2000b) "The Battle Online," *American Journalism Review,* June, p. 26.

Hickey, Neil (1998) "Is Fox News Fair?" *Columbia Journalism Review,* March/April, pp. 30–35.

Hickey, Neil (2000) "Converge Me Up, Scottie: Tribune Beams toward a Multimedia Future," *Columbia Journalism Review,* May/June, pp. 18–22.

Hickey, Neil (2003) "Cable Wars," *Columbia Journalism Review,* January/February, pp. 12–17.

Hitchens, Christopher (1998) "Princess Di, Mother T., and Me," in Mandy Merck, ed., *After Diana: Irreverent Elegies,* London and New York: Verso.

Holson, Laura M. (2003) "Saving The Drama For the Audience," *New York Times,* July 6, C1.

Holt, Linda (1998) "Diana and the Backlash," in Mandy Merck, ed., *After Diana: Irreverent Elegies,* London and New York: Verso.

Horkheimer, Max, and Theodore Adorno (1979) *Dialectic of Enlightenment,* John Cumming, trans., New York: Continuum.

Houpt, Simon (2001) "The War on Dissent," *Globe and Mail,* October 6, R1.

Houston, Frank (1999) "What I Saw in the Digital Sea: After a Two-Year Immersion in Online News, a Journalist Comes up for Air," *Columbia Journalism Review,* July/August, pp. 34–37.

Houston, Frank (2001) "AOL/TW Spells Big," *Columbia Journalism Review,* July/August, pp. 22–27.

Houston, William (2003a) "War Coverage More Objective Here than in U.S.," *Globe and Mail,* March 22, A10.

Houston, William (2003b) "Independent Reporters Jailed, Mistreated," *Globe and Mail,* April 5, A8.

Hoyt, Mike (2000) "With 'Strategic Alliances,' the Map Gets Messy," *Columbia Journalism Review,* January/February, <www.cjr.org/year/00/1/hoyt.asp>.

Hughes, Helen M. (1936) "The Lindbergh Case: A Study of Human Interest and Politics," *American Journal of Sociology*, 42 (2), pp. 32–54.

Hunt, Darnell (1999) *O.J. Simpson Facts and Fictions: News Ritual in the Construction of Reality*, Cambridge: Cambridge University Press.

Ignatieff, Michael (1998) "We are all Diana," *Globe and Mail*, August 29, D4.

InterMedia (1992) "The Global News Agenda," *InterMedia*, January–February and March–April.

Introna, Lucas D., and Helen Nissenbaum (2000) "Shaping the Web: Why the Politics of Search Engines Matters," *The Information Society*, 16 (3), pp. 169–185.

Irving, Mark, and Raymond Whitaker (2003) "Hans Blix: Blair Made a Fundamental Mistake over '45 Minutes to Deploy' Claim," *The Independent*, July 13, p. 15.

Iyengar, Shanto, and Adam Simon (1994) "News Coverage of the Gulf Crisis and Public Opinion: A Study of Agenda-Setting, Priming, and Framing," in W. Lance Bennett and David L. Paletz, eds., *Taken by Storm: The Media, Public Opinion, and U.S. Foreign Policy in the Gulf War*, Chicago: University of Chicago Press.

Jacobs, Ronald (1996) "Producing the News, Producing the Crisis: Narrativity, Television and News Work," *Media, Culture and Society*, Vol. 18 (3), pp. 373–397.

Jacobson, Lee (2000) "Companies Scramble to Build 'Brand Essence,'" *Globe and Mail*, March 2, M1.

James, Caryn (2000) "Breathless Coverage Blurs Divide of Fact and Farce," *New York Times*, November 20, A15.

Jappe, Anselm (1999) *Guy Debord*, Donald Nicholson-Smith, trans., Berkeley: University of California Press.

Jones, Tim (1999) "News Titans Link in Deal with Reach: Washington Post, NBC among Those in Venture," *Chicago Tribune*, November 18, p. 1.

Jones, Tim (2003) "Media Giant's Rally Sponsorship Raises Questions," *Chicago Tribune*, March 19, p. 6.

Kakutani, Michiko (2003) "Shock, Awe and Razzmatazz in the Sequel," *New York Times*, March 25, E1.

Kaplan, Carl S. (2001) "Legal Victory for Internet Advertising Industry," *New York Times*, April 6, <www.nytimes.com/2001/04/06/technology/06CYBERLAW.html>.

Kampfner, John (2003) "The Truth about Jessica," *The Guardian*, May 15, Features Pages, p. 2.

Kear, Adrian, and Deborah Lynn Steinberg (1999) *Mourning Diana: Nation, Culture and the Performance of Grief*, London and New York: Routledge.

Keck, Margaret E. and Kathryn Sikkink (1998) "Transnational Advocacy Networks in the Movement Society," in David S. Meyer, and Sidney Tarrow, eds., *A Social Movement Society: Contentious Politics for a New Century*, Lanham, Maryland: Rowman and Littlefield, pp. 217–238.

Kelley, Matt (2003) "Pentagon Likely to Keep Embedding Plan," *Editor and Publisher*, June 17, <www.editorandpublisher.com/editorandpublisher/headlines/article_display.jsp?vnu_content_id=1915837>.

Kellner, Douglas (1992) *The Persian Gulf TV War*, Boulder, Colorado: Westview Press.

Kellner, Douglas (2002) "September 11, Social Theory and Democratic Politics," *Theory, Culture and Society*, 19 (4), pp. 147–159.

Kellner, Douglas (2003a) "September 11, Spectacles of Terror, and Media Manipulation: A Critique of Jihadist and Bush Media Politics," *Logos*, Winter, <logosonline.home.igc.org/kellner_media.htm>.

Kellner, Douglas (2003b) *From 9/11 to Terror War: The Dangers of the Bush Legacy*, New York: Rowman and Littlefield.

Kempner, Matt (2001) "CNN Garners Top Ratings for Attack Coverage," *The Atlanta Journal and Constitution*, October 3, B4C.

Kenna, Kathleen (2003) "Americans Pay Price for Speaking Out," *Toronto Star*, August 9, A22.

King, John (2003) "Bush Limits Pay Increases for Many Federal Workers," *CNN,* August 27, <edition.cnn.com/2003/ALLPOLITICS/08/27/bush.federal.pay>.

Kirkpatrick, David D. (2001) "Brill Buys Powerful Media," *New York Times,* April 2, B3.

Kirkpatrick, David D. (2003) "Lawsuit Says AOL Investors Were Misled," *New York Times,* April 15, C1.

Kirkpatrick, David D., and Jim Rutenberg (2003) "Turner Plans Role as Gadfly Without Portfolio," *New York Times,* February 20, C1.

Kitzinger, Jenny (1999) "The Moving Power of Moving Images: Television Constructions of Princess Diana," in Tony Walter, ed., *Mourning for Diana,* Oxford and New York: Berg, pp. 65–76.

Klein, Alec (2000) "AOL Restrictions Alleged," *Washington Post,* October 10, E1.

Klein, Alec (2001) "Netscape's New Mission: Web Pioneer Promotes Parent AOL Time Warner's Products," *Washington Post,* August 22, E1.

Koepnick, Lutz (1999) *Walter Benjamin and the Aesthetics of Power,* Lincoln, Ne: University of Nebraska.

Koring, Paul (2000) "McCain's Strategy First Tested by Reagan," *Globe and Mail,* February 11, A8.

Kornblum, Janet (2000) "Newspaper Editors See Standards Slip Online," *USA Today,* May 16, 3D.

Krames, Jeffery A. (2000) "The Big Gamble on a Hillary Book," *New York Times,* December 20, A35.

Kuczynski, Alex (2000) "Several Media Companies Form Web Site Partnership," *New York Times,* February 2, C6.

Kuczynski, Alex (2001) "Brill's Content to Trim Publishing Schedule," *New York Times,* May 5, C15.

Kuhn, Annette (1998) "Special Debate: Flowers and Tears: The Death of Diana, Princess of Wales," *Screen,* 39 (1), pp. 67–68.

Kull, Steven (2003) "Misperceptions, the Media and the Iraq War," Program on International Policy Attitudes (PIPA), October, <www.pipa.org/OnlineReports/Iraq/Media_10_02_03_Report.pdf >.

Kumar, Krishan (1995) *From Post-Industrial to Post-Modern Societies: New Theories of the Contemporary World,* Oxford and Malden, MA: Blackwell.

Kurtz, Howard (1996) *Hot Air: All Talk, All the Time,* New York: Time Books.

Kurtz, Howard (1999a) "NBC's News Machine Marches to War," *Washington Post,* April 21, C1.

Kurtz, Howard (1999b) "Whistle-Stops Candidates Flock to the Talk Shows," *Washington Post,* April 23, C1.

Kurtz, Howard (2000a) "Portrait of Michael Isikoff, Irked," *Washington Post,* February 7, C1.

Kurtz, Howard (2000b) "Bush Cousin Made Florida Vote Call for Fox News," *Washington Post,* November 14, C1.

Kurtz, Howard (2000c) "Don't Touch That Demographic!" *Washington Post,* May 8, C1.

Kurtz, Howard (2000d) "Right Face, Right Time," *Washington Post,* February 1, C1.

Kurtz, Howard (2000e) "Is There Life After McCain?" *Washington Post,* March 13, C1.

Kurtz, Howard (2000f) "John McCain's Life? It's an Open Bus," *Washington Post,* February 14, C1.

Kurtz, Howard (2000g) "Two Campaigns at Full Blast," *Washington Post,* February 28, C1.

Kurtz, Howard (2001) "Is Online Media On Its Way Out?: Web Sites Struggle Financially Despite Millions of Visitors," *Washington Post,* February 21, C1.

Kurtz, Howard (2003a) "Embedded, And Taking Flak," *Washington Post,* March 31, C1.

Kurtz, Howard (2003b) "Embedded Reporter's Role In Army Unit's Actions Questioned by Military," *Washington Post,* June 25, C1.

Kurtz, Howard (2003c) "The Press Gets Pumped," washingtonpost.com, April 3,<www.washingtonpost.com/wp-dyn/articles/A19046-2003Apr3.html>.

Labaton, Stephen (1999) "Wide Belief U.S. Will Let a Vast Deal Go Through," *New York Times,* September 8, C14.

Labaton, Stephen (2000) "U.S. Seeks to Ease Some Restrictions on Broadcasters," *New York Times,* A1.

Labaton, Stephen (2003) "Ideologically Broad Coalition Assails F.C.C. Media Plan," *New York Times,* May 28, C6.

Lafayette, John (2000) "'Nightly News' Ups Its Ad Revenues," *Electronic Media,* July 10, p. 30.

Langer, John (1998) *Tabloid Television: Popular Journalism and the 'Other News,'* London and New York: Routledge.

Lasch, Christopher (1978) *The Culture of Narcissism: American Life in an Age of Diminishing Expectations,* Norton: New York.

Lasica, J.D. (2002) "The Rise of the Digital Networks," *Online Journalism Review,* April 11, <www.ojr.org/ojr/lasica/p1018588363.php>.

Leahy, Michael (2000) "A Fisherman and His 15 Minutes," *Washington Post,* April 27, A1.

Lears, T.J. Jackson (1983) "From Salvation to Self-Realization: Advertising and the Therapeutic Roots of the Consumer Culture, 1880–1930," in Richard W. Fox, and T.J. Jackson Lears, eds., *The Culture of Consumption,* New York: Pantheon.

Leavis, F.R., and D. Thompson (1948) *Culture and Environment,* London: Chatto and Windus.

Ledbetter, James (1999) "Can the Net Save McCain in New York?" *Slate,* December 3, <slate.msn.com/id/57353/>.

Leeman, Sue (1998) "Diana Tour Probes Every Tenuous Link," *Associated Press,* August 13.

Lefebvre, Henri (1991) *Critique of Everyday Life,* John Moore, trans., London and New York: Verso.

Leibovich, Mark (2000) "A Marriage of Mediums," *Washington Post,* January 11, A1.

Leiss, William, Stephen Kline, and Sut Jhally (1990) *Social Communication in Advertising: Persons, Products and Images of Well-Being,* Scarborough: Nelson.

Lentz, Christopher S. (1996) "The Fairness in Broadcasting Doctrine and the Constitution: Forced One-Stop Shopping in the Marketplace of Ideas," *University of Illinois Law Review* (1), pp. 271–317.

Lewis, Justin, Michael Morgan, and Sut Jhally (1998) "Libertine or Liberal? The Real Scandal of What People Know about President Clinton," Department of Communication, University of Massachusetts/Amherst, <www.umass.edu/newsoffice/archive/1998/021098study2.html>.

Li, Kenneth (2001) "What's Behind the Primedia-Brill Deal?" *The Standard,* January 4, <www.thestandard.com/article/display/0,1151,21258,00.html>.

Lloyd, David, and Paul Thomas (1998) *Culture and the State,* London: Routledge.

Lohse, Deborah (2001) "Web Searches Bring up More Pay-for-Placement," *San Jose Mercury News,* February 15.

Luciw, Roma (2000) "Infinite Design's On-line Undertaking," *Globe and Mail,* July 31, B3.

Lukács, Georg (1971) *History and Class Consciousness: Studies in Marxist Dialectics,* Rodney Livingstone, trans., Cambridge, MA.: MIT Press.

Lukes, Steven (1977) *Essays in Social Theory,* London: Macmillan Press.

Lule, Jack (2001) *Daily News, Eternal Stories: The Mythological Role of Journalism,* New York: Guilford Press.

Lule, Jack (2002) "Myth and Terror on the Editorial Page: The New York Times Responds to September 11, 2001," *Journalism and Mass Communication Quarterly,* 79 (2), pp. 275–293.

MacDonald, Gayle (2003) "CNN Medical Reporter Becomes Unlikely Hero," *Globe and Mail,* April 5, A8.

MacGregor, Brent (1997) *Live, Direct and Biased?: Making Television News in the Satellite Age,* London and New York: Arnold.

Mack, Ann M. (2003) "Paid Search Fuels Online Ad Recovery," *Editor and Publisher,* July 30, <www.editorandpublisher.com/editorandpublisher/headlines/article_display.jsp?vnu_content_id=1945044>.

Mahon, Rianne (1980) "Regulatory Agencies: Captive Agents or Hegemonic Apparatuses," in J. Paul Grayson, ed., *Class, State, Ideology, and Change,* Toronto: Holt, Rinehart, and Winston, pp. 154–168.

Maitland, Sara (1998) "The Secular Saint," in Mandy Merck, ed., *After Diana: Irreverent Elegies,* London and New York: Verso.

Manjoo, Farhad (2001) "'Good News' for Arabs on MSNBC," Wired.com, October 17, <www.wired.com/news/conflict/0,2100,47638,00.html>.

Mariano, Gwendolyn (2000) "'Survivor' Draws Record Viewers on TV, Web," CNETNews.com, August 25, <news.cnet.com/news/0-1005-200-2613020.html>.

Mariano, Gwendolyn (2001) "Survivor Pumps Traffic into CBS Site," CNETNews.com, February 9, <news.cnet.com/news/0-1005-200-4772167.html>.

Margolis, Eric (2003) "Powell's 'Proof' is All Smoke and Mirrors," commondreams.org, February 9, <www.commondreams.org/views/03/0209-03.htm>.

Marks, Peter (2000) "All News, All the Time, Even if There Isn't Any," *New York Times,* November 6, A20.

Martin, Lawrence (2003) "Don't Hold Your Breath Waiting for Powell to Say He's Sorry," *Globe and Mail,* May 22, A15.

Martin, Sandra (2003) "Hillary's Tell-Some Book a Hit," *Globe and Mail,* June 12, R3.

Martinson, Jane (2001) "New Media: Prophets of Doom at Online News Profits," *The Guardian,* January 29, Guardian Media Pages, p. 58.

Marx, Karl (1844) "On the Jewish Question," *Deutsch-französische Jahrbücher,* Paris, Im Bureau der Jahrbücher. Reprinted with foreward by Erich Fromm in T.B. Bottomore, ed., *Karl Marx: Early Writings,* London: McGraw-Hill, 1963. Page references are references to 1963 edition.

Marx, Karl (1973) *Grundrisse: Foundations of the Critique of Political Economy,* Martin Nicolaus, trans., New York: Random House. Selections reprinted in Robert C. Tucker, ed., *The Marx-Engels Reader,* New York: Norton and Company, 1978. Page references are to the 1978 edition.

Massing, Michael (1986) "CBS: Sauterizing the news. Go for the moment!" *Columbia Journalism Review,* March/April, p. 32.

Mattelart, Armand (1996) *The Invention of Communication,* Susan Emanuel, trans., Minneapolis: University of Minnesota Press.

McCartney, James (1997) "News Lite," *American Journalism Review,* Vol. 19 (5), pp. 18–25.

McChesney, Robert (1991) "Free Speech and Democracy!: Louis G. Caldwell, the American Bar Association and the Debate Over the Free Speech Implications of Broadcast Regulation, 1928–1938," *The American Journal of Legal History,* 35 (4), pp. 351–392.

McChesney, Robert (1997) *Corporate Media and the Threat to Democracy,* New York: Seven Stories Press.

McChesney, Robert (1999) *Rich Media, Poor Democracy: Communication Politics in Dubious Times,* Urbana: University of Illinois Press.

McChesney, Robert (2003) "September 11 and the Structural Limitations of US Journalism," *Journalism After September 11,* London and New York: Routledge, pp. 91–100.

McConville, Jim, and Chuck Ross (2001) "CNN Out-Foxed on Election," *Electronic Media,* January 29, p. 1.

McCool, Grant (2003) "NY Police Admit Keeping Anti-War Protest Database," *Reuters,* April 10, <www.commondreams.org/headlines03/0410-07.htm>.

McGinness, Joe (1969) *The Selling of the President,* New York: Trident.

McKay, John (1998) "Lloyd and Peter Wary of All-News TV," *Canadian Press,* April 26.

McKenna, Barrie (2002) "Vivendi to Unload Assets," *Globe and Mail,* August 15, B1.

McKenna, Barrie (2003) "U.S. Applauds, But Says the War is Not Over Yet," *Globe and Mail,* April 10, A1.

McKeown, Bob (2001) "How I Won the War," *Saturday Night,* February 24, pp. 26–31.

McNair, Brian (2000) *Journalism and Democracy: An Evaluation of the Political Public Sphere,* London: Routledge.

McQuail, Denis (1996) "Mass Media in the Public Interest: Towards a Framework of Norms for Media Performance," in James Curran, and Michael Gurevitch, eds., *Mass Media and Society,* London: Arnold, pp. 66–80.

McQueen, Trina (1998) "Why We Crave Hot Stuff," *Globe and Mail,* September 26, D3.

Merck, Mandy, ed. (1998) *After Diana: Irreverent Elegies,* London and New York: Verso.

Meyer, David S., and Sidney Tarrow (1998) "A Movement Society: Contentious Politics for a New Century," in David S. Meyer, and Sidney Tarrow, eds., *A Social Movement Society: Contentious Politics for a New Century,* Lanham, Maryland: Rowman and Littlefield, pp. 1–28.

Meyrowitz, Joshua (1985) *No Sense of Place: The Impact of Electronic Media on Social Behavior,* Oxford and New York: Oxford University Press.

Middleberg, Dan, and Steven S. Ross (1998) *Media in Cyberspace Study,*<www.middleberg.com/toolsforsuccess/cyberstudy98.pdf >.

Miladi, Noureddine (2003) "Mapping the Al-Jazeera Phenomenon," in Daya Kishan Thussu, and Des Freedman, eds., *War and the Media: Reporting Conflict 24/7,* London: Sage, pp. 149–160.

Milbank, Dana (2000) "Bush and McCain, Pointless in Pittsburgh," *Washington Post,* May 9, C1.

Milbank, Dana (2003) "White House Didn't Gain CIA Nod for Claim on Iraqi Strikes," *Washington Post,* July 20, A1.

Milbank, Dana and Claudia Deane (2003) "Hussein Link to 9/11 Lingers in Many Minds," *Washington Post,* September 6, A1.

Miller, John (1998) *Yesterday's News: Why Canada's Daily Newspapers Are Failing Us,* Halifax: Fernwood Publishing.

Mitchell, Alanna (1999) "Alberta Student Killed in 'Copycat' School Shooting," *Globe and Mail,* April 29, A1.

Mosco, Vincent (1996) *The Political Economy of Communication,* London: Sage.

Moses, Lucia (2000) "TV or not TV?: Few Newspapers Are Camera-Shy, But Sometimes Two-into-One Just Doesn't Go," *Editor and Publisher,* August 21, p. 22.

Moses, Lucia (2003) "Gen. Franks a Fan of Embedding," *Editor and Publisher,* April 29, <www.editorandpublisher.com/editorandpublisher/headlines/article_display.jsp?vnu_content_id= 1876177>.

MSNBC (1999) "U.S., Again, Mourns, Kennedy Tragedy," MSNBC.com, July 19 <www.msnbc.com/news/290986.asp>.

Nacos, Brigitte L. (2002) *Mass-Mediated Terrorism: The Central Role of the Media in Terrorism and Counterterrorism,* New York: Rowman and Littlefield.

Nagourney, Adam, and Janet Elder (2003) "Threats and Responses: The Poll," *New York Times,* March 11, A1.

Nash, Knowltan (1998) *Trivia Pursuit: How Showbiz Values are Corrupting the News,* Toronto: McClelland and Stewart.

Neal, Terry M. (1999) "Candidates Hit the Electronic Hustings," *Washington Post,* April 26, A1.

Neuman, W. Russell, Marion Just, and Ann Crigler (1992) *Common Knowledge: News and the Construction of Political Meaning,* Chicago: University of Chicago Press.

New York Times (2000) "Excerpts from a Talk with the Vice President," *New York Times,* March 12, A28.

Norris, Pippa (2000) *A Virtuous Circle: Political Communications in Postindustrial Societies,* Cambridge: Cambridge University Press.

O'Brian, Amy (2003) "British Columbians Donate Tonnes of Help: CanWest Global Fire Aid," *Vancouver Sun,* August 5, A2.

Olive, David (2001) "Bell Rings for Fecan: Analysts Are Waiting to See If Ivan Fecan Can Make BCE's Convergence Gamble Pay Off," *National Post,* January 13, D1.

Omaar, Rageh, and Paul Wood (2003) "Eyewitness: Baghdad after Saddam," *BBC News Online,* April 10,<news.bbc.co.uk/go/pr/fr/-/2/hi/middle_east/2935641.stm>.

Onion, Amanda (1999) "Special Report: Littleton—with the Columbine Kids," *Columbia Journalism Review,* May/June, <www.cjr.org/year/99/3/Columbine/index.asp>.

Outing, Steve (2000) "It Takes Killer Content to Generate Killer Revenues," *Editor and Publisher,* June 28, <www.editorandpublisher.com/ephome/news/newshtm/stop/st062800.htm>.

Owen, Bruce M., and Steven S. Wildman (1992) *Video Economics,* Cambridge, MA: Harvard University Press.

Palast, Greg (2002) *The Best Democracy that Money Can Buy: An Investigative Reporter Exposes the Truth about Globalization, Corporate Cons, and High Finance Fraudsters,* London: Pluto Press.

Parker, Richard (1995) *Mixed Signals: The Prospects for Global Television News,* New York: The Twentieth Century Press.

Patelis, Korinna (2000) "The Political Economy of the Internet," in James Curran, ed., *Media Organizations and Society,* London: Arnold, pp. 84-106.

Pavlik, John (2000) "The Impact of Technology on Journalism," *Journalism Studies,* 1 (2), pp. 229-237.

Pavlik, John V., and Steven S. Ross (2000) "Journalism Online: Exploring the Impact of New Media on News and Society," in Alan B. Albarran, and David H. Goff, eds., *Understanding the Web: Social, Political and Economic Dimensions of the Internet,* Ames, Iowa: Iowa State University Press, pp. 117-133.

Pearlstein, Steven (2000) "AOL-Time Warner Analysis: Is Extra-Large Media's Best Fit?" *Washington Post,* December 15, A1.

Pincus, Walter (2003) "Bush Faced Dwindling Data on Iraq Nuclear Bid," *Washington Post,* July 16, A1.

Pogrebin, Abigail (1998) "Chasing Grief," *Brill's Content,* November, <www.brillscontent.com/1998nov/features/chasing.shtml>.

Posner, Michael (1997) "All Funerals, All the Time," *Globe and Mail,* September 13, C1.

Posner, Michael (1998) "Flaming Out: Media at the Stake," *Globe and Mail,* October 10, C1.

Posner, Michael (2001a) "Getting Ready for Primetime," *Globe and Mail,* February 13, R3.

Posner, Michael (2001b) "CBC Expands Media Links," *Globe and Mail,* March 22, R2.

Poster, Mark (1990) *The Mode of Information: Poststructuralism and Social Context,* Chicago: University of Chicago Press.

Postman, Neil (1985) *Amusing Ourselves to Death: Public Discourse in the Age of Show Business,* New York: Penguin.

Priest, Dana, and Dana Milbank (2003) "President Defends Allegations On Iraq," *Washington Post,* July 15, A1.

Priest, Dana, William Booth, and Susan Schmidt (2003) "A Broken Body, a Broken Story, Pieced Together," *Washington Post,* June 17, A1.

Project for Excellence in Journalism (2003) "Embedded Reporters: What are Americans Getting?" Journalism.org, April 3, <www.journalism.org/resources/research/reports/war/embed/default.asp>.

*Province, The* (1999) "Club Monaco Sells Out of Monica's Lipstick," *The Province,* March 7, A6c.

Rampton, Sheldon, and John Stauber (2003) "Trading Fear," *The Guardian,* July 12, Weekend Pages, p. 32.

Rangwala, Glen, and Raymond Whitaker (2003) "20 Lies About the War," *The Hamilton Spectator,* July 14, C1.

Rantanen, Terhi (1997) "The Globalization of Electronic News in the 19th Century," *Media, Culture and Society,* 19 (4), pp. 605-620.

Raphael, Jordan (2000) "All the Iranian News, All the Time," *New York Times,* July 24, C11.

Reguly, Eric (2001) "The Convergence Revolution Can Wait, But Can Investors?," *Globe and Mail,* April 7, B6.

Reuters, and Associated Press (1998) "Lewinsky Agrees to Model Blue Suit," *Globe and Mail,* September 20, A11.

Rich, Frank (2000a) "America Finds Another JonBenet," *New York Times,* April 22, A13.

Rich, Frank (2000b) "The Age of the Mediathon," *New York Times Magazine,* October 29, p. 58.

Rich, Frank (2003) "The Spoils of War Coverage," *New York Times,* April 13, B1.

Richard, Paul (2000) "Big News: The Sagas with Staying Power," *Washington Post,* April 26, C1.

Richtel, Matt (2000) "Internet Work Force Has Its First Brush With Downsizing," *New York Times,* June 22, C1.

Riesman, David (1961) *The Lonely Crowd: A Study of the Changing American Character,* New Haven: Yale University Press.

Robins, Kevin, and Frank Webster (1999) *Times of the Technolculture: From the Information Society to the Virtual Life,* London and New York: Routledge.

Rosaldo, Renato (1989) *Culture and Truth: The Remaking of Social Analysis,* Boston: Beacon Press.

Rosenbaum, David E. (2001) "Since Sept. 11, Lobbyists Put Old Pleas in New Packages, *New York Times,* B1.

Rosenberg, Howard (2000) "Mergers Make for Strained Bedfellows," *Los Angeles Times,* March 15, F1.

Rosenberg, Howard (2001) "CBS Only Has Eyes for Survivor," *Los Angeles Times,* February 12, F1.

Rosenthal, Phil (2003) "Awe Arrives, But Not With Human Angle," *Chicago Sun-Times,* March 22, <www.suntimes.com/output/rosenthal/cst-nws-tv22.html>.

Rosenwein, Rifka (2000) "Why Media Mergers Matter," *Brill's Content,* December/January, pp. 93–95.

Rothstein, Edward (2000) "The New Prophet of a Techno Faith Rich in Profits," *New York Times,* September 23, B9.

Rust, Michael (1997) "Bringing News to the Masses," *Insight on the News,* June 30, p. 10.

Rutenberg, Jim (2000a) "Turner and CNN Uneasily Face a Milestone as Ratings Dip at News Channel," *New York Times,* June 5, C1.

Rutenberg, Jim (2000b) "CNN is Seeking a New Strategy," *New York Times,* August 31, C1.

Rutenberg, Jim (2000c) "The Right Strategy for Fox News Means Rising Ratings and Revenue," *New York Times,* September 18, C1.

Rutenberg, Jim (2000d) "To Stay Afloat, Unlikely Ties in TV News," *New York Times,* November 27, C1.

Rutenberg, Jim (2000e) "Stunts and Thrills at Daybreak: Competitive Hysteria Drives the Morning News Programs," *New York Times,* October 16, C1.

Rutenberg, Jim (2001a) "Media Talk: Lewinsky Agrees to an HBO Documentary," *New York Times,* March 5, C12.

Rutenberg, Jim (2001b) "Hearts, Minds and Satellites," *New York Times,* October 15, C1.

Rutenberg, Jim (2001c) "CNN Plans to Lay Off 400," *New York Times,* January 18, C4.

Rutenberg, Jim (2001d) "AOL Time Warner to Revamp CNNfn," *New York Times,* February 1, C4.

Rutenberg, Jim (2001e) "Mix, Patch, Promote and Lift: A Showman Speeds the Makeover of Ted Turner's Empire," *New York Times,* July 15, C1.

Rutenberg, Jim (2001f) "Hollywood Seeks Role in the War," *New York Times,* October 20, B9.

Rutenberg, Jim (2003a) "Battle Rages Between Fox News and MSNBC," *New York Times,* April 3, C6.

Rutenberg, Jim (2003b) "Cable's War Coverage Suggests a New 'Fox Effect' on Television," *New York Times,* April 16, B9.

Rutenberg, Jim (2003c) "To Interview Former P.O.W., CBS Dangles Stardom," *New York Times,* June 16, A1.

Rutherford, Paul (2000) *Endless Propaganda: The Advertising of Public Goods,* Toronto: University of Toronto Press.

Sachs, Andrea (1995) "Mud and the Mainstream: When the Respectable Press Chases the *National Inquirer,* What's Going on?,"*Columbia Journalism Review,* 34, May/June, pp. 33–38.

Salladay, Robert (2003) "Peace Activism: A Matter of Language," *San Francisco Chronicle,* April 7, A19.

Saunders, Doug (1999) "Distinctions Blur Between Victims and Anchors," *Globe and Mail,* April 22, A14.

Saunders, Doug (2000) "Spirit of Reagan Hovers over GOP Race," *Globe and Mail,* March 3, A11.

Saussure, Frederic (1964) *Course in General Linguistics,* New York: McGraw-Hill.

Scannell, Paddy (1995) "Media Events," *Media, Culture and Society,* 17 (1), pp. 151–157.

Schechner, Richard (1985) *Between Theater and Anthropology,* Philadelphia: University of Pennsylvania Press.

Schecter, Barbara (1999) "Specialty Channels Winning TV Market Share: CTV, CanWest Lose Viewers," *National Post,* January 13, C6.

Schechter, Danny (2001a) "The War-Media Connection," mediachannel.org, September 26, <www.mediachannel.org/views/dissector/fcc.shtml>.

Schechter, Danny (2001b) "Synergy as Propaganda, News as Deception," mediachannel.org, March 28, <www.mediachannel.org/views/dissector/synergy.shtml>.

Schiesel, Seth, and Jim Rutenberg (2001) "Merger Over, the New AOL Will Lay Off More Than 2000," *New York Times,* January 24, C1.

Schiller, Dan (1999) *Digital Capitalism: Networking the Global Market System,* Cambridge, MA: MIT Press.

Schmidt, Susan, and Vernon Loeb (2003) "She Was Fighting to the Death," *Washington Post,* April 3, A1.

Schneider, Mike (2000) "Reporters Must Be Media-Savvy in Newsroom of the Future,"*Associated Press,* March 14, <www.sfgate.com/cgibin/article.cgi?file=/news/archive/2000/03/14/national 0352EST0455.DTL&type=tech_arti>.

Schudson, Michael (1982) "The Politics of Narrative Form: The Emergence of News Conventions in Print and Television," *Daedalus,* Vol. 3 (1), pp. 97–112.

Schudson, Michael (1992) "Was There Ever a Public Sphere? If So, When?: Reflections on the American Case," in Craig Calhoun, ed., *Habermas and the Public Sphere,* Cambridge, MA: MIT Press, pp. 143–163.

Seelye, Katharine Q. (2000) "Gore Discusses Reform With Ventura," *New York Times,* March 12, A28.

Seelye, Katherine Q. (2002) "Pentagon Plays Role in Fictional Terror Drama," *New York Times,* March 31, A1.

Seigel, Jessica (1999) "Hugging the Spotlight," *Brill's Content,* July/August, <www.brillscontent.com /features/aftermath_spotlight1_0899.html>.

Sella, Marshall (2001) "The Red-State Network: How Fox News Conquered Bush Country—and Toppled CNN," *New York Times Magazine,* June 24, p. 6.

Sennett, Richard (1978) *The Fall of Public Man: On the Social Psychology of Capitalism,* New York: Vintage.

Sharkey, Jacqueline E. (2003) "The Television War," *American Journalism Review,* May, p. 18.

Shenon, Philip (2003) "Report on USA Patriot Act Alleges Civil Rights Violations," *New York Times,* July 21, A1.

Shepard, Alicia C. (1999) "White Noise," *American Journalism Review,* January, p. 20.

Sherwood, S. (1994) "Narrating the Social," *Journal of Narratives and Life Histories,* 4 (1–2), pp. 89–120.

Sinclair, Stewart (2000) "Quebecor Deletes 30% of Online Workforce: 65 Jobs," *National Post,* August 16, C1.

Slater, Don (1997) *Consumer Culture and Modernity,* Cambridge: Polity.

Smith, Terence (2000) "Media Mergers," transcript of broadcast story produced for the *NewsHour with Jim Lehrer,* July 17, <www.pbs.org/newshour/bb/media/july-dec00/mergers_7-17.html>.

Sorkin, Andrew Ross (2000) "DoCoMo Handsets Will Soon Carry News," *New York Times,* July 3, C7.

Southerst, John (2000) "Franchisees Have Little to Say About Ads," *Globe and Mail,* February 15, W1.

Sparks, Colin (1991) "Goodbye Hildy Johnson: The Vanishing Serious Press," in Peter Dahlgren, and Colin Sparks, eds., *Communication and Citizenship: Journalism and the Public Sphere,* London and New York: Routledge.

Sparks, Colin (2000) "The Panic Over Tabloid News," in Colin Sparks, and John Tolloch, eds., *Tabloid Tales: Global Debates over Media Standards,* Lanham, Maryland: Rowman and Littlefield, pp. 1–40.

Stanley, Alessandra (2001a) "Opponents of War Are Scarce on Television," *New York Times,* November 9, B4.

Stanley, Alessandra (2001b) "Battling the Skepticism of a Global TV Audience," *New York Times,* November 1, B4.

Stanley, Alessandra, and Jim Rutenberg (2001) "Anchors Use Care to Avoid Speculation on Cause of Crash," *New York Times,* November 13, D9.

Stein, Nicholas (1999) "New Media, Old Values," *Columbia Journalism Review,* July/August, <www.cjr.org/year/99/4/ona.asp>.

Steinberg, Jacques (2003) "Limbaugh Signs on again, Sharing Life's Tough Lessons," *New York Times,* November 18, E3.

Stephens, Mitchell (1988) *A History of News: From the Drum to the Satellite,* New York: Viking.

Stephens, Mitchell (1998) *The Rise of the Image and the Fall of the Word,* New York: Oxford University Press.

Stern, Christopher (2001) "Network Ownership Rule Eased," *Washington Post,* April 20, E3.

Stern, Christopher, and Jonathan Krim (2003) "House Votes to Prevent Change in Media Rule," *Washington Post,* July 24, A1.

Straub, Bill (2001) "'That Woman' Strikes it Rich in Handbags," *Globe and Mail,* August 18, A8.

Street, John (1997) *Politics and Popular Culture,* Philadelphia: Temple University Press.

Streitfeld, David (2000) "Before the Revolution, More Consolidation Likely," *Washington Post,* January 11, E1.

Strobel, Warren P. and Jonathan S. Landay (2001) "Pentagon Hires Image Firm to Explain Airstrikes to World," *San Jose Mercury News,* October 19, <www.commondreams.org/headlines01/1019-05.htm>.

Strupp, Joe (2003) "Was Press Asleep on Pre-War WMD Issue?" *Editor and Publisher,* June 12, <www.editorandpublisher.com/editorandpublisher/headlines/article_display.jsp?vnu_content_id=1910998>.

Sullivan, Paul (1999) "Battling the Global Bogeyman," *Globe and Mail,* December 1, A17.

Swingewood, Alan (1977) *The Myth of Mass Culture,* London: Macmillan Press.

Swisher, Kara (2000) "Decline in AOL's Stock Price Shifts Dynamics of Merger," *Wall Street Journal Interactive Edition,* October 23, <interactive.wsj.com/archive/retreive.cgi?id=SB9722557 40298481293.dj-m>.

Taras, David (1999) *Power and Betrayal in the Canadian Media,* Peterborough, Ontario: Broadview Press.

Tedesco, R. (1996) "NBC Makes Olympian Showing in 'Net Ratings,'" *Broadcasting and Cable,* September 30, p. 83.

Thomas, Evan (2000) "Cashing In on Little Elián," *Newsweek,* May 8, p. 32.

Thompson, John B. (1990) *Ideology and Modern Culture: Critical Social Theory in the Era of Mass Communication,* Stanford: Stanford University Press.

Thompson, John B. (1995) *The Media and Modernity: A Social Theory of the Media,* Stanford: Stanford University Press.

Thompson, John B.(2000) *Political Scandal: Power and Visibility in the Media Age,* Cambridge: Polity Press.

Thorne, Stephen (2000) "There is More Diversity Today Than Ever, says CanWest Global Chief," *Canadian Press,* August 22.

Thorsell, William (1998) "Journalism's Bottom Line: Tell Me Something New," *Globe and Mail,* October 3, D9.

Thussu, Daya Kishan (1999) "Privatizing the Airwaves: The Impact of Globalization on Broadcasting in India," *Media, Culture and Society,* 21 (1), pp. 125–131.

Timms, Dominic (2003) "What the US Papers Say," *The Guardian,* March 20,

Tomkins, Richard (2000) "Dotcoms Devoured: The Accelerating Shake-Out among Internet Companies Demonstrates the Market's Winner-Takes-All Logic with a Vengeance," *Financial Times,* October 23, p. 24.

Tracey, M. (1995) "Non-Fiction Television," in Anthony Smith, ed., *Television: An International History,* Oxford and New York: Oxford University Press.

Tuchman, Gaye (1978) *Making News: A Study in the Construction of Reality,* New York: Free Press.

Tugend, Alina (2003) "Pundits for Hire," American Journalism Review, May, <www.ajr.org/Article.asp?id=2995>.

Tunstall, Jeremy, and Michael Palmer (1991) *Media Moguls,* London: Routledge.

Turner, Victor (1984) "Liminality and the Performative Genres," in John MacAloon, ed., *Rite, Drama, Festival, Spectacle: Rehearsals toward a Theory of Cultural Performance,"* Philadelphia: Institute for the Study of Human Issues.

Ullman, Harlan K., and James P. Wade (1996) *Shock and Awe: Achieving Rapid Dominance,* Washington: NDU Press Book, <www.dodccrp.org/shockIndex.html>.

Underwood, Doug (1993) *When MBAs Rule the Newsroom: How Marketers and Managers are Reshaping Today's Media,* New York: Columbia University Press.

U.S. Department of Commerce (2000) "Falling Through the Net: Toward Digital Inclusion," October, <www.ntia.doc.gov/ntiahome/fttn00/Falling.htm#36>.

Valpy, Michael (2000a) "The Dream, the Vision, the Style, the Man," *Globe and Mail,* September 29, A1.

Valpy, Michael (2000b) "TV's Funeral Industry Besieges the Vatican," *Globe and Mail,* January 22, A1.

Vancouver Sun (2000) "Lewinsky Stunt Falls Flat as Diet Titans Court Media," *Vancouver Sun,* February 12, A5.

Van Natta Jr., Don (2000) "Courting Web-Head Cash," *New York Times,* February 13, D4.

Van Rijn, Nicolaas (2003) "Blix Wants 'the real truth' About Iraq's Weapons Stash," *Toronto Star,* July 1, A3.

Van Zoonen, Liesbet (1991) "A Tyranny of Intimacy: Women, Feminity and Television News," in *Communication and Citizenship: Journalism and the Public Sphere,* Peter Dahlgren, and Colin Sparks, eds., London and New York: Routledge.

Waisbord, Silvio (2003) "Journalism, Risk, and Patriotism," *Journalism After September 11,* in Barbie Zelizer, and Stuart Allan, eds., London and New York: Routledge, pp. 201–219.

Walker, Leslie (2001a) "AOL Time Warner Sites Lead in Time, Visitors," *Washington Post,* February 27, E1.

Walker, Leslie (2001b) "AOL Users Find Ways to Jump Garden Wall," *Washington Post,* March 8, E11.

Walley, Wayne (1992) "Basic Cable Ratings Rise in January," *Electronic Media,* February 17, p. 4.

Wallis, Roger and Stanley J. Baran (1990) *The Known World of Broadcast News: International News and the Electronic Media,* London and New York: Routledge.

Walter, Tony (1999) "The Questions People Asked," in Tony Walter, ed., *Mourning for Diana,* Oxford and New York: Berg, pp. 19–47.

Wan, Allen and Russ Britt (2001) "WSJ.com to Lay Off Some Staff: Soft Ad Market Stings 260-Strong Web Operation," CBS.MarketWatch.com, March 29. <cbs.marketwatch.com/news/story.asp?guid={C8180E73-0CE3-4B7D-B533-F6BD19284489}&siteid=mktw&dist=&archive=true>.

War, Adriene, and Alison Fahey (1991) "Retailers Rallying Round the Flag," *Advertising Age,* February 11, p. 4.

Ward, Stephen (2003) "In Bed With the Military," *Media,* Spring, 10 (1), pp. 6–7.

Warner, Bernhard (2001) "MSNBC Launches Arabic News Site, CNN to Follow," *Reuters,* Oct 16, <www.excite.com>.

Wayne, Leslie (2000) "Voter Profiles Selling Briskly As Privacy Issues Are Raised," *New York Times,* September 9, A1.

Weaver, Doug (2000) "Dallas: Four Brands at Work in 'Coopetition,'" in ASNE (2000) *Extending the Brand: Newspaper Editor's Guide to Partnerships and Diversification in a Converging Media World,* Reston, VA: American Society of Newspaper Editors, Publication Fulfilment, pp. 26–30.

Weaver, Janet (2000) "Orlando: Values are Central to Convergence Strategy," in ASNE (2000) *Extending the Brand: Newspaper Editor's Guide to Partnerships and Diversification in a Converging Media World,* Reston, VA: American Society of Newspaper Editors, Publication Fulfilment, pp. 22–25.

Weber, Samuel (2002) "War, Terrorism, and Spectacle," *South Atlantic Quarterly,* 101 (3), pp. 449–458.

Webster, Frank (2003) "Information Warfare in an Age of Globalization," in Daya Kishan Thussu, and Des Freedman, eds., *War and the Media: Reporting Conflict 24/7,* London: Sage, pp. 57–69.

Weil, Dan (2001) "Limbaugh's New Radio Contract Worth $285 Million," *Cox News Service,* July 19.

Weinraub, Bernard (1999) "Act I in an Opus of Hollywood Deals," *New York Times,* September 1999, C15.

Weise, Elizabeth (2000) "Web sites Pay to Propel Search Engines: Fees for Detailed Listings Raise Doubts about Where the Links are Taking You," *USA Today,* November 14, 3D.

Wernick, Andrew (1991) *Promotional Culture: Advertising,Ideology and Symbolic Expression,* London: Sage.

White, Curtis (2003) "The New Censorship," *Harper's,* August, 307 (1839), pp. 15–20.

White, Erin (2001) "P&G to Use Plugs in TV News Stories to Send Viewers to Its Web Sites," *Wall Street Journal,* March 7, B1.

Whitworth, Damian (2000) "Hillary Plans to Tell Her Side of Lewinsky Affair," *The Times,* November 30, Overseas news.

Whoriskey, Peter (2003) "In Lynch Country, a Puzzled Kind of Pride," *Washington Post,* July 22, A1.

Wilhelm, Anthony G. (2000) *Democracy in the Digital Age: Challenges to Political Life in Cyberspace,* New York and London: Routledge.

Williamson, Judith (1998) "A Glimpse of the Void," in Mandy Merck, ed., *After Diana: Irreverent Elegies,* London and New York: Verso.

Willis, John (2003) "The War, Brought to You by the White House," *The Guardian,* June 20, Leader Pages, p. 21.

Wilson, Elizabeth (1998) "The Unbearable Lightness of Diana," in Mandy Merck, ed., *After Diana: Irreverent Elegies,* London and New York: Verso.

Wilson, Joseph (2003) "What I Didn't Find in Africa," *New York Times,* July 6, Section 4, p. 9.

Winch, Samuel (1997) *Mapping the Cultural Space of Journalism: How Journalists Distinguish News from Entertainment,* Westport, CT: Praeger.

Winseck, Dwayne (2001) "Lost in Cyberspace: Convergence, Consolidation and Power in the Canadian mediascape," Paper presented at the Union for Democratic Communications

Conference, *Democratic Communications in a Branded World,* Carleton University, Ottawa, Canada, May 17–19.

Winter, James (1997) *Democracy's Oxygen: How Corporations Control the News,* Montreal and New York: Black Rose Books.

Winters Lauro, Patricia (2000) "According to a Survey, the Democratic and Republican Parties Have Brand-Name Problems," *New York Times,* November 17, C10.

Witcover, Jules (1998) "Where We Went Wrong," *Columbia Journalism Review,* 36, March/April, pp. 18–25.

Wolff, Michael (2003) "Live From Doha," NewYorkmetro.com, April 7, <www.newyorkmetro.com/nymetro/news/media/columns/medialife/n_8545/index.html>.

Wollen, Peter (2000) "Government by Appearances," *New Left Review,* 3, May/June, pp. 91–106.

York, Geoffrey (2003) "Independent Journalists' Work Severely Hampered," *Globe and Mail,* April 3, A7.

Zaller, John (2001) "Monica Lewinsky and the Mainsprings of American Politics," in W. Lance Bennett and Robert M. Entman, eds., *Mediated Politics: Communication in the Future of Democracy,* New York: Cambridge University Press, pp. 252–278.

Zerbisias, Antonia (2003) "Spinmeisters in Need of Fodder," *Toronto Star,* July 27, D10.

# Index

Sut Jhally & Justin Lewis
*General Editors*

This series publishes works on media and culture, focusing on research embracing a variety of critical perspectives. The series is particularly interested in promoting theoretically informed empirical work using both quantitative and qualitative approaches. Although the focus is on scholarly research, the series aims to speak beyond a narrow, specialist audience.

## ALSO AVAILABLE

- Michael Morgan, Editor
  *Against the Mainstream: The Selected Works of George Gerbner*

- Edward Herman
  *The Myth of the Liberal Media: An Edward Herman Reader*

- Robert Jensen
  *Writing Dissent: Taking Radical Ideas from the Margins to the Mainstream*

To order other books in this series, please contact our Customer Service Department at:

(800) 770-LANG (within the U.S.)
(212) 647-7706 (outside the U.S.)
(212) 647-7707 FAX

or browse online by series at:
WWW.PETERLANGUSA.COM